Readings for Logical Analysis

Readings for Logical Analysis

Second Edition

STEPHEN R. C. HICKS
AND DAVID KELLEY

W · W · NORTON & COMPANY
NEW YORK · LONDON

Previous edition published as THE ART OF REASONING: Readings for Logical Analysis

The text of this book is composed in Monotype Walbaum with the display set in Corvinus Skyline.
Composition by ComCom.
Manufacturing by Haddon Craftsmen.
Book design by Jack Meserole/Antonina Krass.
Cover painting: *Gewagt wägend* (1930) by Paul Klee, courtesy of Paul Klee-Stiftung, Kuntsmuseum Bern.

Library of Congress Cataloging-in-Publication Data

Readings for logical analysis / [edited by] Stephen R.C. Hicks and
    David Kelly. — 2nd ed.
        p.   cm.
    Rev. ed. of: The art of reasoning : readings for logical analysis.
    c1994.
    Includes bibliographical references.
    ISBN 0-393-97214-3 (pbk.)
    1. Reasoning.   2. Logic.   I. Hicks, Stephen Ronald Craig, 1960–   .
II. Kelley, David, 1949–   .   III. Art of reasoning.
BC177.A78   1998
160—DC21   97-25812
                                                            CIP
                                                            Rev.

W. W. Norton & Company, Inc.
500 Fifth Avenue, New York, N.Y. 10110
http://www.wwnorton.com

W. W. Norton & Company Ltd.
10 Coptic Street, London WC1A 1PU

3 4 5 6 7 8 9 0

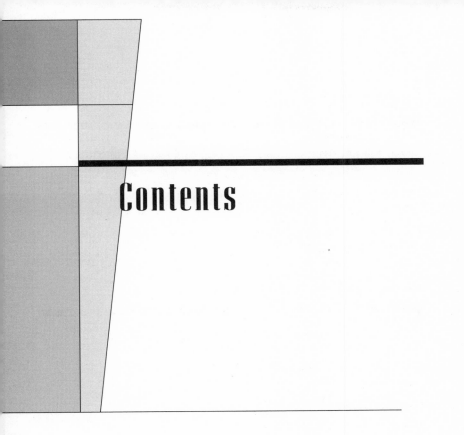

Contents

PART TWO ON THE CAUSES OF CRIME

PART THREE ON THE DEATH PENALTY

PART FOUR ON THE ARTS

PART FIVE   On Science

PART SIX   On Education

PART SEVEN   On Justice and Rights

PART EIGHT On Economic Freedom and Government Regulation

PART NINE On Abortion

PART TEN On the Existence of God

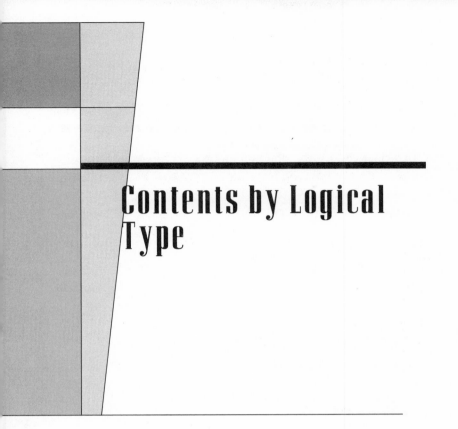

Contents by Logical Type

PART I: CONCEPTS AND PROPOSITIONS

PART II: ARGUMENTS

PART III: DEDUCTIVE LOGIC

PART IV: INDUCTIVE LOGIC

PREFACE

An important need in critical thinking or logic courses is for a variety of examples of real-life argument. Textbooks designed for such courses typically include short examples to illustrate specific points. But many instructors recognize the need for longer passages that call on a wider variety of logical skills. *Readings for Logical Analysis* is designed to fill that need.

The essays in this reader were selected by the following criteria:

1. All of the major types of argument should be represented. For example, arguments relying heavily on analogies, statistical evidence, deduction, Mill's Methods, definitions, and so on, should be included.

2. The selections should vary in length and degree of difficulty. All, however, should be longer than the examples usually found in logic textbooks. Lengths should range from a couple of hundred words (roughly "letters to the editor" length) to two or three thousand words. In some cases the structure of the argument should be transparent. Others should involve detecting assumed premises, separating compound arguments, eliminating repetition, extracting the argument from background material, and connecting points made in different parts of the essay before the overall theme emerges.

3. The selections should be drawn from a wide range of topics. Examples should include the law, the natural sciences, the social sciences, ethics, history, politics, medicine, religion, and philosophy. This will give students a sense for how the same type of argument can be used in different areas of investigation, as well as how such areas sometimes use specialized argumentative techniques.

4. All of the selections should have been published before, and they should either be by well-known, important, or controversial writers, or be about important or controversial topics. Students then will be dealing with real arguments by real people on real issues, not just examples made up as "academic exercises."

5. Examples of both good and bad argumentation should be included. This is in contrast to the "spot the error" approach that characterizes many textbooks, since the examples included there are overwhelmingly selected as examples of mistakes.

6. More selections should be included than can be used in one course, thus giving the instructor the flexibility to vary the selections used from semester to semester.

7. Finally, to the extent that the selections deal with controversial and sensitive issues, the text should be balanced, to reflect major positions across the spectrum.

Our reader is designed with these considerations in mind.

We have included two tables of contents. The first classifies the selections on the basis of subject matter; the second on the basis of the logical techniques they illustrate. In addition, each selection is accompanied by study questions asking the student to identify key logical elements in the passage.

We would like to thank Allen Clawson of W. W. Norton for his careful and friendly editing of this project.

Readings for Logical Analysis

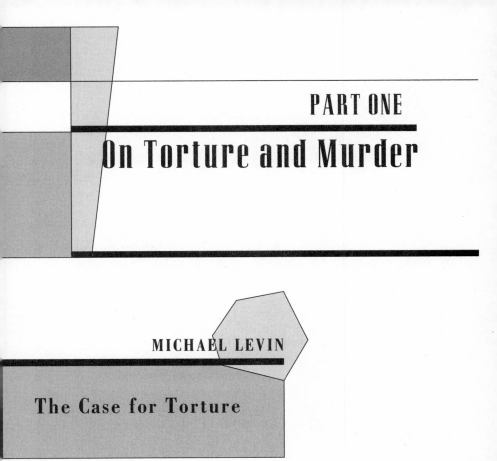

PART ONE

On Torture and Murder

MICHAEL LEVIN

The Case for Torture

Michael Levin, author of Feminism and Freedom *and* Metaphysics and the Mind-Body Problem, *is a professor of philosophy at the City University of New York.*

It is generally assumed that torture is impermissible, a throwback to a more brutal age. Enlightened societies reject it outright, and regimes suspected of using it risk the wrath of the United States. 1

I believe this attitude is unwise. There are situations in which torture is not merely permissible but morally mandatory. Moreover, these situations are moving from the realm of imagination to fact. 2

Death: Suppose a terrorist has hidden an atomic bomb on Man- 3

[Michael Levin, "The Case for Torture." *Newsweek*, June 7, 1982, p. 13.]

hattan Island which will detonate at noon on July 4 unless . . . (here follow the usual demands for money and release of his friends from jail). Suppose, further, that he is caught at 10 a.m. of the fateful day, but—preferring death to failure—won't disclose where the bomb is. What do we do? If we follow due process—wait for his lawyer, arraign him—millions of people will die. If the only way to save those lives is to subject the terrorist to the most excruciating possible pain, what grounds can there be for not doing so? I suggest there are none. In any case, I ask you to face the question with an open mind.

4   Torturing the terrorist is unconstitutional? Probably. But millions of lives surely outweigh constitutionality. Torture is barbaric? Mass murder is far more barbaric. Indeed, letting millions of innocents die in deference to one who flaunts his guilt is moral cowardice, an unwillingness to dirty one's hands. If *you* caught the terrorist, could you sleep nights knowing that millions died because you couldn't bring yourself to apply the electrodes?

5   Once you concede that torture is justified in extreme cases, you have admitted that the decision to use torture is a matter of balancing innocent lives against the means needed to save them. You must now face more realistic cases involving more modest numbers. Someone plants a bomb on a jumbo jet. He alone can disarm it, and his demands cannot be met (or if they can, we refuse to set a precedent by yielding to his threats). Surely we can, we must, do anything to the extortionist to save the passengers. How can we tell 300, or 100, or 10 people who never asked to be put in danger, "I'm sorry, you'll have to die in agony, we just couldn't bring ourselves to . . ."

6   Here are the results of an informal poll about a third, hypothetical, case. Suppose a terrorist group kidnapped a newborn baby from a hospital. I asked four mothers if they would approve of torturing kidnappers if that were necessary to get their own newborns back. All said yes, the most "liberal" adding that she would like to administer it herself.

7   I am not advocating torture as punishment. Punishment is addressed to deeds irrevocably past. Rather, I am advocating torture as an acceptable measure for preventing future evils. So understood, it is far less objectionable than many extant punishments. Opponents of the death penalty, for example, are forever insisting that

executing a murderer will not bring back his victim (as if the purpose of capital punishment were supposed to be resurrection, not deterrence or retribution). But torture, in the cases described, is intended not to bring anyone back but to keep innocents from being dispatched. The most powerful argument against using torture as a punishment or to secure confessions is that such practices disregard the rights of the individual. Well, if the individual is all that important—and he is—it is correspondingly important to protect the rights of individuals threatened by terrorists. If life is so valuable that it must never be taken, the lives of the innocents must be saved even at the price of hurting the one who endangers them.

Better precedents for torture are assassination and pre-emptive attack. No Allied leader would have flinched at assassinating Hitler, had that been possible. (The Allies did assassinate Heydrich.) Americans would be angered to learn that Roosevelt could have had Hitler killed in 1943—thereby shortening the war and saving millions of lives—but refused on moral grounds. Similarly, if nation A learns that nation B is about to launch an unprovoked attack, A has a right to save itself by destroying B's military capability first. In the same way, if the police can by torture save those who would otherwise die at the hands of kidnappers or terrorists, they must. 8

Idealism: There is an important difference between terrorists and their victims that should mute talk of the terrorists' "rights." The terrorist's victims are at risk unintentionally, not having asked to be endangered. But the terrorist knowingly initiated his actions. Unlike his victims, he volunteered for the risks of his deed. By threatening to kill for profit or idealism, he renounces civilized standards, and he can have no complaint if civilization tries to thwart him by whatever means necessary. 9

Just as torture is justified only to save lives (not extort confessions or recantations), it is justifiably administered only to those *known* to hold innocent lives in their hands. Ah, but how can the authorities ever be sure they have the right malefactor? Isn't there a danger of error and abuse? Won't We turn into Them? 10

Questions like these are disingenuous in a world in which terrorists proclaim themselves and perform for television. The name of their game is public recognition. After all, you can't very well intimidate a government into releasing your freedom fighters unless you announce that it is your group that has seized its embassy. 11

"Clear guilt" is difficult to define, but when 40 million people see a group of masked gunmen seize an airplane on the evening news, there is not much question about who the perpetrators are. There will be hard cases where the situation is murkier. Nonetheless, a line demarcating the legitimate use of torture can be drawn. Torture only the obviously guilty, and only for the sake of saving innocents, and the line between Us and Them will remain clear.

12   There is little danger that the Western democracies will lose their way if they choose to inflict pain as one way of preserving order. Paralysis in the face of evil is the greater danger. Some day soon a terrorist will threaten tens of thousands of lives, and torture will be the only way to save them. We had better start thinking about this.

STUDY QUESTIONS

1. Levin argues that torture is justifiable in some cases, but not in others. What conditions does he propose to distinguish the two sorts of cases?

2. Levin's conclusion is that torture is justifiable in some cases. How many different arguments does he use in support of this conclusion?

3. How does Levin respond to the charge that torture would violate the terrorist's rights? Does he think terrorists have rights?

4. What is the point of the "informal poll" Levin reports in paragraph 6? In raising such cases, does Levin run the risk of committing an appeal to emotion?

5. In paragraph 8, Levin compares torture to assassination and preemptive attacks. What points of similarity does he see among the three? Does he overlook any significant differences?

6. Who makes the decision about whether torture is justifiable? In emergency situations, who would decide and ensure that no abuses occur? What if an innocent person is mistakenly tortured? Why, in paragraph 11, does Levin suggest that questions such as these may be "disingenuous"?

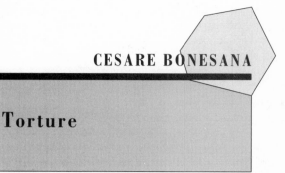

CESARE BONESANA

Torture

*Cesare Bonesana (1738–1794) was the Marchese di Beccarria
and an Italian jurist. The following argument against the use
of torture, especially by legal authorities, is excerpted from his*
Trato dei Delitti e delle Pene *(On Crimes & Punishments),
written in 1764.*

A cruelty consecrated among most nations by custom is the torture   1
of the accused during his trial, on the pretext of compelling him to
confess his crime, of clearing up contradictions in his statements, of
discovering his accomplices, of purging him in some metaphysical
and incomprehensible way from infamy, or finally of finding out
other crimes of which he may possibly be guilty, but of which he is
not accused.

A man cannot be called *guilty* before sentence has been passed   2
on him by a judge, nor can society deprive him of its protection till
it has been decided that he has broken the condition on which it was
granted. What, then, is that right but one of mere might by which
a judge is empowered to inflict a punishment on a citizen whilst his
guilt or innocence are still undetermined? The following dilemma
is no new one: either the crime is certain or uncertain; if certain, no
other punishment is suitable for it than that affixed to it by law; and
torture is useless, for the same reason that the criminal's confession

[Cesare Bonesana, "Torture," excerpt from James A. Farrar, ed., *Crimes and
Punishments*. London: Chatto & Windus, 1880, pp. 148–152.]

is useless. If it is uncertain, it is wrong to torture an innocent person, such as the law adjudges him to be, whose crimes are not yet proved.

3   What is the political object of punishments? The intimidation of other men. But what shall we say of the secret and private tortures which the tyranny of custom exercises alike upon the guilty and the innocent? It is important, indeed, that no open crime shall pass unpunished; but the public exposure of a criminal whose crime was hidden in darkness is utterly useless. An evil that has been done and cannot be undone can only be punished by civil society insofar as it may affect others with the hope of impunity. If it be true that there are a greater number of men who either from fear or virtue respect the laws than of those who transgress them, the risk of torturing an innocent man should be estimated according to the probability that any man will have been more likely, other things being equal, to have respected than to have despised the laws.

4   But I say in addition: it is to seek to confound all the relations of things to require a man to be at the same time accuser and accused, to make pain the crucible of truth, as if the test of it lay in the muscles and sinews of an unfortunate wretch. The law which ordains the use of torture is a law which says to men: "Resist pain; and if Nature has created in you an inextinguishable self-love, if she has given you an inalienable right of self-defence, I create in you a totally contrary affection, namely, an heroic self-hatred, and I command you to accuse yourselves, and to speak the truth between the laceration of your muscles and the dislocation of your bones."

5   This infamous crucible of truth is a still-existing monument of that primitive and savage legal system which called trials by fire and boiling water, or the accidental decisions of combat, *judgments of God*, as if the rings of the eternal chain in the control of the First Cause must at every moment be disarranged and put out for the petty institutions of mankind. The only difference between torture and the trial by fire and water is, that the result of the former seems to depend on the will of the accused, and that of the other two on a fact which is purely physical and extrinsic to the sufferer; but the difference is only apparent, not real. The avowal of truth under tortures and agonies is as little free as it was in those times the prevention without fraud of the usual effects of fire and boiling water. Every act of our will is ever proportioned to the force of the sensible impression which causes it, and the sensibility of every man

is limited. Hence the impression produced by pain may be so intense as to occupy a man's entire sensibility and leave him no other liberty than the choice of the shortest way of escape, for the present moment, from his penalty. Under such circumstances the answer of the accused is as inevitable as the impressions produced by fire and water; and the innocent man who is sensitive will declare himself guilty, when by so doing he hopes to bring his agonies to an end. All the difference between guilt and innocence is lost by virtue of the very means which they profess to employ for its discovery.

Torture is a certain method for the acquittal of robust villains and for the condemnation of innocent but feeble men. See the fatal drawbacks of this pretended test of truth—a test, indeed, that is worthy of cannibals; a test which the Romans, barbarous as they too were in many respects, reserved for slaves alone, the victims of their fierce and too highly lauded virtue. Of two men, equally innocent or equally guilty, the robust and courageous will be acquitted, the weak and the timid will be condemned, by virtue of the following exact train of reasoning on the part of the judge: "I as judge had to find you guilty of such and such a crime; you, AB, have by your physical strength been able to resist pain, and therefore I acquit you; you, CD, in your weakness have yielded to it; therefore I condemn you. I feel that a confession extorted amid torments can have no force, but I will torture you afresh unless you corroborate what you have now confessed." 6

The result, then, of torture is a matter of temperament, of calculation, which varies with each man according to his strength and sensibility; so that by this method a mathematician might solve better than a judge this problem: "Given the muscular force and the nervous sensibility of an innocent man, to find the degree of pain which will cause him to plead guilty to a given crime." 7

STUDY QUESTIONS

1. In his opening paragraph, Bonesana lists five attempted justifications for using torture. Does he address each of them in the rest of the selection?

2. In paragraph 2, Bonesana poses a dilemma for those advocat-

ing the use of torture. Diagram the structure of the dilemma argument, and then explain why he thinks torture is both unsuitable and useless if the crime is certain.

3. How would Bonesana respond to the following objection: "Suppose the crime is certain, and we know the guilty party had accomplices. You [Bonesana] haven't proved that torturing the guilty party wouldn't give us a chance to catch the accomplices"?

4. What do you think Bonesana would say in response to Levin's argument for torture in some cases?

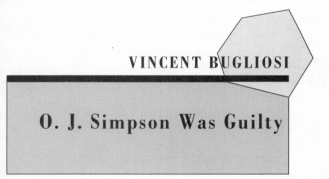

VINCENT BUGLIOSI

O. J. Simpson Was Guilty

Mr. Bugliosi is a lawyer and author of several true-crime books. He was the prosecuting attorney in the Charles Manson case, and based on that experience wrote Helter Skelter, *which won the Édgar Allan Poe Award for best true-crime book of the year. He received his law degree from UCLA Law School.*

1   To distill this case down to its irreducible minimum (and temporarily ignoring all the other evidence pointing inexorably to Simpson's guilt), if your blood is found at the murder scene, as Simpson's was conclusively proved to be by DNA tests, that's really the end of

[Vincent Bugliosi, Excerpt from *Outrage: The Five Reasons Why O. J. Simpson Got Away With Murder.* W. W. Norton & Company, 1996, pp. 20–22.]

the ball game. There is nothing more to say. (And in this case, not only was Simpson's blood found at the murder scene, but the victims' blood was found inside his car and home.) I mean, to deny guilt when your blood is at the murder scene is the equivalent of a man being caught by his wife *in flagrante* with another woman and saying to her (quoting comedian Richard Pryor), "Who are you going to believe? Me or your lying eyes?"

At the crime scene there were five blood drops leading away from the slain bodies of Nicole Brown Simpson and Ronald Goldman toward the rear alley, four of which were immediately to the *left* of bloody size-12 shoe prints (Simpson's shoe size). This indicated, of course, that the killer had been wounded on the left side of his body. And the morning after the murders, Simpson was observed by the police to be wearing a bandage on his left middle finger. When the bandage was removed that afternoon, it was seen that he had a deep cut on the knuckle of the finger.

DNA (deoxyribonucleic acid) is the genetic material found in all human cells that carries the coded messages of heredity unique (with the exception of identical twins) to each individual. DNA, then, is our genetic fingerprint. Each of the approximately 100 trillion cells in a human body contains twenty-three pairs of chromosomes—one of each pair coming from one's father, the other from the mother—which contain DNA molecules. In criminal cases, DNA can be extracted from samples of blood, semen, saliva, skin, or hair follicles found at a crime scene and then compared to DNA drawn from a suspect to determine if there is a "match." DNA testing is a new forensic science, first used in Great Britain in 1985 and in the United States in 1987.

DNA tests on all five blood drops and on three bloodstains found on the rear gate at the crime scene showed that all of this blood belonged to Simpson. Two DNA tests were used, PCR (polymerase chain reaction) and RFLP (restrictive fragment length polymorphism). The PCR test is less precise than the RFLP, but can be conducted on much smaller blood samples as well as samples that have degenerated ("degraded") because of bacteria and/or exposure to the elements. PCR tests were conducted on four out of the five blood drops. Three showed that only one out of 240,000 people had DNA with the markers found in the sample. (A marker is a gene that makes up one portion of the DNA molecule, and the more markers in the sample, the more comparison tests can be conducted, and hence the greater the exclusion of other humans.) The fourth blood drop had markers which one out of 5,200 people could have. Simpson was one of these people. The fifth blood drop had sufficient markers for an RFLP test, and showed that only one out of 170 million people had DNA with those markers. Again, Simpson's blood did. The richest sample was on the rear gate, and an RFLP test showed that only one out of 57 *billion* people had those markers. Simpson was one of them. In other words, just on the blood evidence alone, there's only a one out of 57 billion chance that Simpson is innocent. Fifty-seven billion is approximately ten times the current population of the entire world.

5   Now I realize that Igor in Kiev, Gino in Naples, Colin down Johannesburg way, and Kartac on Pluto might have the same DNA as O. J. Simpson. If you're a skeptic I wouldn't blame you if you checked to see if Igor, Gino, Colin, or Kartac was in Brentwood on the night of the murders, used to beat Nicole within an inch of her life, had blood all over his car, driveway, and home on the night of the murders, had no alibi, and, if charged with the murders, would refuse to take the witness stand to defend himself. Who knows— maybe Simpson isn't the murderer after all. Maybe Igor or one of the others is. You should definitely check this out. And while you're checking it out, someone should be checking you into the nearest mental ward.

6   To elaborate on the irreducible minimum mentioned earlier, there are only three possible explanations other than guilt for one's blood being found at the murder scene, and all three are preposterous on their face. One is that Simpson left his blood there on an earlier occasion. When Simpson was interrogated by LAPD detectives on the afternoon after these murders, he said he had not cut himself the last time he was at the Bundy address a week earlier. But even without that, how can one believe that on some prior occasion Simpson bled, not just on the Bundy premises, but at the precise point on the premises where the murders occurred? In fact, so far-fetched is this possibility that even the defense attorneys, whose stock-in-trade during the trial was absurdity, never proffered it to the jury.

7   And here, not only was Simpson's blood found at the murder scene, but there were the four drops of Simpson's blood found just

to the left of the killer's bloody shoe prints leaving the murder scene. If there is someone who isn't satisfied even by this, I would suggest that this book is perhaps not for you, that you think about pursuing more appropriate intellectual pursuits, such as comic strips. When I was a kid, one of my favorites was *Mandrake the Magician.* You might check to see if Mandrake is still doing his thing.

The second possibility is that Simpson cut himself while killing Ron Goldman and Nicole Brown in self-defense—that is, either Ron or Nicole or both together unleashed a deadly assault on Simpson, and he either took out a knife he had on his own person or wrested Ron's or Nicole's knife away, and stabbed the two of them to death. This, of course, is just too insane to talk about. Again, even the defense attorneys, who apparently possess the gonads of ten thousand elephants, never suggested this possibility. It should be added parenthetically that if such a situation had occurred, Simpson wouldn't have had any reason to worry, since self-defense is a justifiable homicide, a complete defense to murder.

The third and final possibility is that the LAPD detectives planted Simpson's blood not just at the murder scene but to the left of the bloody shoe prints leaving the scene. This is not as insane a proposition as the first two, but only because there are degrees of everything in life. It is still an insane possibility, and if any reader is silly enough to believe that the LAPD detectives decided to frame someone they believed to be innocent of these murders (Simpson) and actually planted his blood all over the murder scene (and, of course, planted the victims' blood in Simpson's car and home), again, this book is probably not for that reader. This book is for people who are very angry that a brutal murderer is among us— with a smile on his face, no less—and want to know how this terrible miscarriage of justice could have occurred. . . .

Let me point out to those who believe in the "possible" existence of either of the aforementioned three innocent possibilities for Simpson's blood being found at the murder scene, that the prosecution only has the burden of proving guilt beyond a *reasonable* doubt, not beyond all possible doubt. So it isn't necessary to have all possible doubts of guilt removed from one's mind in order to reach a conclusion of guilt. Only reasonable doubts of guilt have to be removed. Of course, in this case, *no* doubt remains of Simpson's guilt.

STUDY QUESTIONS

1. To establish the conclusion that O. J. Simpson was guilty of murder, Bugliosi relies on three premises—that Nicole Brown Simpson's blood was found inside O. J. Simpson's car and home, that Ronald Goldman's blood was found inside O. J. Simpson's car and home, and that O. J. Simpson's blood was found at the murder scene. Do these premises support the conclusion additively or independently?

2. To argue that the blood at the murder scene was O. J. Simpson's, Bugliosi offers three types of evidence: the position of four drops of blood, the size of a bloody shoe print, and the results of DNA testing. Using the following propositions, diagram Bugliosi's argument.

   (1) O. J. Simpson's blood was found at the murder scene. [conclusion]

   (2) At the crime scene there were five drops of blood leading away from the victims' bodies.

   (3) Four of these drops of blood were to the left of a bloody shoe print.

   (4) Therefore, the murderer had been wounded on the left side of his body.

   (5) The day after the murders, O. J. Simpson was wearing a bandage on his left middle finger.

   (6) A size 12 shoe made the bloody shoeprint.

   (7) O. J. Simpson wears size 12 shoes.

   (8) The DNA tests used on the five drops of blood showed that only one of 5,200, one of 240,000, and one of 170 million people could leave that blood.

   (9) Tests of O. J. Simpson's blood showed that he is one of those who could leave those drops of blood.

   (10) Blood was also found on the rear gate.

   (11) The DNA test performed on the blood found on the rear gate showed that only one of 57 billion people could leave that blood.

   (12) Tests of O. J. Simpson's blood showed that he is one of those who could leave that blood.

3. After arguing that the blood at the murder scene was O. J. Simpson's, how many possible explanations does Bugliosi consider for the presence of that blood? On what grounds does he reject them?

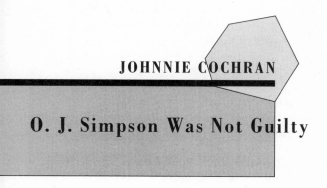

JOHNNIE COCHRAN

O. J. Simpson Was Not Guilty

Born in Louisiana in 1937, Johnnie Cochran is a graduate of UCLA and Loyola Law School. He was a member of O. J. Simpson's defense team, and the following selection is his closing statement to the jury in that trial. Mr. Cochran currently lives in Los Angeles.

Good afternoon, ladies and gentlemen [I began]. The defendant, Mr. Orenthal James Simpson, is now afforded an opportunity to argue the case, but I'm not going to argue with you, ladies and gentlemen. What I'm going to do is discuss the reasonable inferences which I feel can be drawn from this evidence . . . Listen for a moment, will you, please. One of my favorite people in history is the great Frederick Douglass. He said shortly after the slaves were freed, "In a composite nation like ours, as before the law, there should be no rich, no poor, no high, no low, no white, no black, but common country, common citizenship, equal rights and a common destiny." This marvelous statement was made more than one hundred years ago. . . . Now, in this case, you're aware that we represent

[Johnnie L. Cochran, with Tim Rutten. Excerpt from *Journey to Justice*. New York: Ballantine Books, 1996, pp. 338–351.]

Mr. Orenthal James Simpson. The prosecution never calls him Mr. Orenthal James Simpson. They call him the defendant. I want to tell you right at the outset that Mr. Orenthal James Simpson, like all defendants, is presumed innocent. He's entitled to the same dignity and respect as all the rest of us. As he sits over there now, he's cloaked in a presumption of innocence. You will determine the facts and whether or not he's set free to walk out those doors or whether he spends the rest of his life in prison. But he's Orenthal James Simpson. He's not just the defendant, and we on the defense are proud, consider it a privilege to have been part of representing him in this exercise, this journey toward justice. . . .

2   This is not a case for the timid or the weak of heart. This is not a case for the naive. This is a case for courageous citizens who believe in the Constitution. And while I'm talking about the Constitution, think with me for a moment how many times you heard my learned adversary say the defense didn't prove, the defense didn't do this, the defense didn't do that. Remember back in voir dire?[1] What did the judge tell us? We don't have to do anything. We don't have to prove anything. This is the prosecution's burden, and we can't let them turn the Constitution on its head. We can't let them get away from their burden. . . . They must prove beyond a reasonable doubt and to a moral certainty, and we will talk about what a reasonable doubt means. . . .

3   Let me ask each of you a question. Have you ever in your life been falsely accused of something? Ever had to sit there and take it and watch the proceedings and wait and wait and wait, all the while knowing that you didn't do it? . . . Now, last night, as I thought about the arguments of my colleagues, two words came to mind. I asked my wife this morning to get the dictionary out and look up two words. The two words were "speculative," and "cynical."

4   "Cynical" is described as contemptuously distrustful of human nature and motives, gloomy, distrustful view of life. And to "speculate"—to engage in conjecture and to surmise—is to take to be the truth on the basis of insufficient evidence. I mention those two

---

[1]*Voir dire*—"To speak the truth." The phrase refers to a preliminary examination by the court of a witness who has been objected to on grounds of competence, conflict of interest, etc.—Eds.

definitions to you because I felt that much of what we heard yesterday and again this morning was speculative.

Understand this, ladies and gentlemen, that none of us in this courtroom were out at 875 Bundy on June 12, 1994 . . . so that everything we say to you is our best effort to piece together what took place in this case. . . . It is a sad fact that in American society, a large number of people are murdered each year. Violence unfortunately has become a way of life in America. And so when this sort of tragedy does in fact happen, it becomes the business of the police to step up and step in and to take charge of the matter. A good, efficient, competent, noncorrupt police department will carefully set about the business of investigating homicides. They won't rush to judgment. They won't be bound by an obsession to win at all costs. They will set about trying to apprehend the killer or killers and trying to protect the innocent from suspicion. . . .

Your verdict in this case will go far beyond the walls of Department 103 because your verdict talks about justice in America and it talks about the police and whether they're above the law and it looks at the police perhaps as though they haven't been looked at very recently. Remember, I told you this is not for the naive, the faint of heart or the timid. . . .

Continuing on, there's absolutely no evidence at all that Mr. Simpson ever tried to hide a knife or clothes or anything else on his property. You'll recall that Fuhrman—and when I get to Fuhrman, we'll be spending some time on him, as you might imagine. But one of the things he said was that he encountered cobwebs further down that walkway, indicating, if that part is true—and I don't vouch for him at all—there had been nobody down that pathway for quite some time.

And so, Ms. Clark talks about O. J. being very, very recognizable. She talks about O. J. Simpson getting dressed up to go commit these murders. Just before the break, I was thinking—I was thinking last night about this case and their theory and how it didn't make any sense and how it didn't fit and how something is wrong. . . .

It occurred to me how they were going to come here, stand up here, and tell you how O. J. Simpson was going to disguise himself. He was going to put on a knit cap and some dark clothes, and he was going to get in this white Bronco, this recognizable person, and go over and kill his wife. That's what they want you to believe. . . . Let me show you something. This is a knit cap. Let me put this knit cap on. You have seen me for a year. If I put this knit cap on, who am I? I'm still Johnnie Cochran with a knit cap. And if you looked at O. J. Simpson over there—and he has a rather large head—O. J. Simpson in a knit cap from two blocks away is still O. J. Simpson. It's no disguise. It's no disguise. It makes no sense. It doesn't fit. If it doesn't fit, you must acquit. . . .

10   Watch with me now [I invited the jurors], I want you to watch the time counter and understand how important this is. . . . This is Mr. Willie Ford, the police photographer, going up into the bedroom. It's 4:13 on June 13th, 1994. . . . Look at the foot of the bed there, where the socks are supposed to be. You'll see no socks in this video. And you'll recall that Mr. Willie Ford testified about this. I asked him, "Well, where are the socks, Mr. Ford?" And he said, "I didn't see any socks."

11   Now that's interesting, isn't it? These mysterious socks, these socks that no one sees any blood on until August fourth all of a sudden . . . These socks will be their undoing. It just doesn't fit. None of you can deny there are no socks at the foot of that bed at 4:13. Where, then, are the socks, this important piece of evidence?

12   Let's give them the benefit of the doubt. How could the socks be there at 4:35, when you just saw they're not there at 4:13. Who's fooling whom here? They're setting this man up, and you can see it with your own eyes. You're not naive. No one is foolish here. . . .

13   Then we find out [these socks] have EDTA [the preservative injected into blood samples] on them . . . How could it be on there? Why didn't they see blood before that? There's a big fight here. Where is the dirt? How could Mr. Simpson have worn these [black dress] socks with a sweat outfit? Wait a minute. Now you don't have to be from the fashion police to know that . . . You wear those kinds of socks with a suit. Doesn't it make sense that those socks were in the laundry hamper from Saturday night, when Mr. Simpson went to a formal event? They went and took them out of the hamper and staged it there. . . . It just doesn't fit. When it doesn't fit, you must acquit.

14   Dr. Herbert MacDonell [a renowned expert on blood splatters who had testified on Simpson's behalf] came in here and told you that there was no splatter or spatter on these socks. These socks had

compression transfer, and he used his hands to show you somebody took those socks and they put something on them.

Dr. Baden says the perpetrator would be covered with blood. Your common sense tells you that the perpetrator would be covered with blood. . . . How does anyone drive away in that car with bloody clothes with no blood there on the seats, no blood anyplace else? Every police officer who came in talked about how bloody this scene was. . . . It doesn't make any sense. They can't explain it because Mr. Simpson was not in that car and didn't commit these murders. That's the reasonable and logical explanation. None other will do, and it's too late for them to change now these kinds of shifting theories. . . . So the prosecution then has no shoes, no weapon, no clothes. They don't have anything except these socks, which appear all of a sudden under these circumstances. . . .

Now, when you want to think about the depths to which people will go to try to win. . . . I'm going to give you an example. There was a witness in this case named Thano Peratis. This is a man, who's their man, who took O. J. Simpson's blood. He's been a nurse for a number of years. You saw him. He works for the city of Los Angeles. He says that when he took this blood from O. J. Simpson on June 13th, he took between 7.9 and 8.1 cc's of blood. . . . He's sworn to tell the truth both places. Pretty clear, isn't it? Pretty clear . . . Something's wrong here, something's sinister here, something's wrong because if we take their figures and assume they took 8 cc's of blood, there's 6.5 cc's accounted for. There is 1.5 cc's of this blood missing. There's some missing blood in this case. Where is it? . . .

Vannatter, the man who carries the blood. Fuhrman, the man who finds the glove . . . Now, Detective Vannatter has been a police officer for twenty-seven, twenty-eight years, experienced LAPD Robbery-Homicide man who was put on this case because of his experience . . . here you have Mr. Simpson cooperating fully, gives his blood, 8 cc's of blood, we now know . . . The blood is then turned over to Vannatter. He could have gone a couple of floors and booked the blood, as the manual requires. But he didn't do that, did he? . . .

What he does is, he goes way out in this area marked Brentwood Heights. It must be twenty, twenty-five, twenty-seven miles to go way out there carrying the blood in this unsealed gray envelope, supposedly. Why is he doing that? Why is Vannatter carrying Mr. Simpson's blood out there? Why is he doing that? Doesn't make any sense. Violates their own rules . . . Has he ever done it in any other case? No. Name another case where this has happened. . . . It gets even stranger, doesn't it, because supposedly after the blood is carried out to O. J. Simpson's residence, Vannatter gives the blood to Fung, according to what we heard, but Fung then uses some kind of a trash bag, a black trash bag, and gives it to Mazzola, but he doesn't tell her that it's blood. Isn't that bizarre? . . . Mazzola is asked, "Well, do you see—did you see when Vannatter gave the blood to Fung." And she says, "No. I'd sat down on the couch and I was closing my eyes on Mr. Simpson's couch at that moment. I wasn't looking at that moment." . . . Always looking the other way, not looking, doesn't want to be involved, covering for somebody . . . It doesn't fit. . . .

19   Then we come, before we end the day, to Detective Mark Fuhrman. This man is an unspeakable disgrace. He's been unmasked before the whole world for what he is, and that's hopefully positive. His misdeeds go far beyond this case because he speaks of culture that's not tolerable in America. But let's talk about this case. People worry about, this is not the case of Mark Fuhrman. Well, it's not the case of Mark Fuhrman. Mark Fuhrman is not in custody. . . . You know, they were talking yesterday in their argument about, "Well, gee, you think he would commit a felony?" What do you think it was when he was asked the question by F. Lee Bailey. . . .

20   But what I find particularly troubling is that they all knew about Mark Fuhrman and they weren't going to tell you. They tried to ease him by. Of all the witnesses who've testified in this case, how many were taken up to the grand jury room where they have this prep session to ask him all these questions. . . . So they knew. Make no mistake about it. And so when they try and prepare him . . . get him ready and make him seem like a choirboy and make him come in here and raise his right hand as though he's going to tell you the truth and give you a true story here, they knew he was a liar and a racist. . . . There's something about good versus evil. There's something about truth. That truth crushed to earth will rise again. You can always count on that. He's the one who says the Bronco was parked askew, and he sees some spot on the door [at Rockingham]. He makes all of the discoveries. . . .

21   He's got to be the big man because he's had it in for O. J. because of his views since '85. This is the man, he's the guy who climbs over

the fence. He's the guy who goes in and talks to Kato Kaelin while the other detectives are talking to the family. He's the guy who's shining a light in Kato Kaelin's eyes. . . . He's the guy who's off this case who's supposedly there to help this man, our client . . . who then goes out all by himself. Now he's worried about bodies or suspects or whatever. He doesn't even take out his gun. He goes around the side of the house, and lo and behold, he claims he finds this glove and he says the glove is still moist and sticky.

Why would it be moist and sticky unless he brought it over there 22 and planted it there to make this case? And there is a Caucasian hair on that glove. This man cannot be trusted. He is central to the prosecution, and for them to say he's not important is untrue and you will not fall for it, because as guardians of justice here, we can't let it happen. . . .

We'll see you tomorrow . . . thank you, Your Honor. 23

Let's continue where we left off then, with this man Fuhrman. 24 He's said some very interesting things.

He tells you that Rokahr, the photographer, took this photograph 25 [of him pointing to the glove] after seven o'clock in the morning. And the reason he tells you that is because he wants that photograph of him pointing at the glove taken after he supposedly finds the glove at Rockingham. . . . Rokahr then comes here near the end of the case . . . and says these photographs on this contact sheet are all taken while it is dark. . . . Now we know it is not seven o'clock. You see that photograph up there. That is Mark Fuhrman pointing. . . . But he is lying again. He is lying. . . . Remember there is a question he was asked about the gloves, and Lee Bailey asked him about. Well—he says, well—he is talking about gloves and he says "them." He never explained that. He says "them." Does that mean two gloves? He said, "I saw them." Is that two gloves? Why would you say "them"? . . .

These are the facts. I haven't made them up. This is what you 26 heard in this case. This is what we have proved. Some of it came in late; some of it came in early, but our job here is to piece this together so that you can then see this, so when he refers to the glove as "them," that has never been cleared up for you and he can't. . . .

One of the things that has made this country so great is people's 27 willingness to stand up and say, "That is wrong. I'm not going to be part of it. I'm not going to be part of the cover-up." That is what

I'm asking you to do. Stop this cover-up. Stop this cover-up. If you don't stop it, then who? Do you think the police department is going to stop it? Do you think the D.A.'s office is going to stop it? Do you think we can stop it by ourselves? It has to be stopped by you.

28   . . . The jury instruction which you know about now says essentially that a witness willfully false . . . in one material part of his or her testimony is to be distrusted in others. You may reject the whole testimony of a witness who willfully has testified falsely to a material point unless from all the evidence you believe the probability of truth favors his or her testimony in other particulars . . . Why is this instruction so important? . . . First of all, both prosecutors have now agreed that we have convinced them beyond a reasonable doubt, that Mark Fuhrman is a lying, perjuring, genocidal racist, and he has testified falsely in this case on a number of scores. . . . When you go back in the jury room, some of you may want to say, "Well, gee, you know, boys will be boys." This is just like police talk. This is the way they talk. That is not acceptable as the consciences of this community if you adopt that attitude. That is why we have this, because nobody has the courage to say it is wrong.

29   You are empowered to say, "We are not going to take that anymore." I'm sure you will do the right thing about that . . . Lest you feel that a greater probability of truth lies in something else, then you may disregard this testimony. This applies not only to Fuhrman, it applies to Vannatter, and then you see what trouble their case is in. They can't explain to you why Vannatter carried that blood, because they were setting this man up, and that glove, anybody among you think that glove was just sitting there, just placed there, moist and sticky after six and a half hours? The testimony is it will be dried in three or four hours, according to MacDonell. We are not naive. You understand there is no blood on anything else. There is no blood trail. There is no hair and fiber. And you get the ridiculous explanation that Mr. Simpson was running into air conditioners on his own property. . . .

30   So when they take the law into their own hands, they become worse than the people who break the law, because they are the protectors of the law. Who then polices the police? You police the police. You police them by your verdict. . . .

31   And now we have it. There was another man not too long ago in the world who had those same views, who wanted to burn people,

who had racist views and ultimately had power over the people in his country. People didn't care. People said, "He's just crazy. He's just a half-baked painter." They didn't do anything about it. This man, this—scourge—became one of the worst people in the history of this world. Adolf Hitler. Because people didn't care, or they didn't try to stop him. He had the power over his racism and his anti-religion. Nobody wanted to stop him, and it ended up in World War II, the conduct of this man. And so Fuhrman, Fuhrman wants to take all black people now and burn them or bomb them. That is genocidal racism. Is that ethnic purity? What is that? We are paying this man's salary to espouse these views? Do you think he only told Kathleen Bell, whom he just had met? Do you think he talked to his partners about it? Do you think his commanders knew about it? Do you think everybody knew about it and turned their heads? Nobody did anything about it.

Things happen for a reason in your life. Maybe this is one of the reasons we are all gathered together this day, one year and two days after we met. Maybe there is a reason for your purpose. Maybe this is why you were selected. There is something in your background, in your character, that helps you understand this is wrong. Maybe you are the right people at the right time at the right place to say, "No more, we are not going to have this. This is wrong." What they've done to our client is wrong. You cannot believe these people. You can't trust the message. You can't trust the messengers. It is frightening. It is, quite frankly, frightening, and it is not enough for the prosecutors now to stand up and say, "Oh well, let's just back off." . . . This is . . . frightening. It is not just African Americans, it is white people who would associate or deign to go out with a black person or marry one. You are free in America to love whoever you want, so it infects all of us, doesn't it, this one rotten apple, and yet they cover for him. 32

Yet they cover for him . . . 33

And I always think in a circular fashion, that you kind of end up where you started out. The truth is a wonderful commodity in this society. Some people can't stand the truth. But you know what. That notwithstanding, we still have to deal with truth in this society. 34

Carlysle said that no lie can live forever. . . . I happen to really like the Book of Proverbs and in Proverbs it talks a lot about false witnesses. It says that a false witness shall not be unpunished and he that speaketh lies shall not escape. . . . 35

36   And James Russell Lowell said it best about wrong and evil. He said that truth's forever on the scaffold, wrong forever on the throne, yet that scaffold sways the future, and beyond the dim unknown standeth God within the shadows, keeping watch above his own. . . .

37   I will some day go on to other cases, no doubt as will Ms. Clark and Mr. Darden. Judge Ito will try another case someday, I hope, but this is O. J. Simpson's one day in court. By your decision, you control his very life in your hands. Treat it carefully. Treat it fairly. Be fair. Don't be part of this continuing cover-up. Do the right thing, remembering that if it doesn't fit, you must acquit, that if these messengers have lied to you, you can't trust their message, that this has been a search for truth. That no matter how bad it looks, if truth is out there on a scaffold and wrong is in here on the throne, when that scaffold sways the future and beyond the dim unknown standeth the same God—for all people—keeping watch above his own.

38   He watches all of us. He will watch you in your decision.

STUDY QUESTIONS

1. In the preceding selection, Vincent Bugliosi emphasizes the blood evidence against O. J. Simpson. What strategy does Mr. Cochran use to argue against the blood evidence?
2. The peculiarities surrounding the bloody socks are a key part of Cochran's argument that the police attempted to frame O. J. Simpson. How many peculiarities does Cochran discuss? Do they provide additive or independent support for the conclusion that the police attempted to frame Simpson?
3. Diagram the following part of Cochran's argument.
   (1) Detective Fuhrman lied under oath.
   (2) Detective Fuhrman is a racist.
   (3) 1.5 cc's of Simpson's voluntarily given blood sample are not accounted for.
   (4) Detective Vannatter did not follow the usual procedure in passing Simpson's blood sample on to Fung.
   (5) The socks were planted.
   (6) The police attempted to frame Simpson.

4. As Cochran points out in paragraphs 1 and 2, the prosecution bears the burden of proving beyond a reasonable doubt that O. J. Simpson committed the murders. In your judgment, has Cochran shown that a reasonable doubt exists?

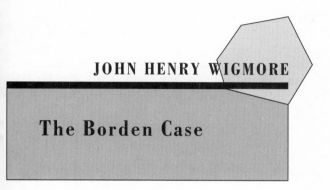

JOHN HENRY WIGMORE

The Borden Case

John Henry Wigmore (1863–1943), professor of law at North-western University, was a legal scholar who specialized in the law of evidence. In the following essay, Wigmore presents the facts of the famous Lizzie Borden murder case.

On the 4th of August, 1892, was committed in the city of Fall River, Massachusetts, the double murder for which Lizzie Andrew Borden was tried in the month of June, 1893, at New Bedford. Not since the trial of Professor Webster for the murder of Dr. Parkman has such widespread popular interest been aroused; but on this occasion the notoriety far exceeded that of the Webster case, and the report of the proceedings was daily telegraphed to all parts of the country. If we look for the circumstances which made the case such a special theme of discussion, they seem to be three: first, the particularly brutal mode in which the killing was done; next, the sex of the accused person and her standing in the community; but principally

1

[John H. Wigmore, "The Borden Case." *American Law Review* 37 (1893), pp. 806–814.]

the fact that the evidence was purely circumstantial and was such as to afford singularly conflicting inferences.

2   In August, 1892, Andrew Jackson Borden was a retired merchant of Fall River, and lived in a house on the east side of Second Street in that city, an important thoroughfare running north and south and faced partly by dwelling houses, partly by business structures. South of the Borden house and closely adjoining was Dr. Kelly's; north of it Mrs. Churchill's; in the rear, but diagonally, Dr. Chagnon's. Mr. Borden was seventy years of age. He was reputed to be worth $300,000 or more, but his family lived in the thrifty and unpretentious style characteristic of New England. The members of the household were Mr. Borden and four others: 1. Mrs. Borden, a short but heavy person, sixty-four years of age, formerly Abby Durfee Gray, now for twenty-five years the second wife of Mr. Borden: 2. Emma Borden, forty-one years of age, a daughter of Mr. Borden's first marriage, and unmarried; 3. Lizzie Andrew Borden, thirty-two years of age, the other child of the first marriage, also unmarried; 4. Bridget Sullivan, a servant who had been with the family nearly three years. Mr. Borden's first wife had died some twenty-eight years before; by the second marriage there was no issue living.

3   In the latter part of July Emma Borden went to visit friends in Fairhaven, an adjacent town. On Wednesday, August 3, however, the number in the household was restored by a brief visit from John V. Morse, a brother of the first wife. He came just after noon, left for a few hours, returned in the evening, sleeping in the house, and went out the next morning. On Tuesday night, August 2, Mr. and Mrs. Borden were taken suddenly ill with a violent vomiting illness; Lizzie Borden was also slightly affected; Bridget Sullivan was not. On Wednesday morning Mrs. Borden consulted a physician as to this illness. On Thursday morning, August 4, the only persons known to be in the house were Mr. and Mrs. Borden, Miss Borden, Mr. Morse, and the servant Bridget Sullivan. Before describing the occurrences of the morning it is necessary to explain the arrangement of the house.

4   The appended plan shows the situation of the rooms on the ground and upper floors.[1] As to the ground floor, it is enough to call attention to the fact that there were three doors only: the front door,

1. See pp. 37–38—Eds.

the kitchen door, and the cellar door; that access from the back door to the front hall might be obtained through the kitchen only, and thence through the sitting-room, or through the dining-room and one or both other rooms, and that in the front hall were two small closets. On the upper floor a doorless partition divided into two small rooms the space over the dining-room. Mr. and Mrs. Borden occupied the room over the kitchen; Lizzie Borden the room over the sitting-room and the front half of the partitioned rooms; and the room over the parlor was used as a guest-room and sewing-room. The door between the rooms of Lizzie Borden and Mr. and Mrs. Borden was permanently locked on both sides (on one by a hook, on the other by a bolt); so that there was no access from the rear part of the upper floor to the front part. Furthermore, the door between the guest-room and Lizzie Borden's room was permanently locked on both sides, and in the latter room a desk stood against the door. In the upper hall over the front door was a clothes closet. As to the condition of the doors below, on August 3 and 4, (1) the front door was locked on Wednesday night by Lizzie Borden, the last one to enter it; the fastening being a spring latch, a bolt, and an ordinary lock; (2) the cellar door (opening into the yard) had been closed on Tuesday and was found locked on Thursday at noon; (3) the kitchen door was locked by Bridget Sullivan on Wednesday night, when she came in (and was found locked by her), but on Thursday morning there was passing in and out, and its condition was not beyond doubt, as we shall see; (4) the door from the bedroom of the Borden couple leading down-stairs was kept locked in their absence from the room. As to the disposition of the inmates of the house on Wednesday, Mr. Morse slept in the guest-chamber, Mr. and Mrs. Borden and Miss Borden in their respective rooms, Bridget Sullivan in the attic at the rear.

On Thursday morning shortly after 6, Bridget Sullivan came down the back stairs, got fuel from the cellar, built the fire, and took in the milk. The kitchen door was thus unlocked, the wooden door being left open, the wire screen door fastened, as usual. Just before 7, Mrs. Borden came down. Then Mr. Borden came down, went out and emptied his slop-pail, and unlocked the barn door. Mr. Morse then came down, and shortly after 7 the three ate breakfast. Mr. Morse left the house at a quarter before 8, Mr. Borden letting him out and locking the door behind him. Lizzie Borden shortly afterwards came down and began her breakfast in the kitchen. At this point Mr. Borden went upstairs to his room, and Bridget went out in the yard, having an attack of vomiting. After a few minutes' absence she returned and found Lizzie Borden absent, Mrs. Borden dusting the dining-room, and Mr. Borden apparently gone down town. Mrs. Borden then directed Bridget to wash the windows on both sides, and left the kitchen, remarking that she had made the bed in the guestroom and was going up to put two pillow-cases on the pillows there. This was the last time that she was seen alive by any witness. Mr. Borden had left the house somewhere between 9 and 9:30.

6   Bridget then set to work at the windows, after getting her implements from the cellar, and here the kitchen door seems to have been unlocked and left so. In cleaning the windows of the sitting-room and the dining-room Bridget found nobody present, both Lizzie Borden and Mrs. Borden being elsewhere. As Bridget went out, Lizzie came to the back door, apparently to hook it; but Bridget seems to have dissuaded her. The washing began with the outside of the windows; Bridget proceeded from the two sitting-room windows (where the screen door, now unlocked, was out of sight) to the parlor-front windows, the parlor side window, and the dining-room windows; and during this time neither Lizzie Borden nor Mrs. Borden appeared on the lower floor. Then Bridget entered by the screen door, hooking it behind her, and proceeded to the washing of the inside of the windows, following the same order as before. While washing the first, some one was heard at the front door. Mr. Borden had come home, and failing to enter the screen door, had come round to the front and was trying the door with his key, but the triple fastening prevented his entrance, and Bridget came and opened it before he was obliged to ring the bell. At this moment a laugh or other exclamation was heard from the daughter on the floor above. She came down shortly to the dining-room where Mr. Borden was, asked if there was any mail, and then volunteered the information, "Mrs. Borden has gone out; she had a note from somebody." It was now 10:45, though by a bare possibility 7 or 8 minutes earlier. Mr. Borden took his key, went up the back stairs (the only way to his room), and came down again just as Bridget had finished the second sitting-room window and was passing to the dining-room. Mr. Borden then sat down in the sitting-room; Bridget began on the dining-room windows; and Lizzie Borden put

an ironing-board on the dining-room table and began to iron handkerchiefs. This conversation ensued:—

"She said, 'Maggie, are you going out this afternoon?' I said, 'I 7
don't know; I might and I might not; I don't feel very well.' She says, 'If you go out, be sure and lock the door, for Mrs. Borden has gone on a sick call, and I might go out too.' Says I, 'Miss Lizzie, who is sick?' 'I don't know; she had a note this morning; it must be in town.'"

Then Bridget, finishing the windows, washed out the cloths in 8
the kitchen; and, while she was there, Lizzie Borden stopped her ironing, came into the kitchen and said:—

"There is a cheap sale of dress goods at Sargent's to-day at 8 cents 9
a yard."

And Bridget said, "I am going to have one." 10

At this point Bridget went upstairs and lay down. In perhaps 3 or 11
4 minutes the City Hall clock struck, and Bridget's watch showed it to be 11 o'clock. Lizzie Borden never finished her ironing. Miss Russell testified (without contradiction) that she afterwards carried the handkerchiefs upstairs, and that there were 4 or 5 finished with 2 or 3 only sprinkled and ready to iron.

The next incident was a cry from below, coming 10 or 15 minutes 12
later:—

"Miss Lizzie hollered: 'Maggie, come down.' I said, 'What is the 13
matter?' She says, 'Come down quick, father's dead. Somebody's come in and killed him.'"

Bridget hurried down-stairs and found the daughter at the back 14
entrance, leaning against the open wooden door, with her back to the screen door. The daughter sent her for Dr. Bowen, and next, on returning, for her friend Miss Russell, Dr. Bowen being absent. While Miss Russell was being sought, Dr. Bowen and the neighbor, Mrs. Churchill, came, the latter first. Mrs. Churchill gave the alarm at a stable near by, and the telephone message reached police headquarters at 11:15. When Bridget came back and mutual suggestion began, as Bridget relates:—

"I says, 'Lizzie, if I knew where Mrs. Whitehead was I would go 15
and see if Mrs. Borden was there and tell her that Mr. Borden was very sick.' She says: 'Maggie, I am almost positive I heard her coming in. Won't you go upstairs to see?' I said: 'I am not going upstairs alone."

16   Mrs. Churchill offered to go with her. They went upstairs, and
as Mrs. Churchill passed up, the door of the guest-room being open,
she saw the clothing of a woman on the floor, the line of sight
running under the bed. She ran on into the room and, standing at
the foot of the bed, saw the dead body of Mrs. Borden stretched on
the floor.[2] It may here be mentioned that the medical testimony
showed, from the temperature of the body, the color and consistency
of the blood, and the condition of the stomach's contents, that Mrs.
Borden's death had occurred between one and two hours earlier,
probably one and one-half hours earlier, than Mr. Borden's,—or not
much later or earlier than 9:30.

17   During this time the other neighbors were with Lizzie Borden,
who had thrown herself on the lounge in the dining-room, not
having been to see her father's or her stepmother's body at any time
since the call for Bridget. At a neighbor's suggestion she went
upstairs to her room, and here without suggestion she afterwards
(within half an hour of the killing) changed her dress and put on a
pink wrapper.

18   Something must now be said in brief description of the manner
in which the two victims had met their death. Mr. Borden's head
bore ten wounds from a cutting instrument wielded with a swing;
the body bore no other injury. The shortest cut was one-half inch
long, the longest was four and one-half inches. Four penetrated the
brain, the skull at the points of penetration being about one-six-
teenth inch thick. The body was found, lying on the right side on
the sofa in the sitting-room, the head nearest the front door, and the
wounds indicated that the assailant stood at or near the head of the
couch and struck down vertically from that direction. Spots of blood
were upon the wall over the sofa (30 to 100), on a picture on the
same wall (40 to 50), on the kitchen door near his feet, and on the
parlor door. On the carpet in front of the sofa, and on a small table
near by, there was no blood. On Mrs. Borden's head and neck (and
not elsewhere) were twenty-two injuries, three ordinary head con-
tusions from falling and nineteen wounds from blows by a cutting
instrument,—of these, one was on the back of the neck and eighteen
on the head. The shortest was one-half inch, the longest three and
one-half inches in length. Four were on the left half of the head,

2. See plan, p. 38.

one being a flap wound made in the flesh by a badly-aimed cut from in front. Some thirteen of these made a hole in the top of the skull, crushing into the brain, this part of Mrs. Borden's skull being about one-eighth inch in thickness and the thinnest part of her skull. There were blood spots on the north wall, on the dressing-case (over 75), and on the east wall. The weapon or weapons employed were apparently hatchets or axes. Upon the premises that day were found two hatchets and two axes. Of these only one offered any opportunity for connection with the killings, for the others had handles so marked with ragged portions that they could not have been cleansed from the blood which they must have received. Of the fourth some mention will be made later.

On Tuesday, Wednesday and Thursday, August 9, 10 and 11, the 19 inquest was held by Judge Blaisdell, and on Thursday evening Lizzie Borden was arrested on charge of committing the murders. The preliminary trial began before Judge Blaisdell, August 25, continuing until September 1, when she was found probably guilty and ordered to be held for the grand jury. The indictment was duly found, and on Monday, June 5, 1893, the trial began in the Superior Court of Bristol County, at the New Bedford Court House. In accord with the law of the State, the Court for such a trial was composed of three judges of the Superior Court of the Commonwealth. Those who officiated on this occasion were Mason, C. J., Blodgett, J., and Dewey, J.

The case for the prosecution was conducted by Hosea M. Knowlton, 20 District Attorney for the County,[3] and Wm. H. Moody, District Attorney of Essex County.[4] The case for the defence was conducted by George D. Robinson,[5] Melvin O. Adams,[6] and Andrew J. Jennings.[7]

We now come to consider the question, what points did the 21 prosecution attempt to make against Lizzie Borden in charging the crime upon her? It endeavored to show, *first,* prior indications, *(a)* Motive, *(b)* Design; *second,* concomitant indications, *(a)* Opportunity, *(b)* Means and Capacity; *third,* posterior indications, *(a)* Consciousness of Guilt. Let us take these in order very briefly.

3. Afterwards Justice of the Massachusetts Supreme Court.
4. Afterwards Justice of the United States Supreme Court.
5. Former Governor of Massachusetts.
6. Eminent at the Boston Bar in the defense of criminal cases.
7. Former partner of Mr. Justice Morton of the Massachusetts Supreme Court.

22   1. *(a) Motive.* The family history was brought in to show that the accused was not on the best of terms with her stepmother. This was evidenced by the testimony of: (1) A dressmaker, who reported that in a conversation held some time previously, when her "mother" was mentioned, she answered: "Don't say 'mother' to me. She is a mean, good-for-nothing old thing. We do not have much to do with her; I stay in my room most of the time." "Why, you come down to your meals?" "Yes, sometimes; but we don't eat with them if we can help it." (2) The servant, who reported that, though she never saw any quarreling, "most of the time they did not eat with the father and mother." (3) The uncle, who did not see Lizzie Borden during the visit from Wednesday noon till Thursday noon: (4) the sister, Emma, who explained the ill-feeling partly on the ground of a small transfer of property by the father to his wife a few years before, and reported that since that time the accused had ceased saying "mother" and addressed her as "Mrs. Borden," and that a gift of other property to the daughters had only partially allayed the ill-feeling; (5) the police officer, who on asking Lizzie Borden on Thursday noon, "When did you last see your mother?" was answered, "She is not my mother. My mother is dead." The general effect of the motive testimony purported to be that the daughters were afraid of the property going to the second wife, to their exclusion, and that this fomented an ill-feeling existing on more or less general grounds of incompatibility.

23   *(b) Design.* No evidence was offered of a specific design to kill with the weapons used. But it was attempted to show a general intention to get rid of the victims: (1) Testimony of a druggist and of by-standers as to an attempted purchase of prussic acid in the forenoon of Wednesday, the day before the killing:—

24   "This party came in there and inquired if I kept prussic acid. I was standing out there; I walked in ahead. She asked me if we kept prussic acid. I informed her that we did. She asked me if she could buy ten cents' worth of me. I informed her that we did not sell prussic acid unless by a physician's prescription. She then said that she had bought this several times, I think; I think she said several times before. I says: 'Well, my good lady, it is something we don't sell unless by a prescription from the doctor, as it is a very dangerous thing to handle.' I understood her to say she wanted it to put on the edge of a seal-skin cape, if I remember rightly. She did not buy

anything, no drug at all, no medicine? No, sir." This was excluded, for reasons to be mentioned later.

(2) Testimony of a conversation on the same Wednesday, during an evening call on Miss Russell, an intimate friend:— 25

The prisoner said: "I have made up my mind, Alice, to take your advice and go to Marion, and I have written there to them that I shall go, but I cannot help feeling depressed; I cannot help feeling that something is going to happen to me; I cannot shake it off. Last night," she said, "we were all sick; Mr. and Mrs. Borden were quite sick and vomited; I did not vomit, and we are afraid that we have been poisoned; the girl did not eat the baker's bread and we did, and we think it may have been the baker's bread." 26

"No," said Miss Russell, "if it had been that, some other people would have been sick in the same way." 27

"Well, it might have been the milk; our milk is left outside upon the steps." 28

"What time is your milk left?" 29

"At 4 o'clock in the morning." 30

"It is light then, and no one would dare to come in and touch it at that time." 31

"Well," said the prisoner, "probably that is so. But father has been having so much trouble with those with whom he has dealings that I am afraid some of them will do something to him; I expect nothing but that the building will be burned down over our heads. The barn has been broken into twice." 32

"That," said Miss Russell, "was merely boys after pigeons." 33

"Well, the house has been broken into in broad daylight when Maggie and Emma and I were the only ones in the house. I saw a man the other night when I went home lurking about the buildings, and as I came he jumped and ran away. Father had trouble with a man the other day about a store. There were angry words, and he turned him out of the house." 34

(3) The suggestion to Bridget that she should go to town and purchase the dress-goods mentioned. 35

2. (a) *Opportunity.* One of the chief efforts of the prosecution was to prove an exclusive opportunity on the part of the accused. The essential result of the testimony bearing on this may be gleaned from what has already been noted. (b) *Means* and *Capacity.* The medical testimony showed that there was nothing in the assaults 36

which a woman of her strength might not have accomplished. The lengthy testimony in regard to the fourth hatchet was directed to showing that it was not incapable of being the weapon used. The handle was broken off; but the presence of ashes on the handle in all other places but the broken end, as well as the appearance of the break, showed that it was a fresh one, and not impossibly one made after the killing; and if thus made, it was not impossible that the hatchet was used in killing, washed, rubbed in ashes, broken off, and the fragment burnt. A strong effort was made by the defense to discredit these results, which rested chiefly on the reports of police officers, but it had little effect.

37   3. *(a) Consciousness of Guilt.* This, with exclusive opportunity, were the main objects of the prosecution's attack. Much that was here offered was excluded, and this exclusion possibly affected the result of the case. The points attempted to be shown were: (1) Falsehoods to prevent detection of the first death; (2) falsehoods as to the doings of the accused; (3) knowledge of the first death; (4) concealment of knowledge of the first death; (5) destruction of suspicious materials.

38   (1) To Bridget and to her father the accused said, as already related, that her mother had received a note and gone out. The same statement she made to Mrs. Churchill and to Marshal Fleet. No note, however, was found; no one who brought a note or sent a note came forward or was heard of; no sound or sight of the sort was perceived by Bridget or any others. The only blot upon an almost perfectly conducted trial was the attempt of the counsel for the defense in argument to show that the information as to the note emanated originally from Bridget and that the accused merely repeated it. This was decidedly a breach of propriety, because it was not merely an argument suggesting the fair possibility of that explanation, but a distinct assertion that the testimony was of that purport, and, therefore, in effect, a false quotation of the testimony. In truth the accused's statement about the note was her own alone and was one of the facts to be explained.

39   (2) Here were charged three falsehoods: *(a)* When the accused was asked where she was at the time of the killing of Mr. Borden, she said that she went out to the barn (to Dr. Bowen) "looking for some iron or irons," (to Miss Russell) "for a piece of iron or tin to fix a screen," (to the mayor and an officer and at the coroner's

inquest)[8] in the barn loft, eating some pears and "looking over lead for sinkers." The inconsistency of the explanations was offered as very suggestive. The day was shown to be a very hot one, and the loft was argued to be too hot for such a sojourn. Moreover Officer Medley testified to going into the barn, in the loft, and finding the floor covered with dust, easily taking an impression from his hand or foot, but on his arrival quite devoid of any traces of the previous presence of another. The trustworthiness of his statements was attacked by witnesses who said that they and others had been there before the officer. The priority of their visits was not placed beyond doubt; but the effect of the officer's statement of course fell from practical proof to a merely probative circumstance.

(b) When the accused was describing her discovery of the father's 40 death, she said (to Officer Mullaly) that she heard "a peculiar noise, something like a scraping noise, and came in and found the door open;" (to the servant) that she heard a groan and rushed in and found her father; (to Mrs. Churchill) that she heard a distress noise, came in, and found her father; (at the inquest) that after eating pears in the loft and looking over lead, she came down, returned to the kitchen, looked in the stove to see if the fire was hot enough for her ironing, found that it was not, put her hat down, started to go upstairs and wait for Bridget's noon-day fire, and thus discovered her father; (to Officer Harrington) that she was up in the loft of the barn and thus did not hear any outcry or noise of any kind; (to Marshal Hilliard) that after half an hour up in the barn, she came in and found her father. Here, again, a substantial inconsistency was charged.

(c) Mr. Borden had on, when found, a pair of congress boots or 41 gaiters; but at the inquest the accused, before this was pointed out, testified that when he came home about 10:45, she assisted him to lie down on the sofa, took off his boots, and put on his slippers.

(3) Her knowledge of the first death was said to have been 42 indicated: *(a)* By the inevitable discovery of the body in the guest-room through the open door, or of the murderer either in passing about or in going up and down the stairs; *(b)* by the noise of the scuffle, if another had done it, and by the thud of the heavy woman's fall; *(c)* by the readiness with which the accused suggested that Mrs.

---

8. Her inquest testimony was excluded, for reasons to be considered later.

Borden must have returned;[9] (1) for as her father had been in the room off the hall from 10:45 to, say, 11, and as she had been out in the barn from 11 till the killing was discovered and others came in, there was no time when the mother could have returned since the father's return, and up to that time the accused herself predicated her absence.

43   (4) If this knowledge existed, then beyond doubt the concealment of it and the pretense of ignorance involved in sending Bridget to get the step-mother was strongly indicative of guilt.

44   (5) Some attempt was made to show a degree of secrecy and obstruction to official investigation of the rooms; but with little or no result. On Sunday morning, however (the officers having informed her on Saturday that she was suspected of the crime), when Emma Borden and Lizzie Borden were in the kitchen and officers were in the yard, Alice Russell came in:—

45   "I saw Miss Lizzie at the other end of the stove, I saw Miss Emma at the sink. Miss Lizzie was at the stove and she had a skirt in her hand, and her sister turned and said: 'What are you going to do?' and Lizzie said, 'I am going to burn this old thing up; it is covered with paint.' I left the room then, and on coming back, Miss Lizzie stood up toward the cupboard door, and she appeared to be either ripping something down or tearing part of this garment. I said to her: 'I wouldn't let anybody see me do that, Lizzie.' She didn't make any answer, but just stepped one step farther back, up toward the cupboard door. . . . Afterwards, I said to them, 'I am afraid, Lizzie, the worst thing you could have done was to burn that dress. I have been asked about your dress.' She said: 'Oh, what made you let me do it? Why didn't you tell me?'"

46   The prosecution naturally attempted, first, to identify this dress as the one worn on the morning of the killing; in this they failed; second, to show at least that the dress worn on that day was missing, and was not the one handed over by the accused, as the dress of that morning. On this point they made out a very strong case. The dress handed over by the accused to the officers as the one worn on Thursday morning, while ironing, and afterwards, was a silk dress, of a dark blue effect; the testimony, however, pointed strongly to

9. This, however, was not argued at the trial. Moreover, no attempt was made to show that Mrs. Borden had no latch-key to the knowledge of the accused.

the wearing of a cotton dress, light blue with a dark figure. Such a dress existed, and had been worn on the day before, but not on Friday or Saturday.

Thus far the prosecution. The defense began with character evidence based on the accused's cooperation in Sunday-school and charitable work and her good standing as a church member. The motive-evidence was not shaken; though the sister of the accused represented the ill-feeling to be of minimum intensity. The design-evidence of prussic acid did not come to the jury. In regard to exclusive opportunity, the defense made no break in the chain of the prosecution, except in showing that the screen door was not closed at all moments during the morning. The evidence as to the possibility of an unseen escape from the house was not potent on either side. But no traces of another person were shown within the house; and no suspicious person was located in the vicinity of the house—if we except some vague reports of a tramp, of a pale, excited young man, and the like, being seen on the street, near by, within a day or an hour of the killing. The attempt failed to show the impossibility of the handleless hatchet having been used—unless we assume (what the defense desired to suggest) that the testimony of all the officers was wilfully false. Coming to the evidence of consciousness of guilt,—the defense could not shake the story of the note; they merely suggested that it might have been a part of the scheme of the murderer to divert suspicion. They searched for the note and they advertised for the sender or carrier, but nothing appeared. The inconsistent stories about going to the barn were explained by the excitement of the moment; the inquest-story—with the most marked divergence—was excluded. Lead was found in the loft; but no fish-line was shown[10] and no screen was identified. It was suggested that perhaps both explanations were true, that both purposes co-existed. The inconsistent stories as to her return and discovery of the murder were in part slid over, in part ignored, and in part discredited.[11]

The discrepancy between the statement about the slippers and the actual foot-coverings did not get to the jury. As to the circum-

47

48

---

10. The lead-for-sinkers statement had not been admitted, but the counsel for the defense took it up in his argument.

11. The inquest-story, going into particulars, had never been admitted; but there were still at least two distinct statements.

stances indicating knowledge, their force was a matter of argument and probability merely; the defense urged the contrary hypotheses which suggest themselves to all. The dress burning was explained by the sister to have taken place in consequence of a suggestion of hers; but Miss Russell's testimony contradicted this. The defense offered to show a custom in the family of burning all old dresses, but this was rejected. Another offer, also rejected, was to show the conduct of a demented-looking man, seen in the woods near the town, a few days after the murder, carrying an axe, and exclaiming "Poor Mrs. Borden!"

49   The stronghold of the defense was the utter absence of all such traces or marks as would presumably be found upon the murderer. No blood was seen upon her by the five or six persons who came in within ten minutes and before she donned the pink wrapper. No garment was found with blood or other traces upon it.[12] No weapon bearing blood or other traces was found within or without the house. One or two of the experts were willing to say that it was practically impossible to deal the twenty-nine blows without receiving more or less blood on the garments and perhaps in the hair (though it does not appear that her head was examined for blood). It is safe to say that this was the decisive fact of the case.

50   It is, of course, impossible to rehearse here all the minor details of evidence and argument offered on either side. It has been necessary to make a summary estimate of the force of certain evidence mentioned.

51   On Tuesday, June 20, at 4:32 in the afternoon, after less than an hour and a half of deliberation, the jury returned a verdict of "not guilty."[13]

12. Except a white skirt having at the back and below a spot of blood as large as a pinhead, the spot being otherwise explainable.

13. It was reported that they were of one mind on the first ballot, and remained an hour in general conversation, at the suggestion of one member, merely to avoid letting the counsel for the Commonwealth suppose that his argument did not receive consideration.

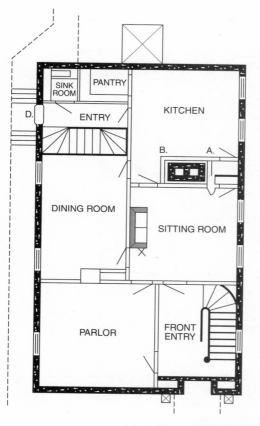

—Adapted from Porter's *Fall River Tragedy*

GROUND FLOOR, BORDEN HOUSE

Mr. Borden's head rested on sofa arm by door—see X—as he took his nap.

A. Lizzie stood here, in angle of coal-closet door, as she burned the dress she had placed on the closet shelf some hours before.
B. Stove in which she burned it.
C. Where Emma was washing the dishes when Lizzie began to burn the dress.

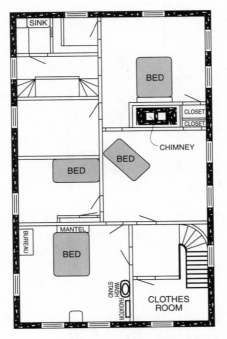

—Adapted from Porter's *Fall River Tragedy*

SECOND FLOOR, BORDEN HOUSE

Note that upstairs guest room can be reached from kitchen entry (D) only by way of the kitchen and sitting room. Shelves at left side of sink room and two sides of pantry; sitting-room closet also filled with shelves. Extremely small broom closet facing stairs at right side of front door is not indicated on this floor plan.

STUDY QUESTIONS

1. Wigmore classifies the evidence in the trial into several categories. Do these categories provide an exhaustive classification for the evidence relevant to a murder charge? Which category of evidence, in general, seems strongest?
2. For each category of evidence, determine whether (a) Lizzie Borden's guilt is consistent with all the evidence, and (b) whether it is the only hypothesis consistent with all the evidence.
3. Diagram the prosecution's overall argument, showing how the various categories of evidence integrate into a case against Lizzie Borden.
4. Do you think Lizzie Borden killed her parents?
5. If you had been on her jury, would you have voted to convict her?

PART TWO

On the Causes of Crime

SIGMUND FREUD

Human Nature Is Inherently Bad

Sigmund Freud (1856–1939) is famous for being the founder of psychoanalysis and for his view of sex as the primary motivating factor in human behavior. He studied medicine at the University of Vienna, and after graduation researched the organic bases of mental disorders. Freud's research led him to the study of hypnosis, which in turn led him to investigate the possibility that our mental lives are shaped primarily by unconscious forces.

[M]en are not gentle creatures who want to be loved, and who at the most can defend themselves if they are attacked; they are, on

[Sigmund Freud, excerpt from *Civilization and Its Discontents*, transl. James Strachey. New York: W. W. Norton, 1962, pp. 58–59.]

the contrary, creatures among whose instinctual endowments is to be reckoned a powerful share of aggressiveness. As a result, their neighbour is for them not only a potential helper or sexual object, but also someone who tempts them to satisfy their aggressiveness on him, to exploit his capacity for work without compensation, to use him sexually without his consent, to seize his possessions, to humiliate him, to cause him pain, to torture and to kill him. *Homo homini lupus*.[1] Who, in the face of all his experience of life and of history, will have the courage to dispute this assertion? As a rule this cruel aggressiveness waits for some provocation or puts itself at the service of some other purpose, whose goal might also have been reached by milder measures. In circumstances that are favourable to it, when the mental counter-forces which ordinarily inhibit it are out of action, it also manifests itself spontaneously and reveals man as a savage beast to whom consideration towards his own kind is something alien. Anyone who calls to mind the atrocities committed during the racial migrations or the invasions of the Huns, or by the people known as Mongols under Jenghiz Khan and Tamerlane, or at the capture of Jerusalem by the pious Crusaders, or even, indeed, the horrors of the recent World War—anyone who calls these things to mind will have to bow humbly before the truth of this view.

2 The existence of this inclination to aggression, which we can detect in ourselves and justly assume to be present in others, is the factor which disturbs our relations with our neighbour and which forces civilization into such a high expenditure [of energy]. In consequence of this primary mutual hostility of human beings, civilized society is perpetually threatened with disintegration. The interest of work in common would not hold it together; instinctual passions are stronger than reasonable interests. Civilization has to use its utmost efforts in order to set limits to man's aggressive instincts and to hold the manifestations of them in check by psychi-cal reaction-formations. Hence, therefore, the use of methods in-tended to incite people into identifications and aim-inhibited rela-tionships of love, hence the restriction upon sexual life, and hence too the ideal's commandment to love one's neighbour as oneself—a commandment which is really justified by the fact that nothing else

1. Man is a wolf to man.—Eds.

runs so strongly counter to the original nature of man. In spite of every effort, these endeavours of civilization have not so far achieved very much. It hopes to prevent the crudest excesses of brutal violence by itself assuming the right to use violence against criminals, but the law is not able to lay hold of the more cautious and refined manifestations of human aggressiveness. . . .

STUDY QUESTIONS

1. Does Freud argue inductively or deductively for his conclusion that humans have an innate "inclination to aggression"? What role does his mentioning of the invasions of the Huns and World War I play in his argument?
2. What does Freud consider "the original nature of man"?
3. Freud states that "instinctual passions are stronger than reasonable interests." Does the existence of long-standing cooperative institutions weaken Freud's claim? Would Freud have to concede that humans also have a "cooperative instinct"?
4. Can you think of explanations for historical atrocities that do not depend upon the existence of human instincts? Does Freud say anything in this passage to rule out such possibilities?

MICHAEL HARRINGTON

Defining Poverty

Michael Harrington, born in 1928 in St. Louis, was a leading American socialist. He was a professor of political science at Queens College, City University of New York, and the author of The Other America, *from which the following excerpt is taken.*

1   In the nineteenth century, conservatives in England used to argue against reform on the grounds that the British worker of the time had a longer life expectancy than a medieval nobleman.

2   This is to say that a definition of poverty is, to a considerable extent, a historically conditioned matter. Indeed, if one wanted to play with figures, it would be possible to prove that there are no poor people in the United States, or at least only a few whose plight is as desperate as that of masses in Hong Kong. There is starvation in American society, but it is not a pervasive social problem as it is in some of the newly independent nations. There are still Americans who literally die in the streets, but their numbers are comparatively small.

3   This abstract approach toward poverty in which one compares different centuries or societies has very real consequences. For the nineteenth century British conservative, it was a way of ignoring the plight of workers who were living under the most inhuman conditions. The twentieth-century conservative would be shocked

[Michael Harrington, excerpt from the Appendix to *The Other America: Poverty in the United States*. New York: Pelican Books, 1971, pp. 187–190.]

and appalled in an advanced society if there were widespread
conditions like those of the English cities a hundred years ago. Our
standards of decency, of what a truly human life requires, change,
and they should.

There are two main aspects of this change. First, there are new
definitions of what man can achieve, of what a human standard of
life should be. In recent times this has been particularly true since
technology has consistently broadened man's potential: it has made
a longer, healthier, better life possible. Thus, in terms of what is
technically possible, we have higher aspirations. Those who suffer
levels of life well below those that are possible, even though they
live better than medieval knights or Asian peasants, are poor.

Related to this technological advance is the social definition of
poverty. The American poor are not poor in Hong Kong or in the
sixteenth century; they are poor here and now, in the United States.
They are dispossessed in terms of what the rest of the nation enjoys,
in terms of what the society could provide if it had the will. They
live on the fringe, the margin. They watch the movies and read the
magazines of affluent America, and these tell them that they are
internal exiles.

To some, this description of the feelings of the poor might seem
to be out of place in discussing a definition of poverty. Yet if this
book indicates anything about the other America, it is that this sense
of exclusion is the source of a pessimism, a defeatism that intensifies
the exclusion. To have one bowl of rice in a society where all other
people have half a bowl may well be a sign of achievement and
intelligence; it may spur a person to act and to fulfill his human
potential. To have five bowls of rice in a society where the majority
have a decent, balanced diet is a tragedy.

This point can be put another way in defining poverty. One of
the consequences of our new technology is that we have created new
needs. There are more people who live longer. Therefore they need
more. In short, if there is technological advance without social
advance, there is, almost automatically, an increase in human
misery, in impoverishment.

And finally, in defining poverty one must also compute the social
cost of progress. One of the reasons that the income figures show
fewer people today with low incomes than twenty years ago is that
more wives are working now, and family income has risen as a

4

5

6

7

8

result. In 1940, 15 per cent of wives were in the labor force; in 1957 the figure was 30 per cent. This means that there was more money and, presumably, less poverty.

9   Yet a tremendous growth in the number of working wives is an expensive way to increase income. It will be paid for in terms of the impoverishment of home life, of children who receive less care, love, and supervision. This one fact, for instance, might well play a significant role in the problems of the young in America. It could mean that the next generation, or a part of it, will have to pay the bill for the extra money that was gained. It could mean that we have made an improvement in income statistics at the cost of hurting thousands and hundreds of thousands of children. If a person has more money but achieves this through mortgaging the future, who is to say that he or she is no longer poor?

10   It is difficult to take all these imponderables together and to fashion them into a simple definition of poverty in the United States. Yet this analysis should make clear some of the assumptions that underlie the assertions in this book:

11   Poverty should be defined in terms of those who are denied the minimal levels of health, housing, food, and education that our present stage of scientific knowledge specifies as necessary for life as it is now lived in the United States.

12   Poverty should be defined psychologically in terms of those whose place in the society is such that they are internal exiles who, almost inevitably, develop attitudes of defeat and pessimism and who are therefore excluded from taking advantage of new opportunities.

13   Poverty should be defined absolutely, in terms of what man and society could be. As long as America is less than its potential, the nation as a whole is impoverished by that fact. As long as there is the other America, we are, all of us, poorer because of it.

STUDY QUESTIONS

1. In paragraphs 11–13, Harrington offers three guidelines for defining poverty. Summarize this information into a single concise definition.

2. Central to Harrington's psychological dimension of poverty is his notion of an "internal exile." Does he use this concept literally or metaphorically? If he uses it metaphorically, does it violate the rule that prohibits metaphorical definitions?

3. In paragraph 9, Harrington suggests that an increase in the number of working wives "will be paid for in terms of the impoverishment of home life." What evidence does he provide for this?

4. How would Harrington respond to the following objection: "Poverty should not be defined relatively, because poverty is a matter of basic needs not being met, and while people's *expectations* have increased, their basic *needs* have stayed the same"?

5. Does Harrington's argument depend on an assumed premise to the effect that one's material circumstances determine one's psychological outlook? Suppose, for instance, that two individuals have the same minimal amount of money and education, but while one feels optimistic about his or her future, the other feels pessimistic. Would Harrington say they are equally poor? Do you agree?

DAVID RUBINSTEIN

Don't Blame Crime on Joblessness

David Rubinstein is a professor of sociology at the University of Illinois at Chicago. The following selection on the relation-

[David Rubinstein, "Don't Blame Crime on Joblessness." *The Wall Street Journal*, November 9, 1992, op-ed page.]

ship between crime and unemployment first appeared in the
op-ed page of The Wall Street Journal.

1   The California Assembly Special Committee on the Los Angeles crisis recently released its findings on the riots of last spring. Unsurprisingly, the report echoes the Kerner Commission of a generation ago by emphasizing lack of economic opportunity as a major cause of the riots and the high crime rates in South Central Los Angeles.

2   The coincidence of crime and unemployment in places like South Central Los Angeles seems to confirm their connection. And it makes sense motivationally. Surely an absence of employment can make crime an attractive option, and so enhanced job opportunities ought to make it less so. University of Chicago economist Gary S. Becker just won the Nobel Prize for this sort of reasoning.

3   But there are profound anomalies in this analysis. First, the place of crime in the life cycle is odd. One would think that limited job options would mean more to a man approaching 30 than to a teen-ager. But conviction rates for men between 25 and 30 are about one-third the rates for boys between 14 and 16. Similarly, a man with a family faces more urgent economic imperatives than a single man, and yet his inclination to crime is far less. It is noteworthy that women, despite various economic barriers, are invariably less prone to crime than men.

4   Also, it is hard to see crimes like rape, drug addiction, most homicides and assaults as substitutes for legitimate employment. Even profit-oriented crime is often of doubtful economic benefit. The take in most petty street crimes is so low that, even with a small chance of arrest for any single crime, a perpetrator will likely be jailed before he equals a year's income from a minimum wage job.

5   With a little ingenuity, the economic interpretation can be stretched to "explain" crimes that lack economic sense. While stabbing someone in a bar fight, using drugs or setting fire to a store are hardly substitutes for gainful employment, such crimes might be interpreted as "ultimately" reflecting the frustrations of blocked opportunities.

6   But all such theories founder on a striking fact: the nearly invisible relationship between unemployment and crime rates. Charting homicide since 1900 reveals two peaks. The first is in 1933. This represents the crest of a wave that began in 1905, continued

through the prosperous '20s and then began to *decline* in 1934 as the Great Depression was deepening. Between 1933 and 1940, the murder rate dropped nearly 40%. Property crimes reveal a similar pattern.

Between 1940 and 1960 the homicide rate remained relatively stable. In the early '60s, a sharp increase began that peaked in 1974, when the murder rate was more than double that of the late 1950s, and far higher than it had been in the depths of the Depression. Between 1963 and 1973 homicides in New York City tripled. Again, property and most other forms of crime followed a similar pattern.

The cause of this remarkable increase in crime certainly was not unemployment—which was, by contemporary standards, enviably low. In 1961, the unemployment rate was 6.6% and the crime rate was 1.9 per 1,000. By 1969, unemployment had dropped to 3.4% while the crime rate nearly doubled to 3.7 per 1,000. The incidence of robbery nearly tripled. Interestingly, the recession of 1980 to 1982 was accompanied by a small but clearly discernible drop in crime. As the economy revived, so did the crime rate.

These patterns are well known to criminologists. A review of several studies by Thomas Orsagh concluded that "unemployment may affect the crime rate, but even if it does, its general effect is too slight to be measured." Another survey by Richard Freeman concluded that the relationship is so weak that, if unemployment were cut by 50%, the crime rate would drop by only 5%. Some criminologists seriously entertain the thesis that crime, like any other form of "business" activity, turns up in good times.

Despite this evidence, the idea that crime can be substantially cut by enhanced employment opportunities remains deeply entrenched, even in the social sciences. Ours is a materialistic culture. We believe that people are driven by calculations of economic gain and that money can solve a host of social problems. But human motivation is far more diverse, and often darker, than this. Just as money spent on health care can do little to counter the effects of destructive life styles, and money spent on schools cannot overcome a lack of motivation to learn, pouring money into America's inner cities to enhance employment opportunities will do little to make them safer.

When considering what to do about crime in places like South Central Los Angeles, it is worth recalling the relationship between

7

8

9

10

11

crime and economic deprivation in a different part of California at a different time: "During the 1960s, one neighborhood in San Francisco had the lowest income, the highest unemployment rate, the highest proportion of families with incomes under $4,000 a year, the least educational attainment, the highest tuberculosis rate, and the highest proportion of substandard housing. . . . That neighborhood was called Chinatown. Yet in 1965, there were only five persons of Chinese ancestry committed to prison in the entire state of California."

12   This quote, taken from *Crime and Human Nature* by James Q. Wilson and Richard Herrnstein, suggests that economic theories tell us more about our misunderstandings of human motivation than about the causes of crime. It also suggests that policy planners would rather speak of factors that are within the reach of government programs than those, like weak families and a culture that fails to restrain, that are truly related to crime.

STUDY QUESTIONS

1. In the first two paragraphs, Rubinstein sketches the argument that he disagrees with. Rewrite that argument into standard form.

2. Rubinstein presents three deductive arguments in paragraph 5—one based on comparing men between ages 25 and 30 with boys between ages 14 and 16; one based on comparing men with families with single men; and one based on comparing women with men. All of these arguments contain assumed premises. Supply the assumed premises and reconstruct the arguments into standard form.

3. In paragraphs 6 to 8, Rubinstein presents a series of statistics correlating the homicide rate and unemployment rates. In concluding that unemployment does not lead to crime, which of Mill's Methods is he using?

4. At the end of his article, Rubinstein hypothesizes that "weak families and a culture that fails to restrain" are actual causes of crime. In support of this hypothesis he offers two analogies in paragraph 10, and in paragraph 11 he mentions San

Francisco's Chinatown in the 1960s. How much support do these give to his hypothesis?

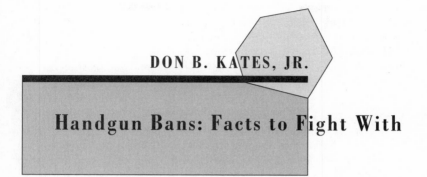

DON B. KATES, JR.

Handgun Bans: Facts to Fight With

Donald Kates, Jr., is an attorney, the author of Firearms and Violence: Issues of Public Policy, *and a leading advocate of the right to own firearms. His most recent book, co-authored with Gary Kleck, is* The Great American Gun Debate. *In the following selection Kates defends handgun ownership on a number of grounds, one of which is the surprising claim that gun ownership may reduce crime.*

The handgun debate has produced a plethora of emotional rhetoric on both sides of the issue, but very little hard research. On one side are the emotional bumper-sticker slogans full of patriotic posturing. On the other are equally emotional and sensationalized horror stories of innocent citizens killed by handguns, supplemented by supposedly neutral but, in fact, "result-oriented" social science research that is either misleading or downright inaccurate.

Gun owners nod enthusiastically at "Guns Don't Kill People, People Do" and "When Guns are Outlawed, Only Outlaws Will Have Guns," but such cliches are virtually useless in intelligent debate with someone who is not committedly pro-gun. Guns *do* kill people, just as knives and hand grenades do. If they didn't kill or

1

2

[Don B. Kates, Jr., "Handgun Bans—Facts to Fight With," in *Guns and Ammo Annual, 1984.* Los Angeles: Petersen, 1984, pp. 4, 6, 8–11.]

injure or at least present that threat, they would be useless as instruments of self-defense. And even if "Only Outlaws Will Have Guns" if guns are outlawed, anti-gun forces have made it clear that they are willing to tolerate firearms possession by hardened criminals if a handgun ban would result in disarming the self-protection owner whom they believe responsible for murder.

3   If this characterization of murderers were accurate, banning handguns would seem an appealingly simple means of reducing domestic and acquaintance homicide. Most killings are not, however, perpetrated by the average noncriminal citizen whose law-obedient mentality (it is believed) would induce him to give up handguns in response to a ban. Refuting "the myth that the typical homicide offender is just an ordinary person" with "no previous criminal record," Professor Gary Kleck of Florida State University's School of Criminology notes F.B.I. figures showing two-thirds of all murderers to have previous felony conviction records.

4   Moreover, a murderer's prior arrest record is likely to substantially underrepresent the real prior violence history. Unlike robbers, who generally strike at strangers, murderers' prior violence may have been directed against relatives or acquaintances, that is, the same kinds of people murderers end up killing. Such prior violent incidents may have never led to arrest or conviction, either because the victim did not press charges or because the police refuse to interfere in "a family affair." A study in Kansas City revealed that in 85 percent of domestic homicide cases, the police have had to be summoned to the home at least once before the killing occurred, and in 50 percent of the cases, the police had stopped beatings five or more times before the actual murder. In short, these people are criminals no less hardened than the professional robbers whom everyone agrees a handgun ban won't disarm. Unlike the average citizen, the typical murderer will not scruple to keep his gun in spite of a ban.

5   Unfortunately, the quality of most research associated with handgun control has been on par with the sort found in UFO magazines. Another example is the tired old line about gun controls working in Europe and Japan. The gun bans of the European countries commonly compared to the U.S. were not enacted to reduce general violence (with which those countries have been little affected), but were enacted to prevent the assassinations and politi-

cal terrorism from which England, Germany, and so forth, still suffer far more than we.

In fact, prohibitionists abruptly stopped referring to England in 6 1971 with the appearance from Cambridge University of the first in-depth study of that country's handgun permit law. This Cambridge study attributes England's comparatively low violence wholly to cultural factors, pointing out that until 1920 England had far fewer gun controls than most American states. Yet England had far less violence at that time than did those states or than England now has. Those who blame greater handgun availability for our greater rates of handgun homicide ignore the fact that rates of murder with knives or without any weapon (i.e., with hands and feet) are also far lower in England. The study's author rhetorically asks whether it is claimed that knives are less available in England than in the U.S. or that the English have fewer hands and feet than Americans. As a subsequent British government publication puts it, although "one reason often given for American homicide is the easy availability of firearms . . . the strong correlation with racial and linked socio-economic variables suggests that the underlying determinants of the homicide rate relate to particular cultural factors."

European comparisons would be incomplete without mention of 7 Switzerland, where violence rates are very low though every man of military age is required to own a handgun or fully automatic rifle. Israeli violence is similarly low, though the populace is even more intensively armed. A comparison with handgun-banning Japan's low homicide rate is plainly inappropriate because of our vastly different culture and heritage and our substantial ethnic heterogeneity. (The only valid comparison reinforces the irrelevancy of gun bans: It is that Japanese-Americans, with full access to handguns, have a slightly lower homicide rate than their gunless counterparts in Japan.) An appropriate comparison to Japan would be Taiwan. Despite even more stringent anti-handgun laws, it has a homicide rate greater than ours and four times greater than Japan's. Similarly the U.S. might well be compared to South Africa, a highly industrialized and ethnically heterogeneous country. Despite one of the world's most stringent "gun control" programs, South Africa's homicide rate, factoring out politically associated killings, is twice ours.

The moral of the story is that nothing about the correlation 8 between levels of handgun ownership and violent crimes could lead one to conclude there is a cause and effect relationship. But it is simply taken for granted by many that there *is* a relationship, and they cite only those countries that have lower crime rates than America to "prove" it.

9   Writers on both sides of the barricade have too often started with conclusions and worked to justify them. For that reason, much of the best research has come not from conservative sources that have traditionally supported the right to own handguns, but from those who have converted to a position favorable to handgun ownership and feel a need to explain their aberrant positions.

10   In order to understand the preponderance of misinformation in the handgun ownership debate, it is necessary to trace some of the ideas that the anti-gun movement has used to justify its position. In my book *Firearms and Violence: Issues of Public Policy* (San Francisco: Pacific Institute for Public Policy Research, 1983), Gary Kleck of the Florida State University School of Criminology and David Bordua of the University of Illinois, Urbana, Department of Sociology have identified what they call "the key assumptions of gun control." The first we will consider for this article is:

People who buy guns for self-defense are the victims of self-deception and a mistaken belief in the protective efficacy of gun ownership. In fact, guns are useless for self-defense or protection of a home or business.

11   Fundamental to systematic discussion of these issues is the distinction between the self-defense value that gun ownership may have and its crime deterrence value. Anti-gun lobbyists are unassailably correct in asserting that a gun owner rarely has the opportunity to defend a home or business against burglars who generally take pains to strike only at unoccupied premises. But this fails to address two important issues of deterrence. Kleck and Bordua calculate that a burglar's small chance of being confronted by a gun-armed defender probably exceeds that of his being apprehended, tried, convicted and actually serving any time. Which, they ask, is a greater deterrent: a slim chance of being punished or a slim chance of being shot?

12   Even more important, fear of meeting a gun-armed defender may be one factor in the care most burglars take to strike at only unoccupied premises. In this connection, remember that it is pre-

cisely because burglary is generally a nonconfrontation crime that victim injury or death is so very rarely associated with it—in contrast to robbery, where victim death is an all too frequent occurrence. If the deterrent effect of victim gun possession helps to make burglary an overwhelmingly nonconfrontational crime, thereby minimizing victim death or injury, that effect *benefits* burglary victims generally, even if the gun owners gain no particular self-defense value thereby.

The most recent evidence of the deterrent value of gun owner- 13 ship appears in a survey taken in 10 major prisons across the United States by the Social and Demographic Research Institute of the University of Massachusetts. It confirms earlier prison surveys in which inmates stated that (1) they and other criminals tried to avoid victims they believed may have been armed and that (2) they favor gun prohibition because, by disarming the victim, it will make their lives safer without affecting their access to illegal guns.

Increasingly, police are concluding and even publicly proclaim- 14 ing that they cannot protect the law-abiding citizens and that it is not only rational to choose to protect oneself with firearms but societally beneficial because it deters violent crimes. Because of the lack of coherent evidence on the subject until the late 1970s, such views necessarily were only intuitively or anecdotally based. They were controverted by the citation of isolated, artificially truncated statistics supposedly showing that citizens rarely are able to kill criminals in self-defense. In fact, civilians justifiably kill about as many violent criminals across the nation as do the police. In California and Miami, private citizens kill twice as many criminals; in Chicago and Cleveland, three times as many.

Even when accurately reported, such statistics are unfair in that 15 they underrepresent the full self-defense value of guns; as with the police, the measure of the success of armed citizens lies not in the number of criminals they kill, but in the total number whom they defeat by wounding, driving off, or arresting. In his paper for *Firearms and Violence,* Professor Wright concludes that incidents of people defending themselves with handguns are even more numerous than incidents of handgun misuse by criminals against citizens. In other words, while there are all too many crimes committed with handguns, there are even more crimes being foiled by law-abiding gun owners.

16   In his extensive study of Atlanta data, Philip Cook concluded that a robber's chance of dying in any one year in that city is doubled by committing only seven robberies because of the risk of counterattack by a potential victim. In addition to illustrating the self-defense value of handgun ownership, that is a pretty good indication of the kind of deterrent effect caused by gun ownership. Cook's work also shows that areas with the strongest anti-gun laws have the highest rates of crime. That in itself does not prove anything except the spurious nature of the data distributed by anti-gun forces that purports to prove the opposite. Since high crime rates often lead governments to seek solutions in gun bans, the correlation between gun control and high crime rates does not necessarily prove that bans cause violence. But more meaningful correlations can be found when examining the opposite case, where the public has actually *increased* the level of gun ownership.

17   The Orlando Police Department, when plagued with a sharply rising number of rapes in the city, undertook a firearms training program for women between October 1966 and March 1967. Kleck and Bordua studied the effects of the program and found that the rape rate in Orlando fell by almost 90 percent from a level of 35.91 per 100,000 inhabitants in 1966 to 4.18 in 1967. The surrounding areas and Florida in general experienced either constant or increasing rape rates during the same period, as did the United States in general. Another benefit from the program seems to have been the corresponding decrease in Orlando burglaries. Though the rape-protection program was well-publicized, the anti-burglary aspect of gun ownership and training was not emphasized in the press. Burglars apparently made a connection between women's willingness and capability to defend their bodies and the increased risk of taking their property.

18   Similar programs have resulted in decreasing store robberies by as much as 90 percent in Highland Park and Detroit, Michigan, and New Orleans. Perhaps the most publicized is that of Kennesaw, Georgia, where the city council passed a kind of reverse gun control act requiring citizens to keep guns in their homes. In the ten months that followed, there was an 89 percent decrease in burglary.

19   These programs have been criticized on the theory that the crime rate has not been lowered but simply shifted to other areas. This does not appear to have been the case in Orlando. There rape fell

by 9 percent in the surrounding communities even as it fell by 90 percent in Orlando in the first year after the handgun training program was publicized. Also, criticisms that gun ownership is causing crime to shift to non-gun-owning areas are based on the perverse idea that defending oneself from rape or burglary is really an offense against others who do not.

It is not likely that women who are willing and able to protect themselves from rapists would have much sympathy with that view, even if it were true. To take the argument to its logical conclusion, one would have to admit that anybody who does anything to discourage crime (locking doors, calling for help, summoning the police, or staying indoors and out of alleys at night) is endangering the others who will not.

The evidence does show gun ownership acts as a deterrent to criminal activity for those who own them *and* those who do not. Opponents of handgun ownership get around that by saying:

Handguns are more dangerous to their owners and the family and friends of the owners than they are to criminals. Handguns kill more people through accident and criminal assault than they save.

Once again, there have been several widely quoted studies supporting this view that have become part of the conscious and subconscious rationale for banning handguns. One study, by Rushforth, purported to show that six times as many Cleveland householders died in gun accidents as killed burglars. It was discredited by Professor James Wright of the University of Massachusetts at Amherst in his paper for the 1981 annual meeting of the American Society of Criminology. Research done with San Francisco City Supervisor Carol Ruth Silver has indicated that between 1960 and 1975 the number of instances where handguns were used for defense exceeded the cases where they were misused to kill by a ratio of 15 to 1.

According to a monitoring of 42 of the nation's largest newspapers between June 1975 and July 1976, 68 percent of the time that police used firearms, they successfully prevented a crime or caught the criminal. On the other hand, the success rate for private citizens was 83 percent. This is not particularly surprising since the police must usually be summoned to the scene of criminal activity while the private gun owner is more likely to be there when it occurs. At the same time, Kleck and Bordua conclude that citizens who resist crimes with weapons are much less likely to be injured than those who attempt to resist without weapons.

24   Anti-gun forces cover themselves in the question of self-defense by asserting that the absence of handguns will lead criminals to use other less dangerous weapons, lowering the death and injury rate in confrontations with criminals. The heart of the argument, as stated by Kleck and Bordua, is:

Guns are five times deadlier than the weapons most likely to be substituted for them in assaults where firearms are not available.

25   To begin with, the above statement does not differentiate between different types of guns. Most anti-gun measures are aimed at handguns because banning all guns is politically unlikely. Furthermore, the statement is based on the assumption that the second choice for a criminal who is denied a handgun would be a knife. In fact, a Massachusetts University survey of 10 major prisons indicates that in the majority of cases, a criminal denied access to a handgun will turn to a sawed-off shotgun or long rifle. Approximately 50 percent of all criminals and 75 percent of those with a history of handgun use said they would use a sawed-off shotgun or rifle. While handguns are slightly more deadly than knives, shotguns and rifles are three to eight times as deadly as handguns. If handguns disappeared but only 19 percent of criminals turned to long guns, the same amount of fatalities could be expected to occur. If 50 percent used shotguns or rifles, there would actually be an increase in assault-related deaths by as much as 300 percent.

26   Another danger associated with the upgrading of firearms due to a handgun ban is the increased risk of accidental wounds and fatalities due to the longer range of shotguns and rifles. This would be the likely consequence of a measure banning handguns but allowing the ownership of long guns for self-defense. A shot from a handgun that misses its target will usually come to rest in a wall much sooner than a shotgun or rifle blast, which is much more likely to continue on to impact whatever is on the other side of the wall. The danger of accidental death increases enormously when long guns replace handguns as the arm kept for home defense. Even now, long guns are involved in 90 percent of all accidental firearms deaths, though they probably represent less than 10 percent of the guns kept loaded at any one time.

27   So we see, handgun ownership is more than a civil liberty, it is

valuable for society as a whole. Given the obvious nature of the analyses, it is surprising that the anti-gun forces in this country have succeeded to the degree they have.

Recent court decisions have made it clear that the government   28
has no responsibility to protect the citizenry. In an important case, *Warren* vs. *District of Columbia*, three women brought suit against the local government because of lack of police action. Two men broke into their home and found one of the women. The other two were upstairs and called the police twice over a period of half an hour. After the woman downstairs had been beaten, raped and sodomized into silence, her roommates believed that the police had arrived. They went downstairs and "for the next 14 hours the women were held captive, raped, robbed, beaten, forced to commit sexual acts upon each other, and made to submit to the sexual demands of [their attackers]." The three women lost their suit and an appeal because, as the courts universally hold, "a government and its agents are under no general duty to provide public services, such as police protection to any particular citizen."

This incident and many others like it took place in the city with   29
the most stringent anti-gun law in the country. The D.C. law required handgun owners to register their guns and then disallowed the ownership of any new arms. Furthermore, the law made it illegal to keep a firearm assembled or loaded in the home for self-defense. There is a real ideological question as to whether a government can disclaim responsibility to protect its citizens *and* take away their means to protect themselves. Pragmatically though, one must admit that the government is basically unable to protect every citizen at all times, regardless of the legal position.

What good are handguns? The evidence has led many to believe   30
that they are the largest single deterrent against crime. A recent study conducted by the Boston Police Department showed that the majority of high-ranking police administrators and police chiefs across the nation actually favor allowing law-abiding citizens to *carry* guns for self-protection. What can be done about the well-intentioned but misinformed foes of the handgun? Perhaps the most important thing would be the self-education of those who already defend that right. Only with intelligent, informed argument can the gun banners be convinced of the foolishness of their position. It is too easy to blame the media for bias or lack of information. Those

who hold a position also have a responsibility to be informed and put those arguments forward. I hope that this article will help to do that.

STUDY QUESTIONS

1. Kates's overall conclusion is that handguns should not be banned. In defending this conclusion, he argues five major claims:
   (1) Handgun bans will not reduce crime;
   (2) Cultural factors, not the legality of handguns, are responsible for the United States' crime rate;
   (3) Handguns have a self-defense value and a deterrence value;
   (4) Handguns are not more dangerous to their owners, friends, and families than they are to criminals;
   (5) If handguns are banned, gun fatalities are likely to increase.
   Identify the major premises Kates uses to support each claim.
2. In paragraphs 5 through 8, Kates is arguing for claim (2), i.e., that comparing the United States with other countries does not help the anti-gun position. Find an example of a negative use of Mill's Methods in this argument.
3. In paragraph 17, Kates is arguing in support of claim (3) by arguing that a firearms-training program for women in Orlando was causally responsible for the decline in the rape rate the following year. Which of Mill's Methods is Kates using in this argument?
4. At the end of paragraph 25, Kates states: "If 50 percent [of criminals] used shotguns or rifles, there would actually be an increase in assault-related deaths by as much as 300 percent." Is this a statistic Kates cites, or is it the conclusion of an argument?
5. In the essay in favor of banning handguns that follows, do John Henry Sloan, et al., raise any arguments that Kates has not addressed in this essay?

JOHN HENRY SLOAN, ET AL.

Handgun Regulations, Crime, Assaults, and Homicide: A Tale of Two Cities

In the following article, a team of medical doctors uses the results of a comparative study of Seattle, Washington, and Vancouver, British Columbia, to argue that good empirical evidence exists to support the conclusion that banning handguns will reduce crime.

Abstract: To investigate the associations among handgun regulations, assault and other crimes, and homicide, we studied robberies, burglaries, assaults, and homicides in Seattle, Washington, and Vancouver, British Columbia, from 1980 through 1986.

Although similar to Seattle in many ways, Vancouver has adopted a more restrictive approach to the regulation of handguns. During the study period, both cities had similar rates of burglary and robbery. In Seattle, the annual rate of assault was modestly higher than that in Vancouver (simple assault: relative risk, 1.18; 95 percent confidence interval, 1.15 to 1.20; aggravated assault: relative risk, 1.16; 95 percent confidence interval, 1.12 to 1.19). However, the rate of assaults involving firearms was seven times higher in Seattle than in Vancouver. Despite similar overall rates of criminal activity and assault, the relative risk of death from homicide, adjusted for age and sex, was significantly higher in Seattle than in Vancouver (relative risk, 1.63; 95 percent confidence inter-

1

2

[John Henry Sloan, Arthur L. Kellermann, Donald T. Reay, James A. Ferris, Thomas Koepsell, Frederick P. Rivara, Charles Rice, Laurel Gray, and James LoGerfo, "Handgun Regulations, Crime, Assaults, and Homicide: A Tale of Two Cities." *New England Journal of Medicine* 319, November 10, 1988, pp. 1256–1262.]

val, 1.28 to 2.08). Virtually all of this excess risk was explained by a 4.8-fold higher risk of being murdered with a handgun in Seattle as compared with Vancouver. Rates of homicide by means other than guns were not substantially different in the two study communities.

3   We conclude that restricting access to handguns may reduce the rate of homicide in a community.

4   Approximately 20,000 persons are murdered in the United States each year, making homicide the 11th leading cause of death and the 6th leading cause of the loss of potential years of life before age 65.[1–3] In the United States between 1960 and 1980, the death rate from homicide by means other than firearms increased by 85 percent. In contrast, the death rate from homicide by firearms during this same period increased by 160 percent.[3]

5   Approximately 60 percent of homicides each year involve firearms. Handguns alone account for three fourths of all gun-related homicides.[4] Most homicides occur as a result of assaults during arguments or altercations; a minority occur during the commission of a robbery or other felony.[2,4] Baker has noted that in cases of assault, people tend to reach for weapons that are readily available.[5] Since attacks with guns more often end in death than attacks with knives, and since handguns are disproportionately involved in intentional shootings, some have argued that restricting access to handguns could substantially reduce our annual rate of homicide.[5–7]

6   To support this view, advocates of handgun control frequently cite data from countries like Great Britain and Japan, where the rates of both handgun ownership and homicide are substantially lower than those in the United States.[8] Rates of injury due to assault in Denmark are comparable to those in northeastern Ohio, but the Danish rate of homicide is only one fifth as high as Ohio's.[5,6] In Denmark, the private ownership of guns is permitted only for hunting, and access to handguns is tightly restricted.[6]

7   Opponents of gun control counter with statistics from Israel and Switzerland, where the rates of gun ownership are high but homicides are relatively uncommon.[9] However, the value of comparing data from different countries to support or refute the effectiveness of gun control is severely compromised by the large number of potentially confounding social, behavioral, and economic factors that characterize large national groups. To date, no study has been

able to separate the effects of handgun control from differences among populations in terms of socioeconomic status, aggressive behavior, violent crime, and other factors.[7] To clarify the relation between firearm regulations and community rates of homicide, we studied two large cities in the Pacific Northwest: Seattle, Washington, and Vancouver, British Columbia. Although similar in many ways, these two cities have taken decidedly different approaches to handgun control.

Methods

STUDY SITES

Seattle and Vancouver are large port cities in the Pacific Northwest. Although on opposite sides of an international border, they are only 140 miles apart, a three-hour drive by freeway. They share a common geography, climate, and history. Citizens in both cities have attained comparable levels of schooling and have almost identical rates of unemployment. When adjusted to U.S. dollars, the median annual income of a household in Vancouver exceeds that in Seattle by less than $500. Similar percentages of households in both cities have incomes of less than $10,000 (U.S.) annually. Both cities have large white majorities. However, Vancouver has a larger Asian population, whereas Seattle has larger black and Hispanic minorities (Table 1).[10,11] The two communities also share many cultural values and interests. Six of the top nine network television programs in Seattle are among the nine most watched programs in Vancouver.[12,13]

FIREARM REGULATIONS

Although similar in many ways, Seattle and Vancouver differ markedly in their approaches to the regulation of firearms (Table 2). In Seattle, handguns may be purchased legally for self-defense in the street or at home. After a 30-day waiting period, a permit can

Table 1 SOCIOECONOMIC CHARACTERISTICS AND RACIAL AND ETHNIC COMPOSITION OF THE POPULATIONS IN SEATTLE AND VANCOUVER

Index	Seattle	Vancouver
1980 Population	493,846	415,220
1985–1986 Population estimate	491,400	430,826
Unemployment rate (%)	5.8	6.0
High-school graduates (%)	79.0	66.0
Median household income (U.S. dollars)	16,254	16,681
Households with incomes $10,000 (U.S.) (%)	30.6	28.9
Ethnic and racial groups (%)		
White (non-Hispanic)	79.2	75.6
Asian	7.4	22.1
Black	9.5	0.3
Hispanic	2.6	0.5
Native North American	1.3	1.5

be obtained to carry a handgun as a concealed weapon. The recreational use of handguns is minimally restricted.[15]

10   In Vancouver, self-defense is not considered a valid or legal reason to purchase a handgun. Concealed weapons are not permitted. Recreational uses of handguns (such as target shooting and collecting) are regulated by the province, and the purchase of a handgun requires a restricted-weapons permit. A permit to carry a weapon must also be obtained in order to transport a handgun, and these weapons can be discharged only at a licensed shooting club. Handguns can be transported by car, but only if they are stored in the trunk in a locked box.[16,17]

11   Although they differ in their approach to firearm regulations, both cities aggressively enforce existing gun laws and regulations, and convictions for gun-related offenses carry similar penalties. For example, the commission of a class A felony (such as murder or robbery) with a firearm in Washington State adds a minimum of two years of confinement to the sentence for the felony.[18] In the

Table 2 REGULATION AND OWNERSHIP OF FIREARMS AND LAW-ENFORCEMENT ACTIVITY IN SEATTLE AND VANCOUVER

	Seattle	Vancouver
Regulations		
Handguns	Concealed-weapons permit is required to carry a gun for self-defense on the street; none is required for self-defense in the home. Registration of handguns is not mandatory for private sales.	Restricted-weapons permit is required for sporting and collecting purposes. Self-defense in the home or street is not legally recognized as a reason for possession of a handgun. Handguns must be registered.
Long guns (rifles, shotguns)	Long guns are not registered.	Firearm-acquisition certificate is required for purchase. Long guns are not registered.
Law enforcement and sentencing		
Additional sentence for commission of a class A felony with a firearm	Minimum of 2 extra years	1 to 14 extra years
Percent of firearm-related homicides that result in police charges (police estimate)	80 to 90%	80 to 90%
Minimum jail sentence for first-degree murder	20 years in prison	25 years in prison (parole is possible after 15 years)
Status of capital punishment	Legal, though no one has been executed since 1963	Abolished
Prevalence of weapons		
Total concealed-weapons permits issued (March 1984 to March 1988)	15,289	—
Total restricted-weapons permits issued (March 1984 to March 1988)	—	4137
Cook's gun prevalence index14	41%	12%

Province of British Columbia, the same offense generally results in
1 to 14 years of imprisonment in addition to the felony sentence.[16]
Similar percentages of homicides in both communities eventually
lead to arrest and police charges. In Washington, under the Sentencing Reform Act of 1981, murder in the first degree carries a minimum sentence of 20 years of confinement.[19] In British Columbia,
first-degree murder carries a minimum sentence of 25 years, with
a possible judicial parole review after 15 years.[20] Capital punishment
was abolished in Canada during the 1970s.[21] In Washington State,
the death penalty may be invoked in cases of aggravated first-degree
murder, but no one has been executed since 1963.

RATES OF GUN OWNERSHIP

12   Because direct surveys of firearm ownership in Seattle and Vancouver have never been conducted, we assessed the rates of gun ownership indirectly by two independent methods. First, we obtained
from the Firearm Permit Office of the Vancouver police department a count of the restricted-weapons permits issued in Vancouver between March 1984 and March 1988 and compared this
figure with the total number of concealed-weapons permits issued
in Seattle during the same period, obtained from the Office of
Business and Profession Administration, Department of Licensing,
State of Washington. Second, we used Cook's gun prevalence index,
a previously validated measure of intercity differences in the prevalence of gun ownership.[14] This index is based on data from 49 cities
in the United States and correlates each city's rates of suicide and
assaultive homicide involving firearms with survey-based estimates of gun ownership in each city. Both methods indicate that
firearms are far more commonly owned in Seattle than in Vancouver (Table 2).

IDENTIFICATION AND DEFINITION OF CASES

13   From police records, we identified all the cases of robbery, burglary,
and assault (both simple and aggravated) and all the homicides that
occurred in Seattle or Vancouver between January 1, 1980, and

December 31, 1986. In defining cases, we followed the guidelines of the U.S. Federal Bureau of Investigation's uniform crime reports (UCR).[22] The UCR guidelines define aggravated assault as an unlawful attack by one person on another for the purpose of inflicting severe or aggravated bodily harm. Usually this type of assault involves the actual or threatened use of a deadly weapon. Simple assault is any case of assault that does not involve the threat or use of a deadly weapon or result in serious or aggravated injuries.

A homicide was defined as the willful killing of one human being by another. This category included cases of premeditated murder, intentional killing, and aggravated assault resulting in death. "Justifiable homicide," as defined by the UCR guidelines, was limited to cases of the killing of a felon by a law-enforcement officer in the line of duty or the killing of a felon by a private citizen during the commission of a felony.[22] Homicides that the police, the prosecuting attorney, or both thought were committed in self-defense were also identified and noted separately.

STATISTICAL ANALYSIS

From both Seattle and Vancouver, we obtained annual and cumulative data on the rates of aggravated assault, simple assault, robbery, and burglary. Cases of aggravated assault were categorized according to the weapon used. Data on homicides were obtained from the files of the medical examiner or coroner in each community and were supplemented by police case files. Each homicide was further categorized according to the age, sex, and race or ethnic group of the victim, as well as the weapon used.

Population-based rates of simple assault, aggravated assault, robbery, burglary, and homicide were then calculated and compared. These rates are expressed as the number per 100,000 persons per year and, when possible, are further adjusted for any differences in the age and sex of the victims. Unadjusted estimates of relative risk and 95 percent confidence intervals were calculated with use of the maximum-likelihood method and are based on Seattle's rate relative to Vancouver's.[23] Age-adjusted relative risks were estimated with use of the Mantel-Haenszel summary odds ratio.[24]

Results

17   During the seven-year study period, the annual rate of robbery in Seattle was found to be only slightly higher than that in Vancouver (relative risk, 1.09; 95 percent confidence interval, 1.08 to 1.12). Burglaries, on the other hand, occurred at nearly identical rates in the two communities (relative risk, 0.99; 95 percent confidence interval, 0.98 to 1.00). During the study period, 18,925 cases of aggravated assault were reported in Seattle, as compared with 12,034 cases in Vancouver. When the annual rates of assault in the two cities were compared for each year of the study, we found that the two communities had similar rates of assault during the first four years of the study. In 1984, however, reported rates of simple and aggravated assault began to climb sharply in Seattle, whereas the rates of simple and aggravated assault remained relatively constant in Vancouver (Fig. 1). This change coincided with the enactment that year of the Domestic Violence Protection Act by the Washington State legislature. Among other provisions, this law required changes in reporting and arrests in cases of domestic violence.[25] It is widely believed that this law and the considerable media attention that followed its passage resulted in dramatic increases in the number of incidents reported and in related enforcement costs in Seattle.[26] Because in Vancouver there was no similar legislative initiative requiring police to change their reporting methods, we restricted our comparison of the data on assaults to the first four years of our study (1980 through 1983) (Fig. 1).

18   During this four-year period, the risk of being a victim of simple assault in Seattle was found to be only slightly higher than that in Vancouver (relative risk, 1.18; 95 percent confidence interval, 1.15 to 1.20). The risk of aggravated assault in Seattle was also only slightly higher than in Vancouver (relative risk, 1.16; 95 percent confidence interval, 1.12 to 1.19). However, when aggravated assaults were subdivided by the type of weapon used and the mechanism of assault, a striking pattern emerged. Although both cities reported almost identical rates of aggravated assault involving knives, other dangerous weapons, or hands, fists, and feet, firearms were far more likely to have been used in cases of assault in Seattle than in Vancouver (Table 3). In fact, all the difference in the relative risk of aggravated assault between these two communities

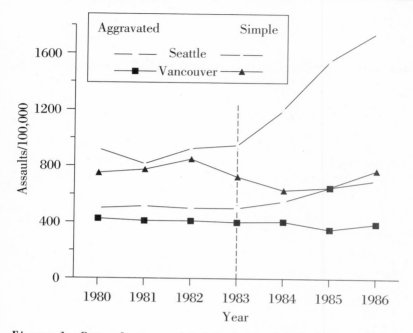

Figure 1 Rates of aggravated and simple assault in Seattle and Vancouver, 1980 through 1986. The dotted line indicates the passage of the Domestic Violence Protection Act in Washington State in 1984.

was due to Seattle's 7.7-fold higher rate of assaults involving firearms (Fig. 2).

Over the whole seven-year study period, 388 homicides occurred in Seattle (11.3 per 100,000 person-years). In Vancouver, 204 homicides occurred during the same period (6.9 per 100,000 person-years). After adjustment for differences in age and sex between the populations, the relative risk of being a victim of homicide in Seattle, as compared with Vancouver, was found to be 1.63 (95 percent confidence interval, 1.28 to 2.08). This difference is highly unlikely to have occurred by chance.

When homicides were subdivided by the mechanism of death, the rate of homicide by knives and other weapons (excluding firearms) in Seattle was found to be almost identical to that in Vancouver (relative risk, 1.08; 95 percent confidence interval, 0.89

Table 3 ANNUAL CRUDE RATES AND RELATIVE RISKS OF AGGRAVATED ASSAULT, SIMPLE ASSAULT, ROBBERY, BURGLARY, AND HOMICIDE IN SEATTLE AND VANCOUVER, 1980 THROUGH 1986*

Crime	Period	Seattle	Vancouver	Relative Risk	95% CI
		(no./100,000)			
Robbery	1980–1986	492.2	450.9	1.09	1.08–1.12
Burglary	1980–1986	2952.7	2985.7	0.99	0.98–1.00
Simple assault	1980–1983	902	767.7	1.18	1.15–1.20
Aggravated assault	1980–1983	486.5	420.5	1.16	1.12–1.19
Firearms		87.9	11.4	7.70	6.70–8.70
Knives		78.1	78.9	0.99	0.92–1.07
Other		320.6	330.2	0.97	0.94–1.01
Homicides	1980–1986	11.3	6.9	1.63	1.38–1.93
Firearms		4.8	1.0	5.08	3.54–7.27
Knives		3.1	3.5	0.90	0.69–1.18
Other		3.4	2.5	1.33	0.99–1.78

*CI denotes confidence interval. The "crude rate" for these crimes is the number of events occurring in a given population over a given time period. The relative risks shown are for Seattle in relation to Vancouver.

to 1.32) (Fig. 3). Virtually all of the increased risk of death from homicide in Seattle was due to a more than fivefold higher rate of homicide by firearms (Table 3). Handguns, which accounted for roughly 85 percent of the homicides involving firearms in both communities, were 4.8 times more likely to be used in homicides in Seattle than in Vancouver.

21   To test the hypothesis that the higher rates of homicide in Seattle might be due to more frequent use of firearms for self-protection, we examined all the homicides in both cities that were ruled "legally justifiable" or were determined to have been committed in self-defense. 32 such homicides occurred during the study period, 11 of which involved police intervention. After the exclusion of justifiable homicide by police, 21 cases of homicide by civilians acting in self-defense or in other legally justifiable ways remained, 17 of which occurred in Seattle and 4 of which occurred in Vancouver (relative risk, 3.64; 95 percent confidence interval, 1.32 to 10.06).

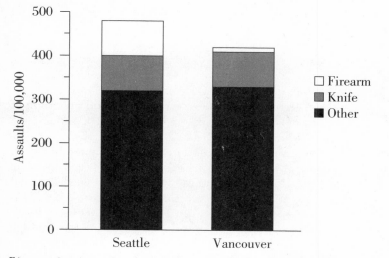

Figure 2 Annual rates of aggravated assault in Seattle and Vancouver, 1980 through 1983, according to the Weapon Used. "Other" includes blunt instruments, other dangerous weapons, and hands, fists, and feet.

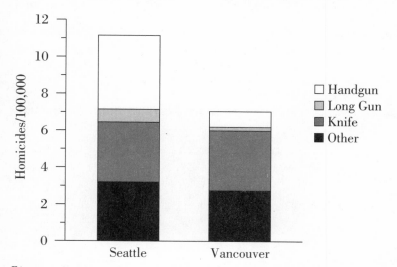

Figure 3 Annual rates of homicide in Seattle and Vancouver, 1980 through 1986, according to the Weapon Used. "Other" includes blunt instruments, other dangerous weapons, and hands, fists, and feet.

Thirteen of these cases (all of which occurred in Seattle) involved firearms. The exclusion of all 21 cases (which accounted for less than 4 percent of the homicides during the study interval) had little overall effect on the relative risk of homicide in the two communities (age- and sex-adjusted relative risk, 1.57; 95 percent confidence interval, 1.22 to 2.01).

22   When homicides were stratified by the race or ethnic group of the victim, a complex picture emerged (Table 4). The homicide rates in Table 4 were adjusted for age to match the 1980 U.S. population. This technique permits fairer comparisons among racial and ethnic groups with differing age compositions in each city. The relative risk for each racial or ethnic group, however, was estimated with use of the Mantel-Haenszel summary odds ratio.[24] This method, in effect, uses a different set off weights for the various age strata, depending on the distribution of persons among the age strata for that racial or ethnic group only. Hence, these estimates of relative risk differ slightly from a simple quotient of the age-adjusted rates.

23   Whereas similar rates of death by homicide were noted for whites in both cities, Asians in Seattle had higher rates of death by homi-

T a b l e 4 ANNUAL AGE-ADJUSTED HOMICIDE RATES AND RELATIVE RISKS OF DEATH BY HOMICIDE IN SEATTLE AND VANCOUVER, 1980 THROUGH 1986, ACCORDING TO THE RACE OR ETHNIC GROUP OF THE VICTIM*

Race or Ethnic Group	Seattle	Vancouver	Relative Risk	95% CI
	(no./100,000)			
White (non-Hispanic)	6.2	6.4	1	0.8–1.2
Asian	15.0	4.1	3.5	2.1–5.7
Excluding Wah Mee murders	9.5	—	2.3	1.4–4.0
Black	36.6	9.5	2.8	0.4–20.4
Hispanic	26.9	7.9	5	0.7–34.3
Native American	64.9	71.3	0.9	0.5–1.5

*CI denotes confidence interval. The relative risks shown are for Seattle in relation to Vancouver.

cide than their counterparts in Vancouver. This difference persisted even after the exclusion of the 13 persons who died in the Wah Mee gambling club massacre in Seattle in 1983. Blacks and Hispanics in Seattle had higher relative risks of death by homicide than blacks and Hispanics in Vancouver, but the confidence intervals were very wide, given the relatively small size of both minorities in Vancouver. Only one black and one Hispanic were killed in Vancouver during the study period. Native Americans had the highest rates of death by homicide in both cities.

Discussion

Previous studies of the effectiveness of gun control have generally compared rates of homicide in nations with different approaches to the regulation of firearms.[7] Unfortunately, the validity of these studies has been compromised by the large number of confounding factors that characterize national groups. We sought to circumvent this limitation by focusing our analysis on two demographically comparable and physically proximate cities with markedly different approaches to handgun control. In many ways, these two cities have more in common with each other than they do with other major cities in their respective countries. For example, Seattle's homicide rate is consistently half to two thirds that reported in cities such as Chicago, Los Angeles, New York, and Houston,[4] whereas Vancouver experiences annual rates of homicide two to three times higher than those reported in Ottawa, Toronto, and Calgary (Canadian Centre for Justice Statistics, Homicide Program, Ottawa: unpublished data).

In order to exclude the possibility that Seattle's higher homicide rate may be explained by higher levels of criminal activity or aggressiveness in its population, we compared the rates of burglary, robbery, simple assault, and aggravated assault in the two communities. Although we observed a slightly higher rate of simple and aggravated assault in Seattle, these differences were relatively small—the rates in Seattle were 16 to 18 percent higher than those reported in Vancouver during a period of comparable case reporting. Virtually all of the excess risk of aggravated assault in Seattle was

24

25

explained by a sevenfold higher rate of assaults involving firearms. Despite similar rates of robbery and burglary and only small differences in the rates of simple and aggravated assault, we found that Seattle had substantially higher rates of homicide than Vancouver. Most of the excess mortality was due to an almost fivefold higher rate of murders with handguns in Seattle.

26   Critics of handgun control have long claimed that limiting access to guns will have little effect on the rates of homicide, because persons who are intent on killing others will only work harder to acquire a gun or will kill by other means.[7,27] If the rate of homicide in a community were influenced more by the strength of intent than by the availability of weapons, we might have expected the rate of homicides with weapons other than guns to have been higher in Vancouver than in Seattle, in direct proportion to any decrease in Vancouver's rate of firearm homicides. This was not the case. During the study interval, Vancouver's rate of homicides with weapons other than guns was not significantly higher than that in Seattle, suggesting that few would-be assailants switched to homicide by other methods.

27   Ready access to handguns has been advocated by some as an important way to provide law-abiding citizens with an effective means to defend themselves.[27–29] Were this true, we might have expected that much of Seattle's excess rate of homicides, as compared with Vancouver's, would have been explained by a higher rate of justifiable homicides and killings in self-defense by civilians. Although such homicides did occur at a significantly higher rate in Seattle than in Vancouver, these cases accounted for less than 4 percent of the homicides in both cities during the study period. When we excluded cases of justifiable homicide or killings in self-defense by civilians from our calculation of relative risk, our results were almost the same.

28   It also appears unlikely that differences in law-enforcement activity accounted for the lower homicide rate in Vancouver. Suspected offenders are arrested and cases are cleared at similar rates in both cities. After arrest and conviction, similar crimes carry similar penalties in the courts in Seattle and Vancouver.

29   We found substantial differences in the risk of death by homicide according to race and ethnic group in both cities. In the United States, blacks and Hispanics are murdered at substantially higher

rates than whites.[2] Although the great majority of homicides in the United States involve assailants of the same race or ethnic group, current evidence suggests that socioeconomic status plays a much greater role in explaining racial and ethnic differences in the rate of homicide than any intrinsic tendency toward violence.[2,30,31] For example, Centerwall has shown that when household crowding is taken into account, the rate of domestic homicide among blacks in Atlanta, Georgia, is no higher than that of whites living in similar conditions.[32] Likewise, a recent study of childhood homicide in Ohio found that once cases were stratified by socioeconomic status, there was little difference in race-specific rates of homicide involving children 5 to 14 years of age.[33]

Since low-income populations have higher rates of homicide, socioeconomic status is probably an important confounding factor in our comparison of the rates of homicide for racial and ethnic groups. Although the median income and the overall distribution of household incomes in Seattle and Vancouver are similar, the distribution of household incomes by racial and ethnic group may not be the same in Vancouver as in Seattle. For example, blacks in Vancouver had a slightly higher mean income in 1981 than the rest of Vancouver's population (Statistics Canada, 1981 Census Custom Tabulation: unpublished data). In contrast, blacks in Seattle have a substantially lower median income than the rest of Seattle's population.[34] Thus, much of the excess risk of homicide among blacks in Seattle, as compared with blacks in Vancouver, may be explained by their lower socioeconomic status. If, on the other hand, more whites in Vancouver have low incomes than whites in Seattle, the higher risk of homicide expected in this low-income subset may push the rate of homicide among whites in Vancouver higher than that for whites in Seattle. Unfortunately, neither hypothesis can be tested in a quantitative fashion, since detailed information about household incomes according to race is not available for Vancouver.

Three limitations of our study warrant comment. First, our measures of the prevalence of firearm ownership may not precisely reflect the availability of guns in the two communities. Although the two measures we used were derived independently and are consistent with the expected effects of gun control, their validity as indicators of community rates of gun ownership has not been conclusively established. Cook's gun prevalence index has been shown to correlate with data derived from national surveys, but it has not been tested for accuracy in cities outside the United States. Comparisons of concealed-weapons permits in Seattle with restricted-weapons permits in Vancouver are probably of limited validity, since these counts do not include handguns obtained illegally. In fact, the comparison of permit data of this sort probably substantially underestimates the differences between the communities in the rate of handgun ownership, since only a fraction of the handguns in Seattle are purchased for use as concealed weapons, whereas all legal handgun purchases in Vancouver require a restricted-weapons permit. Still, these indirect estimates of gun ownership are consistent with one another, and both agree with prior reports.

References

1. Homicide surveillance: 1970–78. Atlanta: Centers for Disease Control, September, 1983.
2. Homicide surveillance: high risk racial and ethnic groups—blacks and Hispanics, 1970 to 1983. Atlanta: Centers for Disease Control, November, 1986.
3. Baker SP, O'Neill B, Karpf RS. The injury fact book. Lexington, Mass.: Lexington Books, 1984.
4. Department of Justice, Federal Bureau of Investigation. Crime in the United States (Uniform Crime Reports). Washington, D.C.: Government Printing Office, 1986.
5. Baker SP. Without guns, do people kill people? Am J Public Health 1985; 75:587–8.
6. Hedeboe J, Charles AV, Nielsen J, et al. Interpersonal violence: patterns in a Danish community. Am J Public Health 1985; 75:651–3.
7. Wright J, Rossi P, Daly K, Weber-Burdin E. Weapons, crime and violence in America: a literature review and research agenda. Washington, D.C.: Department of Justice, National Institute of Justice, 1981.
8. Weiss JMA. Gun control: a question of public/mental health? J Oper Psychiatr 1981; 12:86–8.
9. Bruce-Briggs B. The great American gun war. Public Interest 1976; 45:37–62.
10. Bureau of Census. 1980 Census of population, Washington. Washington, D.C.: Government Printing Office, 1981.
11. Statistics Canada: 1981 census of Canada, Vancouver, British Columbia. Ottawa, Ont.: Minister of Supply and Services, 1983.

12. Seattle local market T.V. ratings, 1985–86. (Based on Arbitron television ratings.) Provided by KING TV, Seattle, Washington.
13. Vancouver local market T.V. ratings, 1985–86. Provided by Bureau of Broadcast Measurement, Toronto.
14. Cook PJ. The role of firearms in violent crime. In: Wolfgang M, ed. Criminal violence. Beverly Hills, Calif.: Sage, 1982:236–90.
15. Revised Code of State of Washington. RCW chapter 9.41.090, 9.41.095, 9.41.070, 1986.
16. Criminal Code of Canada. Firearms and other offensive weapons. Martin's Criminal Code of Canada, 1982. Part II.1 (Sections 81-016.9, 1982).
17. *Idem.* Restricted Weapons and Firearm Control Regulations Sec. 106.2 (11); Amendment Act, July 18, 1977, 1982.
18. Revised Code of State of Washington, Sentence Reform Act Chapter 9 94A.125.1980.
19. Revised Code of State of Washington. Murder I, 9A.32.040.1984.
20. Criminal Code of Canada. Application for judicial review sentence of life imprisonment, 1988 Part XX 669–67, 1(1).
21. *Idem.* Act to Amend Criminal Code B.11 C84, 1976.
22. Department of Justice, Federal Bureau of Investigation. Uniform crime reporting handbook. Washington, D.C.: Government Printing Office, 1984.
23. Rothman KJ, Boice JD Jr. Epidemiologic analysis with a programmable calculator. Boston: Epidemiology Resources, 1982.
24. Armitage P, Berry G. Statistical methods in medical research. 2nd ed. Oxford: Blackwell, 1987.
25. Revised Code of State of Washington. RCW Chapter 10.99.010-.100, 1984.
26. Seattle Police Department. Inspectional service division report, domestic violence arrest costs: 1984–87, Seattle, 1986.
27. Drooz RB. Handguns and hokum: a methodological problem. JAMA 1977; 238:43–5.
28. Copeland AR. The right to keep and bear arms—a study of civilian homicides committed against those involved in criminal acts in metropolitan Dade County from 1957 to 1982. J Forensic Sci 1984; 29:584–90.
29. Kleck G. Crime control through the private use of armed force. Soc Probl 1988; 35:1–21.
30. Loftin C, Hill RH. Regional subculture and homicide: an examination of the Gastil-Hackney thesis. Am Sociol Rev 1974; 39:714–24.
31. Williams KR. Economic sources of homicide: reestimating the effects of poverty and inequality. Am Sociol Rev 1984; 49:283–9.
32. Centerwall BS. Race, socioeconomic status, and domestic homicide, Atlanta, 1971–72. Am J Public Health 1984; 74:813–5.
33. Muscat JE. Characteristics of childhood homicide in Ohio, 1974–84. Am J Public Health 1988; 78:822–4.
34. Seattle City Government. General social and economic characteristics, city of Seattle: 1970–1980. Planning research bulletin no. 45. Seattle: Department of Community Development, 1983.
35. Newton G, Zimring F. Firearms and violence in American life: a staff

report to the National Commission on the Causes and Prevention of Violence. Washington, D.C.: Government Printing Office, 1969.

STUDY QUESTIONS

1. Sloan, et al., conclude that ease of access to handguns is the major causal factor relevant to explaining homicide rates. Which of Mill's Methods does their overall method of argument employ?

2. In paragraph 29, Sloan, et al., hypothesize that socioeconomic factors (and not intrinsic racial differences) are also causally relevant to explaining homicide rates. This hypothesis is based on the results summarized in their Table 4. Which of Mill's Methods leads them to this hypothesis?

3. Notice that while homicide rates are much higher in Seattle than in Vancouver, the unemployment and income statistics given in Table 1 show Seattle and Vancouver to be very similar economically. Why, in paragraph 30, do Sloan, et al., think that these statistics should not lead us to reject the hypothesis that economic factors are relevant?

4. According to Table 1, residents of Vancouver are socioeconomically similar to residents of Seattle. Also according to Table 1, whites make up about the same percentage of the population in Vancouver as they do in Seattle. And according to Table 4, homicide rates for whites in Vancouver and Seattle are nearly identical. Yet whites in Seattle have much easier access to firearms than do whites in Vancouver. Using the negative Method of Difference, what conclusion follows? How do you think Sloan, et al., would respond to this?

5. In his essay against banning handguns (p. 51), did Kates raise any arguments that Sloan, et al., have not dealt with in this essay?

PART THREE

On the Death Penalty

SISSEL SETERAS STOKES

Capital Punishment Is Immoral

*The following selection from the letters-to-the-editor column
of a newspaper is representative of the style and length of such
letters. Since newspaper editors usually set strict word limits,
writers must compress their arguments into as little space as
possible. Consequently, they sometimes state their arguments
as enthymemes, like those supporting Stokes's conclusion below.*

To the editor:
    I am writing as a member of the international human rights   1
organization Amnesty International to express my anxiety and

[Sissel Seteras Stokes, from "Letters to the Editor," *Bloomington* (Indiana)
Herald-Telephone, September 6, 1987.]

concern about the practicing of the death penalty in the state of Indiana.

2   As you are certainly aware, most European countries have abolished the death penalty, with Turkey as the only Western European country to have carried out the death sentence in recent years. In Indiana prisons there are even two juvenile offenders on Death Row. Although a bill has been passed raising the minimum age for passing a death sentence from 10 to 16 years of age, it is still in contravention with agreed international standards stating minimum of 18 years of age for offenders at the time of the crime. I therefore welcome a statement issued by the Indiana Council of Churches expressing the following views:

3   We oppose the death penalty for four reasons:

1. We consider it to be morally wrong.
2. The death penalty is used discriminately. Almost all the executed are poor. A large percentage belongs to minority groups.
3. There is no evidence proving the death penalty of having a deterrent effect.
4. An execution is irrevocable.

STUDY QUESTIONS

1. Stokes mentions that she is a member of Amnesty International. What role does this play in her argument?
2. Stokes also mentions Western European countries and an international agreement. What role do these play in her argument?
3. Like many letters to the editor, this one contains several enthymemes. Reconstruct Stokes's arguments by filling in the assumed premises.

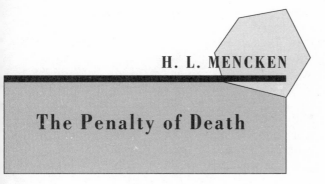

H. L. MENCKEN

The Penalty of Death

Henry Louis Mencken (1880–1956) was an American newspaper reporter, editorialist, and columnist, best known for his salty and boisterous writing style.

Of the arguments against capital punishment that issue from up-lifters, two are commonly heard most often, to wit:

1. That hanging a man (or frying him or gassing him) is a dreadful business, degrading to those who have to do it and revolting to those who have to witness it.
2. That it is useless, for it does not deter others from the same crime.

The first of these arguments, it seems to me, is plainly too weak to need serious refutation. All it says, in brief, is that the work of the hangman is unpleasant. Granted. But suppose it is? It may be quite necessary to society for all that. There are, indeed, many other jobs that are unpleasant, and yet no one thinks of abolishing them—that of the plumber, that of the soldier, that of the garbage-man, that of the priest hearing confessions, that of the sand-hog, and so on. Moreover, what evidence is there that any actual hangman complains of his work? I have heard none. On the contrary, I have known many who delighted in their ancient art, and practiced it proudly.

In the second argument of the abolitionists there is rather more force, but even here, I believe, the ground under them is shaky.

[H. L. Mencken, "The Penalty of Death," from *Prejudices,* Fifth Series. New York: Alfred A. Knopf, 1926; copyright renewed 1954 by H. L. Mencken.]

Their fundamental error consists in assuming that the whole aim of punishing criminals is to deter other (potential) criminals—that we hang or electrocute A simply in order to so alarm B that he will not kill C. This, I believe, is an assumption which confuses a part with the whole. Deterrence, obviously, is *one* of the aims of punishment, but it is surely not the only one. On the contrary, there are at least a half dozen, and some are probably quite as important. At least one of them, practically considered, is *more* important. Commonly, it is described as revenge, but revenge is really not the word for it. I borrow a better term from the late Aristotle: *katharsis*. *Katharsis*, so used, means a salubrious discharge of emotions, a healthy letting off of steam. A school-boy, disliking his teacher, deposits a tack upon the pedagogical chair; the teacher jumps and the boy laughs. This is *katharsis*. What I contend is that one of the prime objects of all judicial punishments is to afford the same grateful relief *(a)* to the immediate victims of the criminal punished, and *(b)* to the general body of moral and timorous men.

4   These persons, and particularly the first group, are concerned only indirectly with deterring other criminals. The thing they crave primarily is the satisfaction of seeing the criminal actually before them suffer as he made them suffer. What they want is the peace of mind that goes with the feeling that accounts are squared. Until they get that satisfaction they are in a state of emotional tension, and hence unhappy. The instant they get it they are comfortable. I do not argue that this yearning is noble; I simply argue that it is almost universal among human beings. In the face of injuries that are unimportant and can be borne without damage it may yield to higher impulses; that is to say, it may yield to what is called Christian charity. But when the injury is serious Christianity is adjourned, and even saints reach for their sidearms. It is plainly asking too much of human nature to expect it to conquer so natural an impulse. A keeps a store and has a bookkeeper, B. B steals $700, employs it in playing at dice or bingo, and is cleaned out. What is A to do? Let B go? If he does so he will be unable to sleep at night. The sense of injury, of injustice, of frustration will haunt him like pruritus. So he turns B over to the police, and they hustle B to prison. Thereafter A can sleep. More, he has pleasant dreams. He pictures B chained to the wall of a dungeon a hundred feet underground, devoured by rats and scorpions. It is so agreeable that it makes him forget his $700. He has got his *katharsis*.

The same thing precisely takes place on a larger scale when there 5
is a crime which destroys a whole community's sense of security.
Every law-abiding citizen feels menaced and frustrated until the
criminals have been struck down—until the communal capacity to
get even with them, and more than even, has been dramatically
demonstrated. Here, manifestly, the business of deterring others is
no more than an afterthought. The main thing is to destroy the
concrete scoundrels whose act has alarmed everyone, and thus made
everyone unhappy. Until they are brought to book that unhappiness
continues; when the law has been executed upon them there is a
sigh of relief. In other words, there is *katharsis*.

I know of no public demand for the death penalty for ordinary 6
crimes, even for ordinary homicides. Its infliction would shock all
men of normal decency of feeling. But for crimes involving the
deliberate and inexcusable taking of human life, by men openly
defiant of all civilized order—for such crimes it seems, to nine men
out of ten, a just and proper punishment. Any lesser penalty leaves
them feeling that the criminal has got the better of society—that
he is free to add insult to injury by laughing. That feeling can be
dissipated only by a recourse to *katharsis*, the invention of the
aforesaid Aristotle. It is more effectively and economically achieved,
as human nature now is, by wafting the criminal to realms of bliss.

The real objection to capital punishment doesn't lie against the 7
actual extermination of the condemned, but against our brutal
American habit of putting it off so long. After all, every one of us
must die soon or late, and a murderer, it must be assumed, is one
who makes that sad fact the cornerstone of his metaphysic. But it is
one thing to die, and quite another thing to lie for long months and
even years under the shadow of death. No sane man would choose
such a finish. All of us, despite the Prayer Book, long for a swift and
unexpected end. Unhappily, a murderer, under the irrational
American system, is tortured for what, to him, must seem a whole
series of eternities. For months on end he sits in prison while his
lawyers carry on their idiotic buffoonery with writs, injunctions,
mandamuses, and appeals. In order to get his money (or that of his
friends) they have to feed him with hope. Now and then, by the
imbecility of a judge or some trick of juridic science, they actually
justify it. But let us say that, his money all gone, they finally throw
up their hands. Their client is now ready for the rope or the chair.
But he must still wait for months before it fetches him.

8   That wait, I believe, is horribly cruel. I have seen more than one man sitting in the death-house, and I don't want to see any more. Worse, it is wholly useless. Why should he wait at all? Why not hang him the day after the last court dissipates his last hope? Why torture him as not even cannibals would torture their victims? The common answer is that he must have time to make his peace with God. But how long does that take? It may be accomplished, I believe, in two hours quite as comfortably as in two years. There are, indeed, no temporal limitations upon God. He could forgive a whole herd of murderers in a millionth of a second. More, it has been done.

STUDY QUESTIONS

1. In paragraph 3, Mencken substitutes the word *katharsis* for "revenge." Do the two words stand for the same concept? If so, what does Mencken's argument gain by making the substitution?

2. In paragraph 2, Mencken draws an analogy between the work of the hangman and the work of the plumber and the garbage-man. In what ways are the jobs not analogous? Do these disanalogies weaken Mencken's point?

3. Mencken says in paragraph 3 that there are "at least a half dozen" aims of punishment. How many does he actually discuss?

4. To what cases does Mencken restrict the use of the death penalty? On what grounds does he restrict it to these cases?

5. How do you think Mencken would respond to the following: "In paragraphs 7 and 8, you [Mencken] show great concern for the condemned criminal. Doesn't this contradict your earlier professed willingness to let the criminal suffer so that his or her victims may get their *katharsis?*"

6. Is Mencken arguing that capital punishment is just and ethical, or is he arguing that it is an acceptable response to understandable (though perhaps unworthy) feelings on the part of most people?

JUSTICE WILLIAM BRENNAN

Furman v. *Georgia* [Capital Punishment Is Unconstitutional]

William Brennan, born in 1906, was educated at the University of Pennsylvania and Harvard. He began his career as a lawyer in New Jersey and in 1956 became a U.S. Supreme Court Justice. In the following selection from a 1972 Supreme Court case, Justice Brennan argues that capital punishment violates the Eighth Amendment to the U.S. Constitution's prohibition of "cruel and unusual" punishment. Brennan has earlier argued that the wording of the Eighth Amendment is not precise, and so he has offered four principles for determining whether a punishment is cruel and unusual:

> *"[A] punishment must not be so severe as to be degrading to the dignity of human beings";*
> *"[T]he State must not arbitrarily inflict a severe punishment";*
> *"[A] severe punishment must not be unacceptable to contemporary society";*
> *"[A] severe punishment must not be excessive."*

In the selection that follows, Brennan proceeds to argue that capital punishment violates all four of these principles.

[Justice Brennan, Section III of concurring opinion in *Furman* v. *Georgia* 408 U.S. 285–305 (1972).]

III

1   ... The question, then, is whether the deliberate infliction of death is today consistent with the command of the Clause that the State may not inflict punishments that do not comport with human dignity. I will analyze the punishment of death in terms of the principles set out above and the cumulative test to which they lead: It is a denial of human dignity for the State arbitrarily to subject a person to an unusually severe punishment that society has indicated it does not regard as acceptable, and that cannot be shown to serve any penal purpose more effectively than a significantly less drastic punishment. Under these principles and this test, death is today a "cruel and unusual" punishment.

2   Death is a unique punishment in the United States. In a society that so strongly affirms the sanctity of life, not surprisingly the common view is that death is the ultimate sanction. This natural human feeling appears all about us. There has been no national debate about punishment, in general or by imprisonment, comparable to the debate about the punishment of death. No other punishment has been so continuously restricted, nor has any State yet abolished prisons, as some have abolished this punishment. And those States that still inflict death reserve it for the most heinous crimes. Juries, of course, have always treated death cases differently, as have governors exercising their commutation powers. Criminal defendants are of the same view. "As all practicing lawyers know, who have defended persons charged with capital offenses, often the only goal possible is to avoid the death penalty." Some legislatures have required particular procedures, such as two-stage trials and automatic appeals, applicable only in death cases. "It is the universal experience in the administration of criminal justice that those charged with capital offenses are granted special considerations." This Court, too, almost always treats death cases as a class apart. And the unfortunate effect of this punishment upon the functioning of the judicial process is well known; no other punishment has a similar effect.

3   The only explanation for the uniqueness of death is its extreme severity. Death is today an unusually severe punishment, unusual in its pain, in its finality, and in its enormity. No other existing punishment is comparable to death in terms of physical and mental

suffering. Although our information is not conclusive, it appears that there is no method available that guarantees an immediate and painless death. Since the discontinuance of flogging as a constitutionally permissible punishment, death remains as the only punishment that may involve the conscious infliction of physical pain. In addition, we know that mental pain is an inseparable part of our practice of punishing criminals by death, for the prospect of pending execution exacts a frightful toll during the inevitable long wait between the imposition of sentence and the actual infliction of death. As the California Supreme Court pointed out, "the process of carrying out a verdict of death is often so degrading and brutalizing to the human spirit as to constitute psychological torture." Indeed, as Mr. Justice [Felix] Frankfurter noted, "the onset of insanity while awaiting execution of a death sentence is not a rare phenomenon." The "fate of ever-increasing fear and distress" to which the expatriate is subjected can only exist to a greater degree for a person confined in prison awaiting death.

The unusual severity of death is manifested most clearly in its finality and enormity. Death, in these respects, is in a class by itself. Expatriation, for example, is a punishment that "destroys for the individual the political existence that was centuries in the development," that "strips the citizen of his status in the national and international political community," and that puts "[h]is very existence" in jeopardy. Expatriation thus inherently entails "the total destruction of the individual's status in organized society." "In short, the expatriate has lost the right to have rights." Yet, demonstrably, expatriation is not "a fate worse than death." Although death, like expatriation, destroys the individual's "political existence" and his "status in organized society," it does more, for, unlike expatriation, death also destroys "[h]is very existence." There is, too, at least the possibility that the expatriate will in the future regain "the right to have rights." Death forecloses even that possibility. 4

Death is truly an awesome punishment. The calculated killing of a human being by the State involves, by its very nature, a denial of the executed person's humanity. The contrast with the plight of a person punished by imprisonment is evident. An individual in prison does not lose "the right to have rights." A prisoner retains, for example, the constitutional rights to the free exercise of religion, 5 to be free of cruel and unusual punishments, and to treatment as a "person" for purposes of due process of law and the equal protection of the laws. A prisoner remains a member of the human family. Moreover, he retains the right of access to the courts. His punishment is not irrevocable. Apart from the common charge, grounded upon the recognition of human fallibility, that the punishment of death must inevitably be inflicted upon innocent men, we know that death has been the lot of men whose convictions were unconstitutionally secured in view of later, retroactively applied, holdings of this Court. The punishment itself may have been unconstitutionally inflicted, yet the finality of death precludes relief. An executed person has indeed "lost the right to have rights." As one 19th century proponent of punishing criminals by death declared, "When a man is hung, there is an end of our relations with him. His execution is a way of saying, 'You are not fit for this world, take your chance elsewhere.'"

6   In comparison to all other punishments today, then, the deliberate extinguishment of human life by the State is uniquely degrading to human dignity. I would not hesitate to hold, on that ground alone, that death is today a "cruel and unusual" punishment, were it not that death is a punishment of long-standing usage and acceptance in this country. I therefore turn to the second principle—that the State may not arbitrarily inflict an unusually severe punishment.

7   The outstanding characteristic of our present practice of punishing criminals by death is the infrequency with which we resort to it. The evidence is conclusive that death is not the ordinary punishment for any crime.

8   There has been a steady decline in the infliction of this punishment in every decade since the 1930s, the earliest period for which accurate statistics are available. In the 1930s, executions averaged 167 per year; in the 1940s, the average was 128; in the 1950s, it was 72; and in the years 1960–1962, it was 48. There have been a total of 46 executions since then, 36 of them in 1963–1964. Yet our population and the number of capital crimes committed have increased greatly over the past four decades. The contemporary rarity of the infliction of this punishment is thus the end result of a long-continued decline. That rarity is plainly revealed by an exami-

nation of the years 1961–1970, the last 10-year period for which statistics are available. During that time, an average of 106 death sentences was imposed each year. Not nearly that number, however, could be carried out, for many were precluded by commutations to life or a term of years, transfers to mental institutions because of insanity, resentences to life or a term of years, grants of new trials and orders for resentencing, dismissals of indictments and reversals of convictions, and deaths by suicide and natural causes. On January 1, 1961, the death row population was 219; on December 31, 1970, it was 608; during that span, there were 135 executions. Consequently, had the 389 additions to death row also been executed, the annual average would have been 52. In short, the country might, at most, have executed one criminal each week. In fact, of course, far fewer were executed. Even before the moratorium on executions began in 1967, executions totaled only 42 in 1961 and 47 in 1962, an average of less than one per week; the number dwindled to 21 in 1963, to 15 in 1964, and to seven in 1965; in 1966, there was one execution, and in 1967, there were two.

When a country of over 200 million people inflicts an unusually severe punishment no more than 50 times a year, the inference is strong that the punishment is not being regularly and fairly applied. To dispel it would indeed require a clear showing of nonarbitrary infliction. 9

Although there are not exact figures available, we know that thousands of murders and rapes are committed annually in States where death is an authorized punishment for those crimes. However the rate of infliction is characterized—as "freakishly" or "spectacularly" rare, or simply as rare—it would take the purest sophistry to deny that death is inflicted in only a minute fraction of these cases. How much rarer, after all, could the infliction of death be? 10

When the punishment of death is inflicted in a trivial number of the cases in which it is legally available, the conclusion is virtually inescapable that it is being inflicted arbitrarily. Indeed, it smacks of little more than a lottery system. The States claim, however, that this rarity is evidence not of arbitrariness, but of informed selectivity: Death is inflicted, they say, only in "extreme" cases. 11

Informed selectivity, of course, is a value not to be denigrated. 12

Yet presumably the States could make precisely the same claim if there were 10 executions per year, or five, or even if there were but one. That there may be as many as 50 per year does not strengthen the claim. When the rate of infliction is at this low level, it is highly implausible that only the worst criminals or the criminals who commit the worst crimes are selected for this punishment. No one has yet suggested a rational basis that could differentiate in those terms the few who die from the many who go to prison. Crimes and criminals simply do not admit of a distinction that can be drawn so finely as to explain, on that ground, the execution of such a tiny sample of those eligible. Certainly the laws that provide for this punishment do not attempt to draw that distinction; all cases to which the laws apply are necessarily "extreme." Nor is the distinction credible in fact. If, for example, petitioner Furman or his crime illustrates the "extreme," then nearly all murderers and their murders are also "extreme."[1] Furthermore, our procedures in death cases, rather than resulting in the selection of "extreme" cases for this punishment, actually sanction an arbitrary selection. For this Court has held that juries may, as they do, make the decision

1. The victim surprised Furman in the act of burglarizing the victim's home in the middle of the night. While escaping, Furman killed the victim with one pistol shot fired through the closed kitchen door from the outside. At the trial, Furman gave his version of the killing:

"They got me charged with murder and I admit, I admit going to these folks' home and they did caught me in there and I was coming back out, backing up and there was a wire down there on the floor. I was coming out backwards and fell back and I didn't intend to kill nobody. I didn't know they was behind the door. The gun went off and I didn't know nothing about no murder until they arrested me, and when the gun went off I was down on the floor and I got up and ran. That's all to it."

The Georgia Supreme Court accepted that version:

"The admission in open court by the accused . . . that during the period in which he was involved in the commission of a criminal act at the home of the deceased, he accidentally tripped over a wire in leaving the premises causing the gun to go off, together with other facts and circumstances surrounding the death of the deceased by violent means, was sufficient to support the verdict of guilty of murder. . . ."

About Furman himself, the jury knew only that he was black and that according to his statement at trial, he was 26 years old and worked at "Superior Upholstery." It took the jury one hour and 35 minutes to return a verdict of guilt and a sentence of death.

whether to impose a death sentence wholly unguided by standards governing that decision. In other words, our procedures are not constructed to guard against the totally capricious selection of criminals for the punishment of death.

Although it is difficult to imagine what further facts would be 13 necessary in order to prove that death is, as my Brother [Potter] Stewart puts it, "wantonly and . . . freakishly" inflicted, I need not conclude that arbitrary infliction is patently obvious. I am not considering this punishment by the isolated light of one principle. The probability of arbitrariness is sufficiently substantial that it can be relied upon, in combination with the other principles, in reaching a judgment on the constitutionality of this punishment.

When there is a strong probability that an unusually severe and 14 degrading punishment is being inflicted arbitrarily, we may well expect that society will disapprove of its infliction. I turn, therefore, to the third principle. An examination of the history and present operation of the American practice of punishing criminals by death reveals that this punishment has been almost totally rejected by contemporary society.

I cannot add to my Brother [Thurgood] Marshall's comprehen- 15 sive treatment of the English and American history of this punishment. I emphasize, however, one significant conclusion that emerges from that history. From the beginning of our Nation, the punishment of death has stirred acute public controversy. Although pragmatic arguments for and against the punishment have been frequently advanced, this longstanding and heated controversy cannot be explained solely as the result of differences over the practical wisdom of a particular government policy. At bottom, the battle has been waged on moral grounds. The country has debated whether a society for which the dignity of the individual is the supreme value can, without a fundamental inconsistency, follow the practice of deliberately putting some of its members to death. In the United States, as in other nations of the western world, "the struggle about this punishment has been one between ancient and deeply rooted beliefs in retribution, atonement or vengeance on the one hand, and, on the other, beliefs in the personal value and dignity of the common man that were born of the democratic movement of the eighteenth century, as well as beliefs in the scientific approach to an understanding of the motive forces of human conduct, which are the result of the growth of the sciences of behavior during the nineteenth and twentieth centuries." It is this essentially moral conflict that forms the backdrop for the past changes in and the present operation of our system of imposing death as a punishment for crime.

16   Our practice of punishing criminals by death has changed greatly over the years. One significant change has been in our methods of inflicting death. Although this country never embraced the more violent and repulsive methods employed in England, we did for a long time rely almost exclusively upon the gallows and the firing squad. Since the development of the supposedly more humane methods of electrocution late in the 19th century and lethal gas in the 20th, however, hanging and shooting have virtually ceased. Our concern for decency and human dignity, moreover, has compelled changes in the circumstances surrounding the execution itself. No longer does our society countenance the spectacle of public executions, once thought desirable as a deterrent to criminal behavior by others. Today we reject public executions as debasing and brutalizing to us all.

17   Also significant is the drastic decrease in the crimes for which the punishment of death is actually inflicted. While esoteric capital crimes remain on the books, since 1930 murder and rape have accounted for nearly 99% of the total executions, and murder alone for about 87%. In addition, the crime of capital murder has itself been limited. As the Court noted in *McGautha* v. *California*, there was in this country a "rebellion against the common-law rule imposing a mandatory death sentence on all convicted murderers." Initially, that rebellion resulted in legislative definitions that distinguished between degrees of murder, retaining the mandatory death sentence only for murder in the first degree. Yet "[t]his new legislative criterion for isolating crimes appropriately by death soon proved as unsuccessful as the concept of 'malice aforethought,'" the common-law means of separating murder from manslaughter. Not only was the distinction between degrees of murder confusing and uncertain in practice, but even in clear cases of first-degree murder juries continued to take the law into their own hands: if they felt that death was an inappropriate punishment, "they simply refused

to convict of the capital offense." The phenomenon of jury nullifi-
cation thus remained to counteract the rigors of mandatory death
sentences. Bowing to reality, "legislatures did not try, as before, to
refine further the definition of capital homicides. Instead they
adopted the method of forthrightly granting juries the discretion
which they had been exercising in fact." In consequence, virtually
all death sentences today are discretionarily imposed. Finally, it is
significant that nine States no longer inflict the punishment of
death under any circumstances, and five others have restricted it to
extremely rare crimes.

Thus, although "the death penalty has been employed through-   18
out our history," in fact the history of this punishment is one of
successive restriction. What was once a common punishment has
become, in the context of a continuing moral debate, increasingly
rare. The evolution of this punishment evidences, not that it is an
inevitable part of the American scene, but that it has proved pro-
gressively more troublesome to the national conscience. The result
of this movement is our current system of administering the punishment, under which death sentences are rarely imposed and death
is even more rarely inflicted. It is, of course, "We, the People" who
are responsible for the rarity both of the imposition and the carrying
out of this punishment. Juries, "express[ing] the conscience of the
community on the ultimate question of life or death," *Witherspoon*
v. *Illinois,* have been able to bring themselves to vote for death in a
mere 100 or so cases among the thousands tried each year where the
punishment is available. Governors, elected by and acting for us,
have regularly commuted a substantial number of those sentences.
And it is our society that insists upon due process of law to the end
that no person will be unjustly put to death, thus ensuring that many
more of those sentences will not be carried out. In sum, we have
made death a rare punishment today.

The progressive decline in, and the current rarity of, the infliction   19
of death demonstrate that our society seriously questions the appropriateness of this punishment today. The States point out that many
legislatures authorize death as the punishment for certain crimes
and that substantial segments of the public, as reflected in opinion
polls and referendum votes, continue to support it. Yet the availability of this punishment through statutory authorization, as well

as the polls and referenda, which amount simply to approval of that authorization, simply underscores the extent to which our society has in fact rejected this punishment. When an unusually severe punishment is authorized for wide-scale application but not, because of society's refusal, inflicted save in a few instances, the inference is compelling that there is a deep-seated reluctance to inflict it. Indeed, the likelihood is great that the punishment is tolerated only because of its disuse. The objective indicator of society's view of an unusually severe punishment is what society does with it, and today society will inflict death upon only a small sample of the eligible criminals. Rejection could hardly be more complete without becoming absolute. At the very least, I must conclude that contemporary society views this punishment with substantial doubt.

20 The final principle to be considered is that an unusually severe and degrading punishment may not be excessive in view of the purposes for which it is inflicted. This principle, too, is related to the others. When there is a strong probability that the State is arbitrarily inflicting an unusually severe punishment that is subject to grave societal doubts, it is likely also that the punishment cannot be shown to be serving any penal purpose that could not be served equally well by some less severe punishment.

21 The States' primary claim is that death is a necessary punishment because it prevents the commission of capital crimes more effectively than any less severe punishment. The first part of this claim is that the infliction of death is necessary to stop the individuals executed from committing further crimes. The sufficient answer to this is that if a criminal convicted of a capital crime poses a danger to society, effective administration of the State's pardon and parole laws can delay or deny his release from prison, and techniques of isolation can eliminate or minimize the danger while he remains confined.

22 The more significant argument is that the threat of death prevents the commission of capital crimes because it deters potential criminals who would not be deterred by the threat of imprisonment. The argument is not based upon evidence that the threat of death is a superior deterrent. Indeed, as my Brother Marshall establishes, the available evidence uniformly indicates, although it does not conclusively prove, that the threat of death has no greater deterrent

effect than the threat of imprisonment. The States argue, however, that they are entitled to rely upon common human experience, and that experience, they say, supports the conclusion that death must be a more effective deterrent than any less severe punishment. Because people fear death the most, the argument runs, the threat of death must be the greatest deterrent.

It is important to focus upon the precise import of this argument. 23 It is not denied that many, and probably most, capital crimes cannot be deterred by the threat of punishment. Thus the argument can apply only to those who think rationally about the commission of capital crimes. Particularly is that true when the potential criminal, under this argument, must not only consider the risk of punishment, but also distinguish between two possible punishments. The concern, then, is with a particular type of potential criminal, the rational person who will commit a capital crime knowing that the punishment is long-term imprisonment, which may well be for the rest of his life, but will not commit the crime knowing that the punishment is death. On the face of it, the assumption that such persons exist is implausible.

In any event, this argument cannot be appraised in the abstract. 24 We are not presented with the theoretical question whether under any imaginable circumstances the threat of death might be a greater deterrent to the commission of capital crimes than the threat of imprisonment. We are concerned with the practice of punishing criminals by death as it exists in the United States today. Proponents of this argument necessarily admit that its validity depends upon the existence of a system in which the punishment of death is invariably and swiftly imposed. Our system, of course, satisfies neither condition. A rational person contemplating a murder or rape is confronted, not with the certainty of a speedy death, but with the slightest possibility that he will be executed in the distant future. The risk of death is remote and improbable; in contrast, the risk of long-term imprisonment is near and great. In short, whatever the speculative validity of the assumption that the threat of death is a superior deterrent, there is no reason to believe that as currently administered the punishment of death is necessary to deter the commission of capital crimes. Whatever might be the case were all or substantially all eligible criminals quickly put to death, unverifiable possibilities are an insufficient basis upon which to conclude that the threat of death today has any greater deterrent efficacy than the threat of imprisonment.[2]

25   There is, however, another aspect to the argument that the punishment of death is necessary for the protection of society. The infliction of death, the States urge, serves to manifest the community's outrage at the commission of the crime. It is, they say, a concrete public expression of moral indignation that inculcates respect for the law and helps assure a more peaceful community. Moreover, we are told, not only does the punishment of death exert this widespread moralizing influence upon community values, it also satisfies the popular demand for grievous condemnation of abhorrent crimes and thus prevents disorder, lynching, and attempts by private citizens to take the law into their own hands.

26   The question, however, is not whether death serves these supposed purposes of punishment, but whether death serves them more effectively than imprisonment. There is no evidence whatever that utilization of imprisonment rather than death encourages private blood feuds and other disorders. Surely if there were such a danger, the execution of a handful of criminals each year would not prevent it. The assertion that death alone is a sufficiently emphatic denunciation for capital crimes suffers from the same defect. If capital crimes require the punishment of death in order to provide moral reinforcement for the basic values of the community, those values can only be undermined when death is so rarely inflicted upon the criminals who commit the crimes. Furthermore, it is certainly doubtful that the infliction of death by the State does in fact strengthen the community's moral code; if the deliberate extinguishment of human life has any effect at all, it more likely tends to lower our respect for life and brutalize our values. That, after all,

2. There is also the more limited argument that death is a necessary punishment when criminals are already serving or subject to a sentence of life imprisonment. If the only punishment available is further imprisonment, it is said, those criminals will have nothing to lose by committing further crimes, and accordingly the threat of death is the sole deterrent. But "life" imprisonment is a misnomer today. Rarely, if ever, do crimes carry a mandatory life sentence without possibility of parole. That possibility ensures that criminals do not reach the point where further crimes are free of consequences. Moreover, if this argument is simply an assertion that the threat of death is a more effective deterrent than the threat of increased imprisonment by denial of release on parole, then, as noted above, there is simply no evidence to support it.

is why we no longer carry out public executions. In any event, this claim simply means that one purpose of punishment is to indicate social disapproval of crime. To serve that purpose our laws distribute punishments according to the gravity of crimes and punish more severely the crimes society regards as more serious. That purpose cannot justify any particular punishment as the upper limit of severity.

There is, then, no substantial reason to believe that the punish- 27
ment of death, as currently administered, is necessary for the protection of society. The only other purpose suggested, one that is independent of protection for society, is retribution. Shortly stated, retribution in this context means that criminals are put to death because they deserve it.

Although it is difficult to believe that any State today wishes to 28
proclaim adherence to "naked vengeance," the States claim, in reliance upon its statutory authorization, that death is the only fit punishment for capital crimes and that this retributive purpose justifies its infliction. In the past, judged by its statutory authorization, death was considered the only fit punishment for the crime of forgery, for the first federal criminal statute provided a mandatory death penalty for that crime. Obviously, concepts of justice change; no immutable moral order requires death for murderers and rapists. The claim that death is a just punishment necessarily refers to the existence of certain public beliefs. The claim must be that for capital crimes death alone comports with society's notion of proper punishment. As administered today, however, the punishment of death cannot be justified as a necessary means of exacting retribution from criminals. When the overwhelming number of criminals who commit capital crimes go to prison, it cannot be concluded that death serves the purpose of retribution more effectively than imprisonment. The asserted public belief that murderers and rapists deserve to die is flatly inconsistent with the execution of a random few. As the history of the punishment of death in this country shows, our society wishes to prevent crime; we have no desire to kill criminals simply to get even with them.

In sum, the punishment of death is inconsistent with all four 29
principles: Death is an unusually severe and degrading punishment; there is a strong probability that it is inflicted arbitrarily; its rejection by contemporary society is virtually total; and there is no reason

to believe that it serves any penal purpose more effectively than the less severe punishment of imprisonment. The function of these principles is to enable a court to determine whether a punishment comports with human dignity. Death, quite simply, does not. . . .

STUDY QUESTIONS

1. In paragraphs 7 to 14, Brennan argues that the death penalty is being inflicted arbitrarily. The following propositions are the main premises and conclusions of his argument. Diagram the argument.
   (1) The use of the death penalty has declined since the 1930s (paragraph 8).
   (2) The death penalty is not regularly and fairly applied (paragraph 9).
   (3) The death penalty is not used in all cases where authorized as a punishment (paragraph 10).
   (4) The use of the death penalty is rare (paragraph 10).
   (5) The death penalty is being inflicted arbitrarily (paragraph 11).
   (6) The rarity of the death penalty is not because of informed selectivity (paragraph 12).
   (7) Crimes and criminals do not admit of a distinction that can be drawn so finely as to explain the execution of such a tiny sample of those eligible (paragraph 12).
   (8) Assumed premise: If the rarity of the death penalty were because of informed selectivity, then we should be able to draw a fine distinction between the extreme crimes and criminals for which the death penalty is used and the less extreme crimes and criminals for which the death penalty is not used.

2. Using question (1) as a model, diagram Brennan's arguments for the conclusions that the death penalty is unusually degrading to human dignity (paragraphs 2 to 6); that society disapproves of the infliction of the death penalty (paragraphs 14 to 19); and that the use of the death penalty is an excessive punishment (paragraphs 20–28).

3. Many people believe that the death penalty is justified be-

cause it serves as a deterrent for potential criminals while also ensuring that convicted criminals will not commit additional crimes. In paragraph 27, Brennan concludes that there is "no substantial reason to believe that the punishment of death, as currently administered, is necessary for the protection of society." Should the burden of proof be on Brennan to prove that society will be just as safe if the death penalty is not used, or should it be on Brennan's opponents to prove that the death penalty makes society safer?

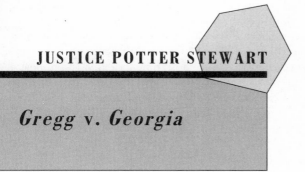

JUSTICE POTTER STEWART

Gregg v. *Georgia*

Justice Stewart, 1915–1981, was born in Jackson, Michigan, and educated at Yale University. He was appointed to the United States Supreme Court by President Eisenhower in 1954. In the following selection, Stewart responds to Justice William Brennan's decision in the 1972 case of Furman v. Georgia *and to legislation enacted by various states in the wake of the* Furman *decision. In his opinion for* Furman v. Georgia, *Justice Brennan argued that capital punishment violates the Eighth Amendment to the Constitution's prohibition of "cruel and unusual punishment."*

Judgment of the Court, and opinion of Mr. Justice Stewart, Mr. Justice Powell, and Mr. Justice Stevens, announced by Mr. Justice Stewart. . . .   1

[Justice Potter Stewart, *Gregg* v. *Georgia* 428 U.S. 153 (1976), excerpts from parts III, IV, and V.]

III

2   . . . The Court on a number of occasions has both assumed and asserted the constitutionality of capital punishment. In several cases that assumption provided a necessary foundation for the decision, as the Court was asked to decide whether a particular method of carrying out a capital sentence would be allowed to stand under the Eighth Amendment. But until *Furman* v. *Georgia,* the Court never confronted squarely the fundamental claim that the punishment of death always, regardless of the enormity of the offense or the procedure followed in imposing the sentence, is cruel and unusual punishment in violation of the Constitution. Although this issue was presented and addressed in *Furman,* it was not resolved by the Court. Four Justices would have held that capital punishment is not unconstitutional *per se;* two Justices would have reached the opposite conclusion; and three Justices, while agreeing that the statutes then before the Court were invalid as applied, left open the question whether such punishment may ever be imposed. We now hold that the punishment of death does not invariably violate the Constitution.

A

3   The history of the prohibition of "cruel and unusual" punishment already has been reviewed at length. The phrase first appeared in the English Bill of Rights of 1689, which was drafted by Parliament at the accession of William and Mary. The English version appears to have been directed against punishments unauthorized by statute and beyond the jurisdiction of the sentencing court, as well as those disproportionate to the offense involved. The American draftsmen, who adopted the English phrasing in drafting the Eighth Amendment, were primarily concerned, however, with proscribing "tortures" and other "barbarous" methods of punishment. . . .

4   . . . A penalty also must accord with "the dignity of man," which is the "basic concept underlying the Eighth Amendment." This means, at least, that the punishment not be "excessive." When a form of punishment in the abstract (in this case, whether capital

punishment may ever be imposed as a sanction for murder) rather than in the particular (the propriety of death as a penalty to be applied to a specific defendant for a specific crime) is under consideration, the inquiry into "excessiveness" has two aspects. First, the punishment must not involve the unnecessary and wanton infliction of pain. Second, the punishment must not be grossly out of proportion to the severity of the crime.

B

Of course, the requirement of the Eighth Amendment must be applied with an awareness of the limited role to be played by the courts. This does not mean that judges have no role to play, for the Eighth Amendment is a restraint upon the exercise of legislative power. . . .

But, while we have an obligation to insure that constitutional bounds are not overreached, we may not act as judges as we might as legislators.

> "Courts are not representative bodies. They are not designed to be a good reflex of a democratic society. Their judgment is best informed, and therefore most dependable, within narrow limits. Their essential quality is detachment, founded on independence. History teaches that the independence of the judiciary is jeopardized when courts become embroiled in the passions of the day and assume primary responsibility in choosing between competing political, economic and social pressures."

Therefore, in assessing a punishment selected by a democratically elected legislature against the constitutional measure, we presume its validity. We may not require the legislature to select the least severe penalty possible so long as the penalty selected is not cruelly inhumane or disproportionate to the crime involved. And a heavy burden rests on those who would attack the judgment of the representatives of the people.

This is true in part because the constitutional test is intertwined with an assessment of contemporary standards and the legislative judgment weighs heavily in ascertaining such standards. "[I]n a democratic society legislatures, not courts, are constituted to re-

spond to the will and consequently the moral values of the people."
The deference we owe to the decisions of the state legislatures under
our federal system is enhanced where the specification of punishments is concerned, for "these are peculiarly questions of legislative
policy." Caution is necessary lest this Court become, "under the
aegis of the Cruel and Unusual Punishment Clause, the ultimate
arbiter of the standards of criminal responsibility . . . throughout the
country." A decision that a given punishment is impermissible
under the Eighth Amendment cannot be reversed short of a constitutional amendment. The ability of the people to express their
preference through the normal democratic processes, as well as
through ballot referenda, is shut off. Revisions cannot be made in
the light of further experience.

C

9   In the discussion to this point we have sought to identify the
principles and considerations that guide a court in addressing an
Eighth Amendment claim. We now consider specifically whether
the sentence of death for the crime of murder is a *per se* violation
of the Eighth and Fourteenth Amendments to the Constitution. We
note first that history and precedent strongly support a negative
answer to this question.

10   The imposition of the death penalty for the crime of murder has
a long history of acceptance both in the United States and in
England. The common-law rule imposed a mandatory death sentence on all convicted murderers. And the penalty continued to be
used into the 20th century by most American States, although the
breadth of the common-law rule was diminished, initially by nar-
rowing the class of murders to be punished by death and subsequently by widespread adoption of laws expressly granting juries
the discretion to recommend mercy.

11   It is apparent from the text of the Constitution itself that the
existence of capital punishment was accepted by the Framers. At
the time the Eighth Amendment was ratified, capital punishment
was a common sanction in every State. Indeed, the First Congress
of the United States enacted legislation providing death as the
penalty for specified crimes. The Fifth Amendment, adopted at the

same time as the Eighth, contemplated the continued existence of the capital sanction by imposing certain limits on the prosecution of capital cases:

> "No person shall be held to answer for a capital, or otherwise infamous crime, unless on a presentment or indictment of a Grand Jury . . . ; nor shall any person be subject for the same offense to be twice put in jeopardy of life or limb; . . . nor be deprived of life, liberty, or property, without due process of law. . . ."

And the Fourteenth Amendment, adopted over three-quarters of a century later, similarly contemplates the existence of the capital sanction in providing that no State shall deprive any person of "life, liberty, or property" without due process of law.

For nearly two centuries, this Court, repeatedly and often expressly, has recognized that capital punishment is not invalid *per se*. . . . 12

Four years ago, the petitioners in *Furman* and its companion 13 cases predicated their argument primarily upon the asserted proposition that standards of decency had evolved to the point where capital punishment no longer could be tolerated. The petitioners in those cases said, in effect, that the evolutionary process had come to an end, and that standards of decency required that the Eighth Amendment be construed finally as prohibiting capital punishment for any crime regardless of its depravity and impact on society. This view was accepted by two Justices. Three other Justices were unwilling to go so far; focusing on the procedures by which convicted defendants were selected for the death penalty rather than on the actual punishment inflicted, they joined in the conclusion that the statutes before the Court were constitutionally invalid.

The petitioners in the capital cases before the Court today renew 14 the "standards of decency" argument, but developments during the four years since *Furman* have undercut substantially the assumptions upon which their argument rested. Despite the continuing debate, dating back to the 19th century, over the morality and utility of capital punishment, it is now evident that a large proportion of American society continues to regard it as an appropriate and necessary criminal sanction.

The most marked indication of society's endorsement of the 15 death penalty for murder is the legislative response to *Furman*. The legislatures of at least 35 States have enacted new statutes that provide for the death penalty for at least some crimes that result in the death of another person. And the Congress of the United States, in 1974, enacted a statute providing the death penalty for aircraft piracy that results in death. These recently adopted statutes have attempted to address the concerns expressed by the Court in *Furman* primarily (i) by specifying the factors to be weighed and the procedures to be followed in deciding when to impose a capital sentence, or (ii) by making the death penalty mandatory for specified crimes. But all of the post-*Furman* statutes make clear that capital punishment itself has not been rejected by the elected representatives of the people.

16   In the only statewide referendum occurring since *Furman* and brought to our attention, the people of California adopted a constitutional amendment that authorized capital punishment, in effect negating a prior ruling by the Supreme Court of California in *People* v. *Anderson* (1972) that the death penalty violated the California Constitution.

17   The jury also is a significant and reliable objective index of contemporary values because it is so directly involved. The Court has said that "one of the most important functions any jury can perform in making . . . a selection [between life imprisonment and death for a defendant convicted in a capital case] is to maintain a link between contemporary community values and the penal system." It may be true that evolving standards have influenced juries in recent decades to be more discriminating in imposing the sentence of death. But the relative infrequency of jury verdicts imposing the death sentence does not indicate rejection of capital punishment *per se*. Rather, the reluctance of juries in many cases to impose the sentence may well reflect the humane feeling that this most irrevocable of sanctions should be reserved for a small number of extreme cases. Indeed, the actions of juries in many States since *Furman* are fully compatible with the legislative judgments, reflected in the new statutes, as to the continued utility and necessity of capital punishment in appropriate cases. At the close of 1974 at least 254 persons had been sentenced to death since *Furman*, and by the end of March 1976, more than 460 persons were subject to death sentences.

As we have seen, however, the Eighth Amendment demands   18
more than that a challenged punishment be acceptable to contemporary society. The Court also must ask whether it comports with
the basic concept of human dignity at the core of the Amendment.
Although we cannot "invalidate a category of penalties because we
deem less severe penalties adequate to serve the ends of penology,"
the sanction imposed cannot be so totally without penological
justification that it results in the gratuitous infliction of suffering.

The death penalty is said to serve two principal social purposes: 19
retribution and deterrence of capital crimes by prospective offenders.

In part, capital punishment is an expression of society's moral   20
outrage at particularly offensive conduct. This function may be
unappealing to many, but it is essential in an ordered society that
asks its citizens to rely on legal processes rather than self-help to
vindicate their wrongs.

> "The instinct for retribution is part of the nature of man, and
> channeling that instinct in the administration of criminal justice
> serves an important purpose in promoting the stability of a society
> governed by law. When people begin to believe that organized
> society is unwilling or unable to impose upon criminal offenders the
> punishment they 'deserve,' then there are sown the seeds of anar-
> chy—of self-help, vigilante justice, and lynch law." *Furman* v.
> *Georgia* (Stewart, J., concurring).

"Retribution is no longer the dominant objective of the criminal
law," but neither is it a forbidden objective nor one inconsistent
with our respect for the dignity of men. Indeed, the decision that
capital punishment may be the appropriate sanction in extreme
cases is an expression of the community's belief that certain crimes
are themselves so grievous an affront to humanity that the only
adequate response may be the penalty of death.

Statistical attempts to evaluate the worth of the death penalty as   21
a deterrent to crimes by potential offenders have occasioned a great
deal of debate. The results simply have been inconclusive. As one
opponent of capital punishment has said:

> "[A]fter all possible inquiry, including the probing of all possible
> methods of inquiry, we do not know, and for systematic and easily

visible reasons cannot know, what the truth about this 'deterrent' effect may be. . . .

"The inescapable flaw is . . . that social conditions in any state are not constant through time, and that social conditions are not the same in any two states. If an effect were observed (and the observed effects, one way or another, are not large) then one could not at all tell whether any of this effect is attributable to the presence or absence of capital punishment. A 'scientific'—that is to say, a soundly based—conclusion is simply impossible, and no methodological path out of this tangle suggests itself."

22   Although some of the studies suggest that the death penalty may not function as a significantly greater deterrent than lesser penalties, there is no convincing empirical evidence either supporting or refuting this view. We may nevertheless assume safely that there are murderers, such as those who act in passion, for whom the threat of death has little or no deterrent effect. But for many others, the death penalty undoubtedly is a significant deterrent. There are carefully contemplated murders, such as murder for hire, where the possible penalty of death may well enter into the cold calculus that precedes the decision to act. And there are some categories of murder, such as murder by a life prisoner, where other sanctions may not be adequate.

23   The value of capital punishment as a deterrent of crime is a complex factual issue the resolution of which properly rests with the legislatures, which can evaluate the results of statistical studies in terms of their own local conditions and with a flexibility of approach that is not available to the courts. Indeed, many of the post-*Furman* statutes reflect just such a responsible effort to define those crimes and those criminals for which capital punishment is most probably an effective deterrent.

24   In sum, we cannot say that the judgment of the Georgia Legislature that capital punishment may be necessary in some cases is clearly wrong. Considerations of federalism, as well as respect for the ability of a legislature to evaluate, in terms of its particular State, the moral consensus concerning the death penalty and its social utility as a sanction, require us to conclude, in the absence of more convincing evidence, that the infliction of death as a punishment for murder is not without justification and thus is not unconstitutionally severe.

Finally, we must consider whether the punishment of death is   25
disproportionate in relation to the crime for which it is imposed.
There is no question that death as a punishment is unique in its
severity and irrevocability. When a defendant's life is at stake, the
Court has been particularly sensitive to insure that every safeguard
is observed. But we are concerned here only with the imposition of
capital punishment for the crime of murder, and when a life has
been taken deliberately by the offender, we cannot say that the
punishment is invariably disproportionate to the crime. It is an
extreme sanction, suitable to the most extreme of crimes.

We hold that the death penalty is not a form of punishment that   26
may never be imposed, regardless of the circumstances of the
offense, regardless of the character of the offender, and regardless
of the procedure followed in reaching the decision to impose it.

IV

[A . . .]

B

We now turn to consideration of the constitutionality of Georgia's   27
capital-sentencing procedures. In the wake of *Furman*, Georgia
amended its capital punishment statute, but chose not to narrow the
scope of its murder provisions. Thus, now as before *Furman*, in
Georgia "[a] person commits murder when he unlawfully and with
malice aforethought, either express or implied, causes the death of
another human being." All persons convicted of murder "shall be
punished by death or by imprisonment for life."

Georgia did act, however, to narrow the class of murderers subject   28
to capital punishment by specifying 10 statutory aggravating circumstances, one of which must be found by the jury to exist beyond
a reasonable doubt before a death sentence can ever be imposed. In
addition, the jury is authorized to consider any other appropriate

aggravating or mitigating circumstances. The jury is not required to find any mitigating circumstances in order to make a recommendation of mercy that is binding on the trial court, but it must find a *statutory* aggravating circumstance before recommending a sentence of death.

29   These procedures require the jury to consider the circumstances of the crime and the criminal before it recommends sentence. No longer can a Georgia jury do as Furman's jury did: reach a finding of the defendant's guilt and then, without guidance or direction, decide whether he should live or die. Instead, the jury's attention is directed to the specific circumstances of the crime: Was it committed in the course of another capital felony? Was it committed for money? Was it committed upon a peace officer or judicial officer? Was it committed in a particularly heinous way or in a manner that endangered the lives of many persons? In addition, the jury's attention is focused on the characteristics of the person who committed the crime: Does he have a record of prior convictions for capital offenses? Are there any special facts about this defendant that mitigate against imposing capital punishment (*e.g.,* his youth, the extent of his cooperation with the police, his emotional state at the time of the crime). As a result, while some jury discretion still exists, "the discretion to be exercised is controlled by clear and objective standards so as to produce non-discriminatory application."

30   As an important additional safeguard against arbitrariness and caprice, the Georgia statutory scheme provides for automatic appeal of all death sentences to the State's Supreme Court. That court is required by statute to review each sentence of death and determine whether it was imposed under the influence of passion or prejudice, whether the evidence supports the jury's finding of a statutory aggravating circumstance, and whether the sentence is disproportionate compared to those sentences imposed in similar cases.

31   In short, Georgia's new sentencing procedures require as a prerequisite to the imposition of the death penalty, specific jury findings as to the circumstances of the crime or the character of the defendant. Moreover, to guard further against a situation comparable to that presented in *Furman,* the Supreme Court of Georgia compares each death sentence with the sentences imposed on similarly situated defendants to ensure that the sentence of death in a particular case is not disproportionate. On their face these proce-

dures seem to satisfy the concerns of *Furman*. No longer should there be "no meaningful basis for distinguishing the few cases in which [the death penalty] is imposed from the many cases in which it is not. . . ."

V

The basic concern of *Furman* centered on those defendants who were being condemned to death capriciously and arbitrarily. Under the procedures before the Court in that case, sentencing authorities were not directed to give attention to the nature or circumstances of the crime committed or to the character or record of the defendant. Left unguided, juries imposed the death sentence in a way that could only be called freakish. The new Georgia sentencing procedures, by contrast, focus the jury's attention on the particularized nature of the crime and the particularized characteristics of the individual defendant. While the jury is permitted to consider any aggravating or mitigating circumstances, it must find and identify at least one statutory aggravating factor before it may impose a penalty of death. In this way the jury's discretion is channeled. No longer can a jury wantonly and freakishly impose the death sentence; it is always circumscribed by the legislative guidelines. In addition, the review function of the Supreme Court of Georgia affords additional assurance that the concerns that prompted our decision in *Furman* are not present to any significant degree in the Georgia procedure applied here. 32

For the reasons expressed in this opinion, we hold that the statutory system under which Gregg was sentenced to death does not violate the Constitution. Accordingly, the judgment of the Georgia Supreme Court is affirmed. . . . 33

STUDY QUESTIONS

   1. At the end of paragraph 4, Justice Stewart offers two criteria by which to decide whether a punishment is "cruel and

unusual." How do these compare to the four criteria Justice Brennan offered in the *Furman* case?

2. In *Furman*, Brennan argued against capital punishment, in part, on the grounds that it is "unacceptable to contemporary society"; he used as evidence the fact that juries rarely impose capital punishment even when it is an available option. What strategies does Stewart adopt in paragraphs 14 through 17 in responding to Brennan?

3. Unlike Brennan, Stewart holds that retribution is an appropriate purpose for a criminal justice system. In paragraph 20, he argues, using the following propositions, that sometimes capital punishment is appropriate as a form of retribution. Diagram the argument.

(1) Humans have an instinct for retribution.

(2) If people do not believe the criminal justice system will impose upon criminals the punishments they deserve, the seeds of anarchy are sown.

(3) Having retribution as one of the aims of the criminal justice system promotes social stability.

(4) Some crimes are extreme affronts to humanity.

(5) Therefore, sometimes capital punishment is the only adequate response.

4. Stewart believes that the seeming arbitrariness of the use of the death penalty was central to the *Furman* case. In paragraphs 27 through 31, how many newly enacted safeguards against arbitrariness does Stewart mention?

5. In the *Furman* decision, Brennan offered four arguments to support the conclusion that the death penalty is cruel and unusual. Has Stewart responded to each of those arguments?

PART FOUR

On the Arts

JOHN ENRIGHT

What Is Poetry?

*John Enright, born in 1952, is a poet and computer consultant
living in Chicago. A volume of his poetry,* Starbound and
Other Poems, *was published by Axton Press in 1995. Many
attempts have been made to define poetry, and the difficulty of
the task can be seen in the fact that none of the attempts has
met with widespread acceptance. In the following selection,
Enright critiques a few of those previous definitions and defends his own.*

Poetry, among the arts, has a history of being poorly, even mysteri-
ously, defined. Part of the problem is that many of those offering

[John Enright, excerpt from "What Is Poetry?" *Objectively Speaking* (Autumn
1989).]

definitions have been poets; and too many of their definitions have been more poetical than precise. Emily Dickinson, for instance, on being asked her criterion for poetry, wrote: "[i]f I read a book and it makes my whole body so cold that no fire can warm me, I know that it is poetry. If I feel physically as if the top of my head were taken off, I know that is poetry." This is vivid and forceful, but it tells us much more about Emily Dickinson than it does about poetry.

2   Dylan Thomas called poetry " . . . the rhythmic, inevitably narrative movement from an over-clothed blindness to a naked vision." In his inclusion of the word "rhythmic," Thomas's definition is a step up from Dickinson's, for he indicates one of poetry's distinguishing marks.

3   An all-too-common failing of proposed definitions of poetry is that they could apply equally well to other art forms. Witness Shelley's: "[p]oetry is the record of the best and happiest moments of the best and happiest minds." Poe did better: "I would define the poetry of words as the rhythmical creation of beauty." This excludes most of the other arts, but does not sharply distinguish poetry from *song*, which also uses words and rhythm.

4   A formal definition combines a genus and a differentia—the general class to which a thing belongs, and the characteristics that make it different from the rest of the things in that class.

5   The proper genus of poetry is art form. We differentiate art forms from one another by the specific material media of the forms. The medium of poetry is language, but novels and vocal songs also depend upon language. The unique medium of poetry is *language utilizing the musical elements intrinsic to the language*. In contrast, prose makes little use of language's musical potential, and song turns upon a musical element which is extrinsic to language: melody.

6   Two classical definitions of poetry, "musical speech" and "rhythmical speech," are not far off the mark. The trouble with "musical speech" is that it does not differentiate poetry from song. The trouble with "rhythmic speech" is that rhythm is *not* the only musical element that poetry employs. There is *much* more to the music of language than beat.

7   An objection to be expected here is that I am simply defining poetry as *verse*, and that I must consequently accept as poetry commercial jingles, such as: "Hold the pickles, hold the let-

tuce!/Special orders don't upset us." However, the purpose of defining poetry's genus as "art form" was precisely to forestall such classification. An art form must project a deeply held view of life—which the above Burger King jingle does not.

It *is* true that much of modern "poetry" cannot qualify as real   8
poetry by this definition. But I consider this to be a virtue rather than a fault. . . .

STUDY QUESTIONS

1. Enright quotes Emily Dickinson, Dylan Thomas, and Percy Bysshe Shelley. Using the criteria for good definitions, critique the quotations as definitions of poetry.
2. Consider several poems that you know. Do all of them utilize *"the musical elements intrinsic to the language,"* as Enright claims?
3. What is the distinction Enright makes between poetry and verse? Do you agree with Enright that the commercial jingle he quotes isn't poetry, merely verse?
4. In what way does Enright's proposed definition of poetry depend on an assumed definition of art?
5. Paragraph 5 states that poetry's genus is art form, and paragraph 7 that an art form must project "a deeply held view of life." This means that Enright's definition of poetry excludes a large body of writing that other people might classify under this concept. How should one decide which attributes are essential to poetry?

JESSE HELMS

Amendment 420 [The NEA Should Not Fund Obscenity]

Mr. Helms is a United States senator from North Carolina. Helms was outraged to learn that taxpayer money was used to support the work of Andres Serrano, Robert Mapplethorpe, and others. Mr. Serrano, for example, had received a grant from the National Endowment for the Arts for a project that consisted of a crucifix placed in a bottle filled with his urine. The following is Helms's proposal to the U.S. Senate to eliminate government funding for art that is judged to be obscene or indecent.

Amendment No. 420

(Purpose: To prohibit the use of appropriated funds for the dissemination, promotion, or production of obscene or indecent materials or materials denigrating a particular religion)

1   MR. HELMS. Mr. President, I send an amendment to the desk and ask for its immediate consideration.

2   The PRESIDING OFFICER. The clerk will report.

3   The legislative clerk read as follows:

[Jesse Helms, Amendment 420: The NEA Should Not Fund Obscenity. U.S. Senate, July 26, 1989. Reprinted in Bolton, Richard, ed. *Culture Wars*, New Press, 1992, pp. 73–77.]

The Senator from North Carolina [Mr. Helms] proposes an   4
amendment numbered 420.

Mr. HELMS. Mr. President, I ask unanimous consent that read-   5
ing of the amendment be dispensed with.

The PRESIDING OFFICER. Without objection, it is so ordered.   6

The amendment is as follows: 7

On page 94, line 16, strike the period and insert the following: 8
"provided that this section will become effective one day after the
date of enactment.

Sec. limitations.

None of the funds authorized to be appropriated pursuant to this   9
Act may be used to promote, disseminate, or produce—

1. obscene or indecent materials, including but not limited to
   depictions of sadomasochism, homoeroticism, the exploitation
   of children, or individuals engaged in sex acts; or
2. material which denigrates the objects or beliefs of the adherents of a particular religion or nonreligion; or
3. material which denigrates, debases, or reviles a person, group
   or class of citizens on the basis of race, creed, sex, handicap, age,
   or national origin.

Mr. HELMS. Mr. President, this amendment has been agreed to   10
on both sides, I believe. I very much appreciate it.

Mr. President, I believe we are all aware of the controversy   11
surrounding the use of Federal funds, via the National Endowment
for the Arts [NEA], to support so-called works of art by Andres
Serrano and Robert Mapplethorpe. My amendment would prevent
the NEA from funding such immoral trash in the future. Specifically, my amendment prohibits the use of the NEA's funds to
support obscene or indecent materials, or materials which denigrate
the objects or beliefs of a particular religion.

I applaud the efforts of my distinguished colleagues from West   12
Virginia, Mr. BYRD, and from Idaho, Mr. McCLURE, to address
this issue in both the Appropriations Subcommittee on the Interior,
and the full Appropriations Committee. Cutting off funding to the
Southeastern Center for Contemporary Art [SECCA] in Winston-
Salem and the Institute for Contemporary Art in Philadelphia will

certainly prevent them from misusing Federal funds for the next 5 years. However, as much as I agree with the measures, the committee's efforts do not go far enough because they will not prevent such blasphemous or immoral behavior by other institutions or artists with Government funds. That is why I have offered my amendment.

13   Frankly, Mr. President, I have fundamental questions about why the Federal Government is involved in supporting artists the taxpayers have refused to support in the marketplace. My concern in this regard is heightened when I hear the arts community and the media saying that any restriction at all on Federal funding would amount to censorship. What they seem to be saying is that we in Congress must choose between: First, absolutely no Federal presence in the arts; or second, granting artists the absolute freedom to use tax dollars as they wish, regardless of how vulgar, blasphemous, or despicable their works may be.

14   If we indeed must make this choice, then the Federal Government should get out of the arts. However, I do not believe we are limited to those two choices and my amendment attempts to make a compromise between them. It simply provides for some common sense restrictions on what is and is not an appropriate use of Federal funding for the arts. It does not prevent the production or creation of vulgar works, it merely prevents the use of Federal funds to support them.

15   Mr. President, I remind my colleagues that the distinguished Senator from New York and I called attention to Mr. Serrano's so-called work of art, which portrays Jesus Christ submerged in a bottle of the artist's urine, on May 18. We pointed out that the National Endowment for the Arts had not only supported a $15,000 award honoring Mr. Serrano for it, but they also helped promote and exhibit the work as well.

16   Over 25 Senators—Democrats and Republicans—expressed their outrage that day by cosigning a letter to Hugh Southern, the Endowment's acting chairman, asking him to review their procedures and to determine what steps are needed to prevent such abuses from recurring in the future. Mr. Southern replied on June 6 that he too was personally offended by Mr. Serrano's so-called art, but that—as I have heard time after time on this issue—the Endowment is prevented by its authorizing language from promoting or suppressing particular points of view.

Mr. Southern's letter goes on to endorse the Endowment's panel   17
review system as a means of ensuring competence and integrity in
grant decisions, and he states that the Endowment will review their
processes to be sure they are effective and maintain the highest
artistic integrity and quality.

However, Mr. President, shortly after receiving Mr. Southern's   18
response, I became aware of yet another example of the competence,
integrity and quality of the Endowment's panel review system. It is
a federally supported exhibit entitled: "Robert Mapplethorpe: The
Perfect Moment." The Corcoran Gallery of Art had planned to open
the show here in Washington on July 1, but abruptly canceled it
citing the danger the exhibit poses to future Federal funding for the
arts. The Washington Project for the Arts subsequently agreed to
make their facilities available and opened the show last Friday, July
21.

Mr. President, the National Endowment, the Corcoran, and oth-   19
ers in the arts community felt the Mapplethorpe exhibit endangered Federal funding for the arts because the patently offensive
collection of homoerotic pornography and sexually explicit nudes
of children was put together with the help of a $30,000 grant from
the Endowment. The exhibit was assembled by the University of
Pennsylvania's Institute for Contemporary Art as a retrospective
look at Mr. Mapplethorpe's work after his recent death from AIDS.
It has already appeared in Philadelphia and Chicago with the
Endowment's official endorsement.

I have a catalog of the show and Senators need to see it to believe   20
it. However, the catalog is only a survey, not a complete inventory,
of what was in the Endowment's show. If Senators are interested, I
have a list and description of the photographs appearing in the show
but not the catalog because even the catalog's publishers knew they
were too vulgar to be included—as sick as that book is.

Vanity Fair magazine ran an article on another collection of   21
Mapplethorpe's works which appears at the Whitney Museum of
Modern Art in New York. This collection included many of the
photographs currently in the NEA funded exhibit. There are un-
speakable portrayals which I cannot describe on the floor of the
Senate.

Mr. President, this pornography is sick. But Mapplethorpe's sick   22
art does not seem to be an isolated incident. Yet another artist

exhibited some of this sickening obscenity in my own State. The Duke Museum of Art at Duke University had a show deceptively titled "Morality Tales: History Painting in the 1980's." One painting, entitled "First Sex," depicts a nude woman on her back, legs open, knees up, and a little boy leaning against her leg looking into her face while two sexually aroused older boys wait in the background. Another work shows a man urinating on a boy lying in a gutter. Other, more despicable, works were included as well.

23   I could go on and on, Mr. President, about the sick art that has been displayed around the country. These shows are outrageous. And, like Serrano's blasphemy, the most outrageous thing is that some of the shows like Mapplethorpe's are financed with our tax dollars. Again, I invite Senators to see what taxpayers got for $30,000 dollars.

24   Mr. President, how did the Endowment's vaunted panel review system approve a grant for this pornography? It was approved because the panel only received a description, provided by the Endowment's staff, which read as follows:

25   "To support a mid-career summary of the work of photographer Robert Mapplethorpe. Although all aspects of the artist's work—the still-lifes, nudes, and portraits—will be included, the exhibition will focus on Mapplethorpe's unique pieces where photographic images interact with richly textured fabrics within carefully design frames."

26   Mr. President, what a useless and misleading description. No legitimate panel of experts would know from this description that the collection included explicit homoerotic pornography and child obscenity. Yet none of the descriptions for other projects funded by the Endowment at the time were any better. Indeed, Mr. Jack Neusner—who sat on the panel approving the Mapplethorpe exhibit—was mystified as to how he had approved a show of this character. He knows now that he was misled.

27   Mr. President, I was hopeful Washington would be spared this exhibit when the Corcoran canceled it. I only wish the Corcoran had canceled the show out of a sense of public decency and not as part of a calculated attempt to shield themselves and the Endowment from criticism in Congress.

28   Some accuse us of censorship because we threaten to cut off Federal funding, yet they are the ones who refuse to share the

contents of their exhibits with the taxpayers' elected representatives. For example, the Southeastern Center for Contemporary
Art in Winston-Salem refused to send me copies of requested works
despite their earlier promises to the contrary. If what such institutions promote and exhibit is legitimate art, then why are they afraid
for the taxpayers and Congress to see what they do?

Mr. President, there is a fundamental difference between Gov- 29
ernment censorship—the preemption of publication or production—and governmental refusal to pay for such publication and
production. Artists have a right, it is said, to express their feelings
as they wish: only a philistine would suggest otherwise. Fair enough,
but no artist has a preemptive claim on the tax dollars of the
American people; time for them, as President Reagan used to say,
"to go out and test the magic of the marketplace."

Congress attaches strings to Federal funds all the time. Churches 30
must follow strict Federal guidelines in order to participate in
Federal programs for the poor and needy—even when those guidelines violate their religious tenets. For example, a U.S. District Court
in Alabama recently held that a practicing witch employed by the
Salvation Army in a women's shelter could not be fired because the
shelter was federally funded.

Mr. President, there have been instances where public outrage 31
has forced artists to remove works from public display. For instance,
shortly after Mayor Harold Washington's death, a work portraying
him as a transvestite was forcibly removed from a show in Chicago.
Another work on display at Richmond's airport was voluntarily
removed after the night crew complained about a racial epithet
which had been inscribed on it. There was little real protest from
the arts community in these instances.

Mr. President, at a minimum, we need to prohibit the Endow- 32
ment from using Federal dollars to fund filth like Mr. Serrano's and
Mr. Mapplethorpe's. If it does not violate criminal statutes and the
private sector is willing to pay for it, fine! However, if Federal funds
are used, then Congress needs to ensure the sensitivities of all
groups—regardless of race, creed, sex, national origin, handicap, or
age—are respected.

Federal funding for sadomasochism, homoeroticism, and child 33
pornography is an insult to taxpayers. Americans for the most part
are moral, decent people and they have a right not to be denigrated,

offended, or mocked with their own tax dollars. My amendment would protect that right.

34   Mr. President, if Senators want the Federal Government funding pornography, sadomasochism, or art for pedophiles, they should vote against my amendment. However, if they think most voters and taxpayers are offended by Federal support for such art, they should vote for my amendment.

STUDY QUESTIONS

1. In paragraphs 32 and 33, Senator Helms makes the argument diagrammed here:

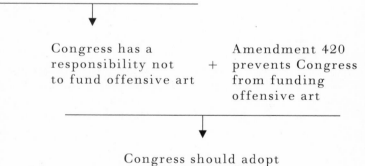

What premise(s) is/are assumed in the above argument?

2. Helms uses the following concepts (and others) to describe various works: *art, obscene, denigrating, blasphemous, sick, offensive, degrading, pornographic, vulgar.* While some of the concepts may be synonyms, construct a genus and species classification scheme to capture the relationship between as many of them as you can.

3. In paragraphs 13, 14, and 29, Helms responds to the charge
   that his amendment is a form of censorship. What definition
   of censorship does his response involve? Does that definition
   seem correct to you?

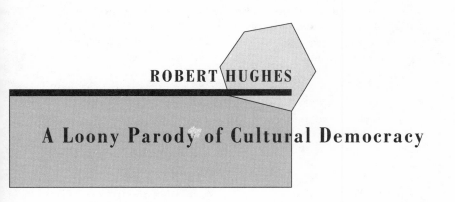

ROBERT HUGHES

A Loony Parody of Cultural Democracy

Robert Hughes is art critic for Time *magazine. In the following article, Hughes argues against Jesse Helms's Amendment
420 and defends government funding for the arts.*

Senator Jesse Helms, that noted paleo-conservative, has taken up   1
the cudgels against the most distinguished and useful vehicle of
patronage in American cultural life, the National Endowment for
the Arts. Neoconservatives want to keep the NEA because they
would like to run it. Paleos like Helms don't greatly care whether
it exists or not; if attacking it can serve a larger agenda, fine.

Last year NEA money totaling $45,000 was used by the Corcoran   2
museum for an exhibition by the photographer Robert Mapplethorpe and by an institution that gave an award to the artist
Andres Serrano. One of Serrano's pieces was a photo of a plastic
crucifix immersed in the artist's urine—a fairly conventional piece
of postsurrealist blasphemy, which, though likely to have less effect
on established religion than a horsefly on a tank, was bound to irk

[Robert Hughes, "A Loony Parody of Cultural Democracy," *Time*, August 14,
1989.]

some people. Mapplethorpe's show was to contain some icy, polished and (to most straights and one surmises, at least a few Republican gays) deeply repulsive photos of S and M queens doing this and that to one another.

3   As soon as the dewlaps of Senator Helms' patriarchal wrath started shaking at its door, the Corcoran caved in and canceled Mapplethorpe's show. Unappeased, the ayatullah of North Carolina proposed a measure that would forbid the NEA to give money to "promote, disseminate or produce" anything "obscene or indecent" or derogatory of "the objects or beliefs of the adherents of a particular religion or non-religion"—which, taken literally, comprises any image or belief of any kind, religious or secular.

4   In effect, this would make the NEA hostage to every crank, ideologue and God botherer in America. A grant for an exhibition of Gothic ivories could be pulled on the grounds that the material was offensive to Jews (much medieval art is anti-Semitic), to Muslims (what about those scenes of false prophets in hell with Muhammad?) or, for that matter, to atheists offended by the intrusion of religious propaganda into a museum. A radical feminist could plausibly argue that her "nonreligious" beliefs were offended by the sexism of Rubens' nudes or Picasso's *Vollard Suite.* Doubtless a fire worshiper would claim that the presence of extinguishers in a theater was repugnant to his god.

5   In short, what the amendment proposes is a loony parody of cultural democracy in which everyone becomes his or her own Cato the Censor. Clearly, Jesse Helms has no doubt that the NEA must be punished if it strays from what he fancies to be the center line of American ethical belief. The truth is, of course, that no such line exists—not in a society as vast, various and eclectic as the real America. Helms' amendment might have played in Papua, where a government spokesman defended the banning of Martin Scorsese's *The Last Temptation of Christ* on the grounds that "our people traditionally set much store on dreams and hallucinations." But in the U.S., no.

6   The problem is compounded by the fact that the NEA is not a ministry of culture. It does not commission large works to reflect glory on the state, or set firm policy for other institutions. Its $169 million budget is tiny—less than one-third the projected price of one Stealth bomber, or, to put it another way, only ten times the

recent cost of a single painting by Jasper Johns. The French government spends three times the NEA's budget each year on music, theater and dance alone ($560 million in 1989). German government spending on culture runs at around $4.5 billion, repeat, billion a year.

The extreme conservative view is that support of the contemporary arts is not the business of government. Never mind that quite a few people who were not exactly radicals, from Rameses II to Louis XIV and Pope Urban VIII, thought otherwise and thus endowed the world with parts of the Egypt, the Paris and the Rome we have today. New culture is optional—slippery stuff, ambiguous in its meanings, uncertain in its returns. Away with it! Let the corporations underwrite it!

The fetish of supply-side culture was one of the worst legacies of the Reagan years. Though the Great Communicator was frustrated in his attempt to abolish the Endowment in 1981, he made sure that more government money went to military bands than to the entire budget of the NEA. Oom-pah-pah culture to fit a time of oom-pah-pah politics. After all, who could say that the arts needed support outside the marketplace at a time when star orchestra conductors were treated like sacred elephants and the art market was turning into a freakish potlatch for new money?

Conversely, why bother to support what market Darwinism seems to condemn to obscurity? "I have fundamental questions," Helms grated, "about why the federal government is supporting artists the taxpayers have refused to support in the marketplace." But this was exactly what the NEA was created, in 1965, to do—and it was the wisest of decisions. Lots of admirable art does badly at first; its rewards to the patron are not immediate and may never come. Hence the need for the NEA. It is there to help the self-realization of culture that is not immediately successful.

Corporate underwriting has produced some magnificent results for American libraries, museums, ballets, theaters and orchestras—for institutional culture, across the board. But today it is shrinking badly, and it requires a delicate balance with government funding to work well. Corporations' underwriting money comes out of their promotion budgets and—not unreasonably, since their goal is to make money—they want to be associated with popular, prestigious events. It's no trick to get Universal Widget to underwrite a Renoir show, or one of those PBS nature series (six hours of granola TV, with bugs copulating to Mozart). But try them with newer, more controversial, or more demanding work and watch the faces in the boardroom drop. Corporate is nervous money; it needs the NEA for reassurance as a Good Housekeeping Seal of Approval. Our problem, despite conservative rant, is too little government support for the arts, not too much. Even if we had a ministry of culture to parade the roosters, we would still need the NEA to look after the eggs.

STUDY QUESTIONS

1. Mr. Hughes says that Jesse Helms is using a "cudgel" on the NEA (paragraph 1), that he is acting in a "patriarchal" manner (paragraph 3), and calls him an "ayatullah" (paragraph 3). Hughes selected these metaphors for their rhetorical force, but what is their literal content—that is, what criticism of Helms do they imply?
2. In paragraphs 7 through 9, Hughes responds to the view, argued by Robert Samuelson and suggested by Jesse Helms in their articles, that the funding of art is not a legitimate purpose of government. What are the premises of his argument?
3. Part of Hughes's argument is diagrammed here.

(1) Governments have successfully funded great art

(2) The market will not adequately fund new and original art

(3) The amount of funding of art by the US government is small compared to that of other governments

(4) The U.S. government should fund art

Identify the premises that Hughes offers to support premises (1)–(3).

4. What does the title of Hughes's article mean?

ROBERT SAMUELSON

Highbrow Pork Barrel

Mr. Samuelson is a columnist who writes regularly for na-tional publication. He is the author of The Good Life and Its Discontents *(1996). In the following article, Samuelson argues that federal funding for the arts should be ended.*

I once suggested that Congress consider creating a National Endow-ment for Rodeo. The proposal's point was to show that rodeo subsidies are as worthy as "art" subsidies. Going beyond the irony, I urged abolishing the National Endowment for the Arts (NEA). This prompted the usual fan mail. One reader speculated that my cultural tastes ran to watching women's mud wrestling. Suppose they did. Should government then subsidize what I consider art?

The recent furor over allegedly obscene art financed by the NEA has only confirmed the wisdom of my view. Genuine art is about self-expression. It flows from individual imagination, ingenuity, joy and rage. By definition, it is undefinable. Standards are always subjective. In a democratic society there is a permanent conflict between artistic freedom and political accountability for "art" sup-ported by public money.

[Robert Samuelson, "Highbrow Pork Barrel," *Washington Post*, August 16, 1989.]

3   Sen. Jesse Helms, Republican of North Carolina, is correct when he says taxpayers shouldn't have to pay for art that most Americans find offensive or indecent. (The current cause célèbre: a picture of a crucifix floating in urine, funded by an NEA grant.) But Helms' critics are also correct when they decry censorship and warn against government imposing standards of conformity and respectability. There's an easy escape from this impasse. Get government out of the arts. Then artists could create without fear, and congressmen would have no cause for complaint.

4   Now I was not born yesterday. I know that the chances of Congress erasing the NEA are about one in 25,000. But we can at least see it for what it is—highbrow pork barrel. By this, I mean that the NEA spends public monies to pay for what are basically private pleasures and pursuits. I do not mean that no good comes from these grants. But the good goes primarily to the individual artists and art groups that receive the grants and to their relatively small audiences. Public benefits are meager.

5   There's a serious issue here, as political scientist Edward Banfield has argued. What are the legitimate uses of national government? Our federal government is the mechanism by which we tax ourselves to meet collective national needs. Subsidizing "art" fails this elementary test. It does not meet an important national need. Neither do subsidies for "good" television or the "humanities": the missions of the Corporation for Public Broadcasting and the National Endowment for the Humanities.

6   Suppose someone actually proposed a National Endowment for Rodeo with a $169 million budget, which is the 1989 budget for the NEA. Grants would go to individual rodeo riders ("to foster bull-riding skills") and to rodeo shows ("to make rodeos more available to the public"). Questions would arise. Why do rodeo riders and fans merit special treatment? Do they create some public benefit?

7   It's considered uncouth to ask similar questions of public support for opera, sculpture, painting or television. But, of course, the same questions apply. Grants from the NEA go mainly to individual artists or arts organizations. In 1988 the New York Philharmonic received $286,000; the San Francisco Opera Association got $330,000; the Denver Center for Performing Arts got $75,000. There were grants of about $10,000 each to 55 small literary magazines, and 89 sculptors got grants of about $5,000 apiece.

What justifies the subsidies? The idea that our artistic future   8
depends on federal handouts to free artists from commercial pressures falters on two counts. It overlooks the complexity of creative
motivation and ignores the corrupting influences of government
grantsmanship. Herman Melville did not need an NEA grant to
write; Winslow Homer did not need an NEA grant to paint. Art
consumers benefit from the NEA, because their ticket prices are
indirectly subsidized. But these are mainly higher-income people
who deserve no subsidy. In 1987 only a quarter of the public
attended opera or musical theater, reports pollster Louis Harris. But
half of those with incomes exceeding $50,000 attended. Museum
and theater attendance reflect similar income patterns.

Public-television subsidies are also highbrow pork barrel. On   9
average, public TV draws about 4 percent of prime-time viewers.
The "MacNeil/Lehrer NewsHour" receives the largest grant from
the Corporation for Public Broadcasting (CPB), $4.3 million in
1989. It's a superb program, but what public purpose does it serve?
Can anyone claim there isn't enough news? My guess is that its
audience consists heavily of news junkies, who read newspapers and
magazines, and watch CNN. The program doesn't inform the uni-
formed but better informs the well-informed.

No great (or even minor) national harm would occur if Congress   10
axed these cultural agencies. Museums wouldn't vanish; the NEA
provides a tiny share of their funds. Neither would public television
stations; they rely on the CPB for only about 11 percent of their
money. The CPB's children's programs with distinct instructional
value could be moved to the Department of Education. In any case,
"Sesame Street" would survive. Oscar the Grouch and his pals are
a tiny industry appearing on toys and clothes.

Some arts groups would retrench, and others would die. Many   11
would find new funding sources; in 1987 private giving for cultural
activities totaled $6.4 billion. The great undercurrents of American
art would continue undisturbed, because they're driven by forces—
the search to understand self and society, the passion of individual
artists—far more powerful than the U.S. Treasury. And the $550
million spent by the three main cultural agencies could be used for
more legitimate public needs: for example, reducing the budget
deficit or improving Medicaid.

As I said, this won't happen. The obscenity tempest probably   12 won't even provoke a serious examination of government and the arts. Arts and public-broadcasting advocates cast any questioning of federal financing as an assault on the Temples of Culture by the Huns. Like all groups feeding at the federal trough, they've created a rhetoric equating their self-interest with the national interest.

13   Most congressmen accept these fictitious claims because Congress enjoys the power and, on occasion, finds the agencies useful whipping boys. It's a marriage of convenience that, however, dishonest, seems fated to endure.

STUDY QUESTIONS

1. Central to Mr. Samuelson's argument is his premise about the legitimate uses of government. In paragraph 5 he offers a definition of legitimate government. In your judgment, is this definition satisfactory? If so, on what grounds does Samuelson then conclude that government subsidies for art are illegitimate?

2. Part of Samuelson's argument for the conclusion that NEA funding is "highbrow pork" is diagrammed here.

Government funding supports the San Francisco Opera Association (paragraph 7)	+	Those who enjoy opera are mainly higher-income people (paragraph 8)

Government funding for the arts is highbrow pork (paragraph 4)

How many other such examples does Samuelson use as premises in support of his conclusion?

3. Do the premises in the following part of Samuelson's argument work additively or independently to support the conclusion?

(1) Government funding is a small part of most cultural agencies' budgets (paragraph 10).
(2) Many great artists in the past created without government funding (paragraph 8).
(3) Therefore, the future of art does not depend on government funding.
4. In paragraphs 12 and 13, Samuelson is skeptical that funding for the NEA will be examined seriously. What are the reasons for his skepticism?

STEVEN DURLAND

Censorship, Multiculturalism, and Symbols

Steven Durland is editor of High Performance *magazine. In this selection, Durland hypothesizes that the controversy over NEA funding is at root an attack on members of minority groups by racist, homophobic, and sexist white males who dominate American society.*

Eventually you will have to ask: who is doing the art that's getting censored? Mapplethorpe was gay, Serrano is Hispanic. Scott Tyler is black. The San Diego billboard group is multicultural, promoting a black cause. While this censorship crisis may be a surprise to many, any multicultural, gay or feminist artist can give you a litany of examples. Were I to make the charge that these acts of censorship were motivated by racism, homophobia or sexism, I'm sure most of

1

[Steven Durland, excerpt from "Censorship, Multiculturalism, and Symbols," *High Performance* (Fall 1989)]

the perpetrators would argue vehemently that such was not the case. And I think they'd honestly believe it when they say it. So what gives?

2   What gives is that the voice of the dominant culture has never understood what it *actually* means when it so graciously legislates racial, sexual and gender equality. Subconsciously, they think they're giving everyone a chance to be just like them. A chance to live like white men. A chance to make art in the great Euro-Western tradition. They've failed to realize that few want to be like them. Rather, they want the freedom to be themselves, living their own religions, and their own histories, and their own cultures. Just like it says in the Constitution. And that is definitely a threat to a country that, in spite of its "Bill of Rights," imagines itself to be white, Christian, heterosexual and male.

3   There are some overriding art world ironies here. For years national, state and local funding agencies have made it a priority to assure that at least token funding go to representatives of these groups. You seldom hear of a peer panel review any more that doesn't make a point of noting sex and ethnicity in the distribution of money. What the people at the top have failed to realize, though, is that when you give a voice to people who've been denied for so long, what you're going to find out is that these people are really pissed* (pun intended) off. No "Thank you, massa" here. They will immediately take the opportunity to point out racist governments and sexist religions and Christian hypocrisy. Sure it may be raw. But it's exercising the same right, used with a much greater sense of real "American" morality, that the dominant culture has used for so long to keep women in the home, blacks in their place, and gays on their death beds.

4   It's a fact that only ten percent of the families in the U.S. are representative of "male provider, woman in the home with the kids." Perhaps these men with their "women in the homes" have more time to write letters, and that's why this small population is dominating our cultural debate. I don't know. They've certainly managed a voice that vastly outnumbers their membership. Per-

---

*A reference to a work by Andres Serrano, which was a crucifix suspended in a bottle of Serrano's urine.—Eds.

haps, in this particular instance, the art world is to blame for its own problems. Any elected official would recognize in an instant that no matter how much artists protest, when it's time to go to the polls, Wildmon's* supporters are going to make their wives go out and vote, while the poorly networked and apolitical members of the art world are deconstructing sitcoms. A sad thought when you consider that the art world potentially has much more clout. . . .

The final, overriding irony in all this, is that all parties in-   5
volved—the artists, the conservative right, the Congress—are in the position of not being able to do anything about the things that are really upsetting them. To compensate, each group, in their own way, is attacking what is perceived to be a symbol of its antagonism. For the artists, those symbols may be the crucifixes of religious zealots, the flags of racist governments, or the sexual mores of oppressive cults. (Excuse me, but why *aren't* fanatic Christians who give lots of money to dubious ministers considered cultists? Where are the de-programmers when you need them?) For the conserva-tive right, the art they attack is, for them, symbolic of a general breakdown in moral fiber. For Congress, this is their Grenada: a symbolic show of power directed toward a tiny, defenseless agency in a government over which they've lost control.

For the artists, working with symbols is the stock in trade. For   6
the others, it's a cop out. The artists have done their job. They've called attention to some of our social, cultural and political failings. If Helms or Wildmon wants to "kill the messenger," they're just not doing their job.

To quote Hilton Kramer, "What we're being asked to support   7
and embrace in the name of art is an attitude toward life." He's right. But unlike Mr. Kramer, I would see it as very positive to support an attitude—even a government supported policy—that champions freedom of expression. Especially when we're faced with the alternatives—the ones we generally associate with such names as Hitler, Stalin, Khomeini and Deng Xiaoping. Need we add Helms to that list?

---

*A reference to Donald Wildmon of Mississippi, a social activist and leader of the American Family Association. Mr. Wildmon has been active in opposing works of art deemed obscene or irreligious.—Eds.

STUDY QUESTIONS

1. In the first paragraph, Mr. Durland concludes that various artists were censored because they were members of minority groups. Does he argue deductively or inductively for his conclusion?

2. The heart of Durland's argument is presented in paragraphs 2 and 3, the main parts of which are extracted here. Diagram the argument.
   (1) The dominant culture has long suppressed minority cultures.
   (2) The minority cultures do not want to be like the dominant culture.
   (3) Therefore, if the dominant culture stops suppressing the minority cultures, the minority cultures will criticize the dominant culture.
   (4) The dominant culture believes that freedom means only the freedom to be like the dominant culture.
   (5) Therefore, the dominant culture will not like the criticism.
   (6) Therefore, the dominant culture will try to censor the criticism.
   (7) Mapplethorpe, Serrano, and others were members of minority groups.
   (8) Mapplethorpe, Serrano, and others were critical of the dominant culture.
   (9) Therefore, Mapplethorpe, Serrano, and others were censored by the dominant culture.

3. In his final paragraph, Durland compares Jesse Helms to several powerful 20th century dictators. In your judgment, would Helms's amendment take us closer to dictatorship?

MARSHA FAMILIARO ENRIGHT

Why Does Music Cause Emotion?

Marsha Familiaro Enright received a bachelor's degree in biology from Northwestern University in Chicago and a master's degree in psychology from the New School for Social Research in New York City. She is currently President of Council Oak Montessori Elementary School.

I. Introduction

Why does man make music?   1

Music is an art without an apparent object—there are no scenes   2
to look at, no sculptured marbles to touch, no stories to follow—and
yet it can cause some of the most passionate and intense feelings
possible. How does this happen—how can sounds from resonant
bodies produce emotion in man?

Further, what is the possible biological function and evolutionary   3
origin of this process by which sound elicits feeling? One researcher
in the psychology of music summarized the problem as follows:
"Musical messages seem to convey no biologically relevant information, as do speech, animal utterances and environmental
sound—yet people from all cultures do react to musical messages.
What in human evolution could have led to this? Is there, or has

[Excerpts from Marsha Familiaro Enright, "Con Molto Sentimento." *Objectivity* 2:3 (1996), 117–151.]

there been, a survival value for the human race in music?" (Roederer 1984, 351).

4   Many in the course of history have thought that music is a kind of language, the language of feeling. And research confirms the everyday experience that music causes emotional states which can seriously affect our actions. Konecni (1982) found that subjects who had been insulted by confederates working for the experimenter were quite aggressive about shocking those confederates. But subjects who had merely been exposed to loud, complex music were almost as aggressive about shocking confederates as the insulted subjects had been! In another experiment, subjects were able to shape their moods by their musical choices, and thereby optimize their moods. Depending on the way they felt when they came to the experimental session (anxious or angry or happy), and how they wanted to feel afterwards, they could pick music that changed the way they felt entirely—once again supporting the idea that the sounds of music have a direct effect on emotions.

5   In this article, I have gathered evidence from several areas of the research literature in search of an answer to the question of music's evolutionary origin and biological function. I believe this evidence indicates that music evolved out of the sonority and prosody of vocal communication and that musical elaboration of those elements has a special biological communication function. Prosody evidently facilitates linguistic syntax (Shapiro and Nagel 1995). In other words, music grew out of man's ability to communicate his feelings through sound.

6   More neuropsychological knowledge is needed to prove my thesis—but I leave the reader to turning over the evidence I have assembled, along with his own knowledge of music, in considering the question: Why does man make music?

II. Neuropsychological Data on Language and Music

7   Why should certain kinds of sounds be able to directly evoke emotion? By what means, what neuropsychological processes?

As have so many in the history of music theory, Roederer (1984) 8
wonders whether the answer lies in the unique human capacity for
language. Human infants have high motivation to acquire language, as evidenced by the assiduous way they attend to, imitate,
and practice language. Language activities are very pleasurable; if
they were not, human infants would not be motivated to perform
language-related activities as much as they do. On this evidence, I
venture to say that humans have built-in developmental pleasure-
pain processes for producing and listening to language. Language
acquisition is a cognitive activity that is highly motivated and
important to survival. Are the emotions aroused for language acquisition the evolutionary link between sound and emotion? That is,
are humans moved by sound as a result of a biological need to be
interested in acquiring language?

> "Experiments show that there are strong similarities in the way in
> which people perceive structure in music and in language . . . [but]
> overall, the syntax of music has much more latitude than that of
> language. Thus, in the syntaxes of music and language, we must
> remember that music is far more flexible and ambiguous than
> language" (Aiello 1994a, 46–49).

Furthermore, neuropsychological evidence seems to be at odds with 9
the proposal that language is the basis of music. The areas of the
brain which primarily process speech are, apparently, mostly different from those which process music. Investigations into the brain
areas that process speech and music have found that, in most infants,
the left hemisphere responds more to speech sounds and the right
to musical tones, as indicated by a type of EEG called auditory
evoked potentials (Molfese 1977). Measures of how much attention
a neonate paid to left- or right-ear stimuli (as indicated by "high
amplitude non-nutritive sucking") indicated that most infants responded more to language sounds presented to their right ears (left
hemispheres) and to musical sounds presented to their left ears
(right hemispheres) (Entus 1977; Glanville, Best, and Levenson
1977), although Vargha-Khadem and Corballis (1979) were not
able to replicate Entus' findings. Best, Hoffman, and Glanville
(1982) found a right-ear advantage for speech in infants older than
two months during tasks in which infants had to remember and
discriminate phonetic sounds and musical timbres. Infants younger

than two months showed an ear advantage only for musical notes, and that advantage was for the left ear. In older children and adult nonmusicians, damage to the left hemisphere usually impairs language functions but tends to spare musical abilities, including singing. Damage to the right hemisphere, particularly the right temporal lobe, tends to leave language functions intact, but impairs musical abilities and the production and comprehension of language tone and of emotion expressed through language or other sounds (Joanette, Goulet, and Hannequin 1990).

10   Zatorre (1979) found a left-ear advantage for the discrimination of melodies versus speech in a dichotic listening task with both musicians and nonmusicians. He found cerebral blood-flow evidence that right temporal lobe neurons are particularly important in melodic and pitch discriminations (Zatorre, Evans, and Meyer 1994). Tramo and Bharucha (1991), following the work of Gordon (1970), found that the right hemisphere seems to process the perception of harmonics (tested by the detection of complex relationships among simultaneous musical sounds). Damage to the right temporal lobe impairs the ability to recognize timbre, and time cues within tones that determine the recognition of timbre (Samson and Zatorre 1993). These authors suggest that "the same acoustical cues involved in perception of musical timbre may also serve as linguistic cues under certain circumstances" (ibid., 239). There are now indications that timbre and phonetic information are processed through some common stage beyond peripheral acoustic processing. Research is underway to determine whether voice identification also proceeds through this same timbre-phoneme nonperipheral stage (Pitt 1995).

11   In a critical review, Zatorre (1984) notes that right-sided damage can produce deficits in tasks that process patterns of pitch and timbre differences. Adults with partial or complete excisions of the right temporal lobe were found to be significantly impaired in the perception of pitch (Zatorre 1988). Kester et al. (1991) found that musical processing was most affected by right temporal lobectomy. In a review of the literature on the infant's perception of tone sequences, or melodies, Trehub (1990) found that human infants do not use local pitch strategies characteristic of nonhuman species, that is, they do not depend on the recognition of particular, or absolute pitches, to identify tone sequences. Rather, like human

adults, they use global and relational means to encode and retain contours of melodies, with little attention to absolute pitch. (Although, interestingly, Kessen, Leving, and Wendrich (1979) found that infants paid very close attention to experimenters' singing and could imitate pitch quite well.) In other words, human infants have the ability to recognize exact pitches, but the exact key in which a melody is played makes little difference for human infant recognition of melody, while animals depend on the particular pitch in which their "song" is sung to recognize it. This seems to imply that even human infants are extracting the abstract pattern of the sounds, rather than using the sounds as signs (specific perceptual markers) of events. In reviewing the research on infants' perception of music, Trehub (1987) suggests that infants have the skills for analyzing complex auditory stimuli. These skills may correspond to musical universals, as indicated by infants' preference for major triadic chord structures.

The evidence indicates that human infants have the ability to recognize and process music in a fairly complex way, at a very early age. Furthermore, music processing in most infants and adults seems to occur primarily in the right hemisphere. And infants, like adults, appear to find music interesting: they tend to pay attention to it, they like to engage in imitations of adult pitches, and they learn to sing as soon as they learn to speak (Cook 1994).

III. Neuropsychological Data on Emotions

How does the data on the neuropsychological processes involved in music relate to the data on the neuropsychological processes involved in emotions?

It is well established that for most people, right-hemisphere damage causes difficulties with the communication and comprehension of emotion (Bear 1983; Ross 1984). Apparently, the right hemisphere mediates the processing of many types of emotionally laden information: visual, facial, gestural, bodily, and auditory. The evidence suggests that the right hemisphere has a special relationship with the emotional functions of the human mind, specifically in being able to process and project emotional meaning through perceptual information (Kolb and Whishaw 1990).

15   Rate, amplitude, pitch, inflection, timbre, melody, and stress contours of the voice are means by which emotion is communicated (in nonhuman as well as human species), and the right hemisphere is superior in the interpretation of these features of voice (Joseph 1988). Samson and Zatorre (1993) found similar cortical areas responding to pitch and timbre in humans and animals. In dichotic listening tasks, Zurif and Mendelsohn (1972) found a right-ear advantage for correctly matching meaningless, syntactically organized sentences with meaningful ones by the way the sentence was emotionally intoned. The subjects could apparently match such nonsense sentences as "Dey ovya ta ransch?" with "How do you do?" by the intonation the speaker gave the sentence. Heilman, Scholes, and Watson (1975) found that subjects with right temporal-parietal lesions tended to be impaired at judging the mood of a speaker. Heilman et al. (1984) also compared subjects with right temporal-lobe damage to both normals and asphasics in discriminating the emotional content of speech. He presented all three types of subjects with sentences wherein the verbal content of the speakers was filtered out and only the emotional tone was left, and found those with temporal-lobe damage to be impaired in their emotional discriminations. In a similar study, Tompkins and Flowers (1985) found that the tonal memory scores (how well the subjects could remember specific tones) for right-brain-damaged subjects were lower than those of other subjects, implying that right-brain damage leads to a problem with the perceptual encoding of sound, but not necessarily with the comprehension of emotional meaning per se.

16   The human voice conveys varied, complex, and subtle meaning through timbre, pitch, stress contour, tempo, and so forth and thereby communicates emotion. "What is clear is that the rhythmic and the musical are not contingent additions to language. . . . The 'musical' aspect of language emphasizes the way that all communication has an irreducibly particular aspect which cannot be subtracted from it" (Bowie 1990, 174–75). Best, Hoffman, and Glanville (1982) found that the ability to process timbre appears in

neonates and very young infants, apparently before the ability to process phonetic stimuli. Through the "music" in voice, we comprehend the feelings of others and we communicate ours to them. This is an important ability for the well-being of the human infant, who has not yet developed other human tools for communicating its needs and comprehending the world around it—a world in which the actions and feelings of its caretakers are of immense importance to its survival.

Emotion is conveyed through language in at least two ways: through the specifically verbal content of what is said, and through the "musical" elements in voice, which are processed by the right hemisphere. One of the characteristic features of traditional poetry is the dense combination of the meaning of words with the way they sound, which, when done well, results in emotionally moving artwork (Enright 1989). Mothers throughout the world use nursery rhymes, a type of poetry, to amuse and soothe infants and young children, that is, to arouse emotions they find desirable in the children. "Music can articulate the 'unsayable,' which is not representable by concepts or verbal language" (Bowie 1990, 184). "Men have not found the words for it nor the deed nor the thought, but they have found the music" (Rand 1943, 544).

Was nature being functionally logical and parsimonious to combine, in the right hemisphere, those functions which communicate emotion with those that comprehend emotion? As social animals, humans have many ways of communicating and comprehending emotions: facial expression, gesture, body language, and voice tone. I propose that music's biopsychological origins lie in the ability to recognize and respond directly to the feelings of another through tone of voice, an important ability for infant and adult survival. (The tone of voice of an angry and menacing person has a very different implication than that of a sweet and kind person.) If inflection and nuance enhance the effect of spoken language, in music they create the meaning of the notes. Unlike words, notes and rests do not point to ideas beyond themselves; their meaning lies precisely in the quality of the sounds and silences, so that the exact renderings of the notes, the nuances, the inflection, the intensity and energy with which notes are performed become their musical meaning (J. M. Lewers, quoted in Aiello 1994a, 55).

19   Furthermore, I propose that the sound triggers literally those physiological processes which cause the corresponding emotion "action programmes," "essentic forms," or whatever one wishes to call these processes. This would explain the uniquely automatic quality in our response to music. In other words, I am proposing that the biopsychological basis of the ability of sound to cause emotions in man originates in man's ability to emotionally respond to the sounds of another's voice. Theoretically, this ability lies in the potential for certain kinds of sounds to set off a series of neurological processes resulting in emotions, which events are similar to those occurring during the usual evocation of emotions. Thus, as so many in the history of musical theory have conjectured, music does result from language—but not language's abstract, denotative qualities.

20   However, I should posit that it is not the ontogeny of language per se that caused the development of music in humans. Many nonhuman animals communicate emotion and subsequently direct and orchestrate actions of their species through voice tone, and there is considerable evidence that humans do likewise, which argues that this ability arose before the emergence of language. Returning to my earlier discussion of motivation in the infant acquisition of language, it seems more likely that the pleasures and emotions communicated through voice (which motivate the acquisition of language) are another biological application of the ability of voice tone to emotionally affect us, rather than an initial cause of emotion in voice. Humans were already set to be affected by voice tone when we acquired the ability to speak. Pleasure associated with vocalizing likely developed into pleasure in language acquisition.

IV. Future Research

21   My hypothesis on the evolutionary basis of music in our ability to respond to emotion in tone of voice would need a vast array of experiments to be proved, including further inquiry into the neurological structures which process voice tone and music. Presumably, if the hypothesis is true, a significant overlap would be found in the areas that process voice tone and the areas that process music. . . .

STUDY QUESTIONS

Ms. Enright's article presents and argues five conclusions.

(1) That language is processed in the left hemisphere of the brain, while emotion and music are processed in the right (paragraphs 9–11, 14–15).

(2) That the communication of emotion in language is a function of structures of sound such as pitch, inflection, timbre, and so on (paragraph 15).

(3) That the communication of emotion between parent and pre-linguistic infant is biologically important to the infant's survival and development (paragraph 16).

(4) That the ability of pre-linguistic infants to understand the emotional content of speech-sounds carried in pitch, inflection, timbre, and so on evolved to help ensure the survival and development of those infants (paragraph 18).

(5) That music's ability to cause emotion is a consequence of humans' ability to understand the content carried in the structures of sound that communicate emotion in language (paragraphs 18–19).

1. Are the experimental results Enright describes in paragraphs 9–11 sufficiently numerous and diverse to make reasonable the conclusion that music is processed in the right hemisphere of the brain?

2. Are they sufficient to make reasonable the conclusion reached in paragraph 12 that infants can respond to music before they can understand language?

3. In her first four paragraphs, Enright explains why it has traditionally been difficult to explain our responses to music. What are the difficult things that she thinks a satisfactory explanation of music has to account for? In your judgment, does her hypothesis of paragraphs 18 and 19 succeed as an explanation?

4. At the end of the article, Enright indicates that further research is necessary to establish her hypothesis more completely. Given what you know, imagine one experiment that may help accomplish this.

STEPHEN JAY GOULD

Sex, Drugs, Disasters, and the Extinction of Dinosaurs

Stephen Jay Gould, born in New York City in 1941, is Profes-
sor of Geology at Harvard University. He is the author of nu-
merous popular essays on science, many of which have been
collected into books such as The Panda's Thumb, Hen's
Teeth and Horse's Toes, *and* The Flamingo's Smile, *from*
which the following essay is taken.

Science, in its most fundamental definition, is a fruitful mode of   1
inquiry, not a list of enticing conclusions. The conclusions are the
consequence, not the essence.

[Stephen J. Gould, "Sex, Drugs, Disasters, and the Extinction of Dinosaurs,"
in *The Flamingo's Smile: Reflections in Natural History.* New York: W. W. Norton,
1985, pp. 417–426.]

2   My greatest unhappiness with most popular presentations of
science concerns their failure to separate fascinating claims from
the methods that scientists use to establish the facts of nature.
Journalists, and the public, thrive on controversial and stunning
statements. But science is, basically, a way of knowing—in P. B.
Medawar's apt words, "the art of the soluble." If the growing corps
of popular science writers would focus on *how* scientists develop and
defend those fascinating claims, they would make their greatest
possible contribution to public understanding.

3   Consider three ideas, proposed in perfect seriousness to explain
that greatest of all titillating puzzles—the extinction of dinosaurs.
Since these three notions invoke the primally fascinating themes of
our culture—sex, drugs, and violence—they surely reside in the
category of fascinating claims. I want to show why two of them rank
as silly speculation, while the other represents science at its grandest
and most useful.

4   Science works with testable proposals. If, after much compilation
and scrutiny of data, new information continues to affirm a hypothesis, we may accept it provisionally and gain confidence as
further evidence mounts. We can never be completely sure that a
hypothesis is right, though we may be able to show with confidence
that it is wrong. The best scientific hypotheses are also generous and
expansive: they suggest extensions and implications that enlighten
related, and even far distant, subjects. Simply consider how the idea
of evolution has influenced virtually every intellectual field.

5   Useless speculation, on the other hand, is restrictive. It generates
no testable hypothesis, and offers no way to obtain potentially
refuting evidence. Please note that I am not speaking of truth or
falsity. The speculation may well be true; still, if it provides, in
principle, no material for affirmation or rejection, we can make
nothing of it. It must simply stand forever as an intriguing idea.
Useless speculation turns in on itself and leads nowhere; good
science, containing both seeds for its potential refutation and implications for more and different testable knowledge, reaches out. But,
enough preaching. Let's move on to dinosaurs, and the three proposals for their extinction.

   1. Sex: Testes function only in a narrow range of temperature (those
   of mammals hang externally in a scrotal sac because internal body

temperatures are too high for their proper function). A worldwide rise in temperature at the close of the Cretaceous period caused the testes of dinosaurs to stop functioning and led to their extinction by sterilization of males.

2. Drugs: Angiosperms (flowering plants) first evolved toward the end of the dinosaurs' reign. Many of these plants contain psychoactive agents, avoided by mammals today as a result of their bitter taste. Dinosaurs had neither means to taste the bitterness nor livers effective enough to detoxify the substances. They died of massive overdoses.

3. Disasters: A large comet or asteroid struck the earth some 65 million years ago, lofting a cloud of dust into the sky and blocking sunlight, thereby suppressing photosynthesis and so drastically lowering world temperatures that dinosaurs and hosts of other creatures became extinct.

Before analyzing these three tantalizing statements, we must establish a basic ground rule often violated in proposals for the dinosaurs' demise. *There is no separate problem of the extinction of dinosaurs.* Too often we divorce specific events from their wider contexts and systems of cause and effect. The fundamental fact of dinosaur extinction is its synchrony with the demise of so many other groups across a wide range of habitats, from terrestrial to marine.

The history of life has been punctuated by brief episodes of mass extinction. A recent analysis by University of Chicago paleontologists Jack Sepkoski and Dave Raup, based on the best and most exhaustive tabulation of data ever assembled, shows clearly that five episodes of mass dying stand well above the "background" extinctions of normal times (when we consider all mass extinctions, large and small, they seem to fall in a regular 26-million-year cycle). The Cretaceous debacle, occurring 65 million years ago and separating the Mesozoic and Cenozoic eras of our geological time scale, ranks prominently among the five. Nearly all the marine plankton (single-celled floating creatures) died with geological suddenness; among marine invertebrates, nearly 15 percent of all families perished, including many previously dominant groups, especially the ammonites (relatives of squids in coiled shells). On land, the dinosaurs disappeared after more than 100 million years of unchallenged domination.

In this context, speculations limited to dinosaurs alone ignore the larger phenomenon. We need a coordinated explanation for a system of events that includes the extinction of dinosaurs as one component. Thus it makes little sense, though it may fuel our desire to view mammals as inevitable inheritors of the earth, to guess that dinosaurs died because small mammals ate their eggs (a perennial favorite among untestable speculations). It seems most unlikely that some disaster peculiar to dinosaurs befell these massive beasts—and that the debacle happened to strike just when one of history's five great dyings had enveloped the earth for completely different reasons.

8   The testicular theory, an old favorite from the 1940s, had its root in an interesting and thoroughly respectable study of temperature tolerances in the American alligator, published in the staid *Bulletin of the American Museum of Natural History* in 1946 by three experts on living and fossil reptiles—E. H. Colbert, my own first teacher in paleontology; R. B. Cowles; and C. M. Bogert.

9   The first sentence of their summary reveals a purpose beyond alligators: "This report describes an attempt to infer the reactions of extinct reptiles, especially the dinosaurs, to high temperatures as based upon reactions observed in the modern alligator." They studied, by rectal thermometry, the body temperatures of alligators under changing conditions of heating and cooling. (Well, let's face it, you wouldn't want to try sticking a thermometer under a 'gator's tongue.) The predictions under test go way back to an old theory first stated by Galileo in the 1630s—the unequal scaling of surfaces and volumes. As an animal, or any object, grows (provided its shape doesn't change), surface areas must increase more slowly than volumes—since surfaces get larger as length squared, while volumes increase much more rapidly, as length cubed. Therefore, small animals have high ratios of surface to volume, while large animals cover themselves with relatively little surface.

10   Among cold-blooded animals lacking any physiological mechanism for keeping their temperatures constant, small creatures have a hell of a time keeping warm—because they lose so much heat through their relatively large surfaces. On the other hand, large animals, with their relatively small surfaces, may lose heat so slowly that, once warm, they may maintain effectively constant temperatures against ordinary fluctuations of climate. (In fact, the resolution of the "hot-blooded dinosaur" controversy that burned so

brightly a few years back may simply be that, while large dinosaurs possessed no physiological mechanism for constant temperature, and were not therefore warm-blooded in the technical sense, their large size and relatively small surface area kept them warm.)

Colbert, Cowles, and Bogert compared the warming rates of small   11
and large alligators. As predicted, the small fellows heated up (and cooled down) more quickly. When exposed to a warm sun, a tiny 50-gram (1.76-ounce) alligator heated up one degree Celsius every minute and a half, while a large alligator, 260 times bigger at 13,000 grams (28.7 pounds), took seven and a half minutes to gain a degree. Extrapolating up to an adult 10-ton dinosaur, they concluded that a one-degree rise in body temperature would take eighty-six hours. If large animals absorb heat so slowly (through their relatively small surfaces), they will also be unable to shed any excess heat gained when temperatures rise above a favorable level.

The authors then guessed that large dinosaurs lived at or near   12
their optimum temperatures; Cowles suggested that a rise in global temperatures just before the Cretaceous extinction caused the dino-saurs to heat up beyond their optimal tolerance—and, being so large, they couldn't shed the unwanted heat. (In a most unusual statement within a scientific paper, Colbert and Bogert then explic-itly disavowed this speculative extension of their empirical work on alligators.) Cowles conceded that this excess heat probably wasn't enough to kill or even to enervate the great beasts, but since testes often function only within a narrow range of temperature, he proposed that this global rise might have sterilized all the males, causing extinction by natural contraception.

The overdose theory has recently been supported by UCLA   13
psychiatrist Ronald K. Siegel. Siegel has gathered, he claims, more than 2,000 records of animals who, when given access, administer various drugs to themselves—from a mere swig of alcohol to mas-sive doses of the big H. Elephants will swill the equivalent of twenty beers at a time, but do not like alcohol in concentrations greater than 7 percent. In a silly bit of anthropocentric speculation, Siegel states that "elephants drink, perhaps, to forget . . . the anxiety produced by shrinking rangeland and the competition for food."

Since fertile imaginations can apply almost any hot idea to the   14
extinction of dinosaurs, Siegel found a way. Flowering plants did not evolve until late in the dinosaurs' reign. These plants also

produced an array of aromatic, amino-acid-based alkaloids—the major group of psychoactive agents. Most mammals are "smart" enough to avoid these potential poisons. The alkaloids simply don't taste good (they are bitter); in any case, we mammals have livers happily supplied with the capacity to detoxify them. But, Siegel speculates, perhaps dinosaurs could neither taste the bitterness nor detoxify the substances once ingested. He recently told members of the American Psychological Association: "I'm not suggesting that all dinosaurs OD'd on plant drugs, but it certainly was a factor." He also argued that death by overdose may help explain why so many dinosaur fossils are found in contorted positions. (Do not go gentle into that good night.)[1]

15   Extraterrestrial catastrophes have long pedigrees in the popular literature of extinction, but the subject exploded again in 1979, after a long lull, when the father-son, physicist-geologist team of Luis and Walter Alvarez proposed that an asteroid, some 10 km in diameter, struck the earth 65 million years ago (comets, rather than asteroids, have since gained favor. Good science is self-corrective).

16   The force of such a collision would be immense, greater by far than the megatonnage of all the world's nuclear weapons. In trying to reconstruct a scenario that would explain the simultaneous dying of dinosaurs on land and so many creatures in the sea, the Alvarezes proposed that a gigantic dust cloud, generated by particles blown aloft in the impact, would so darken the earth that photosynthesis would cease and temperatures drop precipitously. (Rage, rage against the dying of the light.)[2] The single-celled photosynthetic oceanic plankton, with life cycles measured in weeks, would perish outright, but land plants might survive through the dormancy of their seeds (land plants were not much affected by the Cretaceous extinction, and any adequate theory must account for the curious pattern of differential survival). Dinosaurs would die by starvation and freezing; small, warm-blooded mammals, with more modest requirements for food and better regulation of body temperature, would squeak through. "Let the bastards freeze in the dark," as bumper stickers of our chauvinistic neighbors in sunbelt states

1. A reference to a poem of this title by the Welsh poet Dylan Thomas (1914–1953).—Eds.
2. A reference to the same poem.—Eds.

proclaimed several years ago during the Northeast's winter oil crisis.

All three theories, testicular malfunction, psychoactive overdosing, and asteroidal zapping, grab our attention mightily. As pure phenomenology, they rank about equally high on any hit parade of primal fascination. Yet one represents expansive science, the others restrictive and untestable speculation. The proper criterion lies in evidence and methodology; we must probe behind the superficial fascination of particular claims.

How could we possibly decide whether the hypothesis of testicular frying is right or wrong? We would have to know things that the fossil record cannot provide. What temperatures were optimal for dinosaurs? Could they avoid the absorption of excess heat by staying in the shade, or in caves? At what temperatures did their testicles cease to function? Were late Cretaceous climates ever warm enough to drive the internal temperatures of dinosaurs close to this ceiling? Testicles simply don't fossilize, and how could we infer their temperature tolerances even if they did? In short, Cowles's hypothesis is only an intriguing speculation leading nowhere. The most damning statement against it appeared right in the conclusion of Colbert, Cowles, and Bogert's paper, when they admitted: "It is difficult to advance any definite arguments against this hypothesis." My statement may seem paradoxical—isn't a hypothesis really good if you can't devise any arguments against it? Quite the contrary. It is simply untestable and unusable.

Siegel's overdosing has even less going for it. At least Cowles extrapolated his conclusion from some good data on alligators. And he didn't completely violate the primary guideline of siting dinosaur extinction in the context of a general mass dying—for rise in temperature could be the root cause of a general catastrophe, zapping dinosaurs by testicular malfunction and different groups for other reasons. But Siegel's speculation cannot touch the extinction of ammonites or oceanic plankton (diatoms make their own food with good sweet sunlight; they don't OD on the chemicals of terrestrial plants). It is simply a gratuitous, attention-grabbing guess. It cannot be tested, for how can we know what dinosaurs tasted and what their livers could do? Livers don't fossilize any better than testicles.

The hypothesis doesn't even make any sense in its own context. Angiosperms were in full flower ten million years before dinosaurs

[17]

[18]

[19]

[20]

went the way of all flesh. Why did it take so long? As for the pains of a chemical death recorded in contortions of fossils, I regret to say (or rather I'm pleased to note for the dinosaurs' sake) that Siegel's knowledge of geology must be a bit deficient: muscles contract after death and geological strata rise and fall with motions of the earth's crust after burial—more than enough reason to distort a fossil's pristine appearance.

21   The impact story, on the other hand, has a sound basis in evidence. It can be tested, extended, refined and, if wrong, disproved. The Alvarezes did not just construct an arresting guess for public consumption. They proposed their hypothesis after laborious geochemical studies with Frank Asaro and Helen Michael had revealed a massive increase of iridium in rocks deposited right at the time of extinction. Iridium, a rare metal of the platinum group, is virtually absent from indigenous rocks of the earth's crust; most of our iridium arrives on extraterrestrial objects that strike the earth.

22   The Alvarez hypothesis bore immediate fruit. Based originally on evidence from two European localities, it led geochemists throughout the world to examine other sediments of the same age. They found abnormally high amounts of iridium everywhere— from continental rocks of the western United States to deep sea cores from the South Atlantic.

23   Cowles proposed his testicular hypothesis in the mid-1940s. Where has it gone since then? Absolutely nowhere, because scientists can do nothing with it. The hypothesis must stand as a curious appendage to a solid study of alligators. Siegel's overdose scenario will also win a few press notices and fade into oblivion. The Alvarezes' asteroid falls into a different category altogether, and much of the popular commentary has missed this essential distinction by focusing on the impact and its attendant results, and forgetting what really matters to a scientist—the iridium. If you talk just about asteroids, dust, and darkness, you tell stories no better and no more entertaining than fried testicles or terminal trips. It is the iridium— the source of testable evidence—that counts and forges the crucial distinction between speculation and science.

24   The proof, to twist a phrase, lies in the doing. Cowles's hypothesis has generated nothing in thirty-five years. Since its proposal in 1979, the Alvarez hypothesis has spawned hundreds of studies, a major conference, and attendant publications. Geologists are fired

up. They are looking for iridium at all other extinction boundaries. Every week exposes a new wrinkle in the scientific press. Further evidence that the Cretaceous iridium represents extraterrestrial impact and not indigenous volcanism continues to accumulate. As I revise this essay in November 1984 (this paragraph will be out of date when the book is published), new data include chemical "signatures" of other isotopes indicating unearthly provenance, glass spherules of a size and sort produced by impact and not by volcanic eruptions, and high-pressure varieties of silica formed (so far as we know) only under the tremendous shock of impact.

My point is simply this: Whatever the eventual outcome (I suspect it will be positive), the Alvarez hypothesis is exciting, fruitful science because it generates tests, provides us with things to do, and expands outward. We are having fun, battling back and forth, moving toward a resolution, and extending the hypothesis beyond its original scope.

As just one example of the unexpected, distant cross-fertilization that good science engenders, the Alvarez hypothesis made a major contribution to a theme that has riveted public attention in the past few months—so-called nuclear winter. In a speech delivered in April 1982, Luis Alvarez calculated the energy that a ten-kilometer asteroid would release on impact. He compared such an explosion with a full nuclear exchange and implied that all-out atomic war might unleash similar consequences.

This theme of impact leading to massive dust clouds and falling temperatures formed an important input to the decision of Carl Sagan and a group of colleagues to model the climatic consequences of nuclear holocaust. Full nuclear exchange would probably generate the same kind of dust cloud and darkening that may have wiped out the dinosaurs. Temperatures would drop precipitously and agriculture might become impossible. Avoidance of nuclear war is fundamentally an ethical and political imperative, but we must know the factual consequences to make firm judgments. I am heartened by a final link across disciplines and deep concerns—another criterion, by the way, of science at its best:[3] A recognition of

---

3. This quirky connection so tickles my fancy that I break my own strict rule about eliminating redundancies from these essays and end both this and the next piece with this prod to thought and action.

the very phenomenon that made our evolution possible by exterminating the previously dominant dinosaurs and clearing a way for the evolution of large mammals, including us, might actually help to save us from joining those magnificent beasts in contorted poses among the strata of the earth.

STUDY QUESTIONS

1. What definition of "science" does Gould propose?
2. On what grounds does Gould contrast good scientific hypotheses with useless speculations?
3. In paragraph 7, why is the hypothesis that small animals ate the dinosaurs' eggs dismissed as an untestable speculation?
4. Why are paragraphs 5 through 7 important to Gould's later evaluation of the proposed explanations of the extinction of the dinosaurs?
5. In paragraph 18, Gould argues that if you can't find any definite arguments against a given hypothesis, then the hypothesis has no value. Why does he believe this to be the case?
6. Reconstruct the "Sex" hypothesis and the "Drugs" hypothesis. In order to explain the extinction of the dinosaurs, what propositions do they depend upon? Is Gould right that none of those propositions is testable?
7. In what ways is the "Disaster" hypothesis both more testable and a more comprehensive explanation of the extinction of the dinosaurs?
8. In the end, how should we view the "Sex" and "Drugs" hypotheses? After all, couldn't they be true, even though they're not testable?

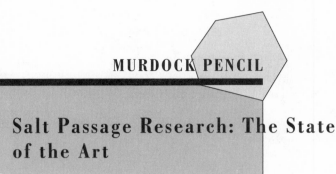

MURDOCK PENCIL

Salt Passage Research: The State of the Art

Murdock Pencil, Professor of Social Darwinism at the Old School for Social Science Research, is the pseudonym of Michael Paconowsky, of the Institute for Communication Research at Stanford University. In the following selection, Paconowsky parodies social science research.

Conclusive evidence on the effects of the utterance "Please pass the salt" is found to be sadly lacking.

Strongly rooted in the English speech community is the belief that the utterance, "Please pass the salt," is efficacious in causing salt to move from one end of a table to the source of the utterance. In his *Canterbury Tales*, Chaucer notes:

> Shee I askked
> The salde to passe.
> Ne surprised was I
> Tha shee didde (4. p. 318).[1]

Similarly, Dickens writes:

> Old Heep did not become disgruntled at my obstinence. "Please pass the salt, Davey," he repeated coldly. I vacillated for a moment longer. Then I passed the salt, just as he knew I would (5. p. 278).

[Murdock Pencil, "Salt Passage Research: The State of the Art." *Journal of Communication* (Autumn 1976), pp. 31–36.]

1.   I asked her to pass the salt.
                    I was not surprised that she did.

2   The question of whether the movement of salt is causally dependent on the utterance of the phrase, "Please pass the salt," has occupied the attention of numerous philosophers (3, 9, 20). Empirical resolution of the validity of this belief, however, was not undertaken until the classic work of Hovland, Lumsdaine, and Sheffield (8) on the American soldier. Since then, numerous social scientists have explored the antecedent conditions that give rise to this apparent regularity. In this article, we will summarize those efforts that shed some light on the complex phenomenon known as salt passage.

3   Many social observers have noticed the apparent regularity with which salt travels from one end of the table to the source of the utterance "Please pass the salt." Hovland, Lumsdaine, and Sheffield (8), however, were the first to demonstrate empirically that the salt passage phenomenon was mediated by the presence of other people at the table. In a comparison of "others present" with "no others present" conditions, they found that when there were other people present at the table, there was a greater likelihood that the utterance, "Please pass the salt," would result in salt movement toward the source of the utterance. When there were *no other people* at the table, the utterance, "Please pass the salt," had no apparent effect. To test the possibility of a time delay involved in the "no others present" condition, Hovland, *et al.* arranged for 112 Army recruits, each sitting alone at one end of a table with salt at the other end, to repeat the utterance, "Please pass the salt," every five minutes for 12 hours. The average distance the salt traveled was .5 inch, which the experimenters explained was due to measurement error. The result of these two studies was, therefore, to demonstrate the importance of the presence of other people in the salt passage phenomenon.

4   Once the presence of other people was established as a necessary condition for salt passage as a consistent response to the utterance, "Please pass the salt," researchers began focusing on source and receiver characteristics that would affect salt passing behavior. Osgood and Tannenbaum (16) predicted greater compliance with salt passage utterances by high credible sources than by low credible sources. Newcomb (14) predicted greater compliance with sources who were perceived to have similar, rather than dissimilar, attitudes. Rokeach (17) predicted greater compliance for low dogmatic, rather than high dogmatic, people. McClelland (12) predicted

greater compliance for high N achievers than low N achievers. Surprisingly, no significant differences were found along any of these dimensions. Differences due to race were found, however, in the original Hovland, *et al.* study (8). Black soldiers were more likely to pass the salt to white soldiers, while white soldiers were less likely to pass the salt to black soldiers.[2]

> *Because source and receiver characteristics seemed to have little effect on the extent of salt passage, research attention turned its focus to the effects of message variables as the causal mechanism underlying this phenomenon.*

Janis and Feshbach (10) found that other utterances were just as effective as "Please pass the salt" in achieving salt passage compliance. No significant differences in the extent of compliance were found due to the utterances, "Please pass the salt," "Would you mind passing the salt?" "Could I have the salt down here, buddy?" and "Salt!" Janis and Feshbach noted that in every successful utterance, the word "salt" was found. They concluded that the frequency of the sound waves associated with the phonemes in "salt" was in fact the causal mechanism underlying the salt passage phenomenon.

5

Zimbardo (21) subjected this hypothesis to an explicit test. He had students from an introductory psychology class sit at a table near a salt shaker while a confederate would say either "Salt!" or "Assault!" He hypothesized that compliance would be as great in the "Salt!" as in the "Assault!" condition. Zimbardo found, however, that the utterance "Assault!" was met with more calls for clarification than the utterance "Salt!" and the utterance "Assault!" had to be repeated more frequently before the salt would move.[3]

6

2. However, in a replication of the original Hovland, *et al.* study, Triandis (19) uncovered the opposite tendency due to race. That is, Triandis found that white soldiers were more likely to pass the salt to black soldiers, while black soldiers were more likely to tell the white soldiers to get the salt themselves.

3. In a replication and extension of the Zimbardo experiment, Kelley (11) found that if the confederate had a steak in front of him. "Assault!" was just as effective as "Salt!" in causing salt passage. Kelley concluded that receivers make attributions as to the meaning of utterances based on environmental cues that they perceive.

The search for the source of regularity in salt passing behavior was extended to situational variables.

7   Asch (1) tested the effects of pressure to conform on salt passage. In an experiment, a subject was seated at a table with seven confederates. The subject and six of the confederates had salt shakers in front of them, one confederate did not. The confederate without the salt shaker said, "Please pass the salt." Asch found that, when one confederate passed the salt, the subject was more likely not to pass the salt; but when all the confederates passed the salt, the subject was more likely to conform to peer pressure and also pass the salt. Asch concluded that conformity was an essential aspect of salt passage.

8   Festinger (6) tested the effects of substance uncertainty on salt passage. Subjects were placed at a table where salt was loosely piled on a napkin, while sugar was placed in a salt shaker. When a confederate said, "Please pass the salt," the overwhelming number of subjects passed the sugar. From this study, Festinger concluded that the salt shaker, not the salt itself, was the crucial factor in salt passage.

9   Bem (2) extended Festinger's study by placing two shakers on the table, both clearly marked with the word "SALT." One shaker had salt in it; the other, however, was filled with pepper. Bem reasoned that, if the salt *shaker* were the crucial factor, both the pepper and salt should be passed about an equal number of times. Surprisingly, Bem found that when prompted with the utterance, "Please pass the salt," people more frequently passed the shaker with salt in it than passed the shaker with pepper in it. Bem concluded that, in salt passage, there is an interaction effect between substance in the shaker and the shaker itself.

10   Festinger (7) tested the effects of payment on subject evaluation of salt passage. In a "high reward" condition, subjects were given $20 for passing the salt. In a "low reward" condition, subjects were given $1 for passing the salt. Subjects' evaluations of how much they liked salt passing were then obtained. No significant differences in salt passage liking were found between the two groups. Subjects paid $20, however, expressed more interest in participating in another session of the experiment than did their $1 counterparts. Festinger concluded that subjects in the $1 condition were probably more trustworthy than subjects in the $20 condition.

Milgram (13) tested the effects of threats on salt passage. In a "no threat" condition, subjects were not forewarned about any consequences of passing salt to a confederate. In a "high threat" condition, subjects were told that if they passed the salt, they would be struck by lightning. Subjects were seated in metal chairs attached to lightning rods. Thunder in the distance was simulated. Significant differences were found in salt passage compliance between "no threat" and "high threat" groups. Interestingly, in the "high threat" group, there was differential response to the threat of lightning. For golfers and persons who had previously undergone electroschock therapy, there was less reluctance to exposure to possible lightning bolts. Milgram concluded that, for most people, salt passage is contingent on a supportive environment.

In a descriptive study Schramm (18) reported that the utterance, "Please pass the salt," was more efficacious in England, Canada, and the United States, than it was in Argentina, Pakistan, and Korea.

Schramm noted the high correlation between the countries where "Please pass the salt" was effective and the degree of exposure of the populace to mass media. He concluded that salt passage is related to an index of the number of color television sets, tape cassettes, and Moog synthesizers in a country. Schramm, however, made no claims about the causal ordering of the variables.

Orne (15) studied the motivations to comply among salt passers. After exposing subjects to the treatments of typical salt passage studies, he asked them for their motivations in salt passage. Options were

a. I passed the salt because I thought I would be rewarded.

b. I passed the salt to reduce cognitive dissonance.

c. I passed the salt because the behavior was consistent with previously made public commitments to salt passing.

d. I passed the salt because that's what I thought I was supposed to do.

Over 90 percent of all subjects chose response d, strong evidence of the presence of high demand characteristics in the situation. Responses a, b, and c were more popular among students with social science backgrounds. Orne cautioned, nonetheless, that the high demand characteristics of these situations may call into question the findings of previous research.

Why does salt move from one end of a table to another when someone says, "Please pass the salt?"

15   Through the efforts of social science researchers, we are able to offer some educated guesses as to the causes of salt passage. Unfortunately, we do not yet have a complete understanding of this complex phenomenon. Findings tend to be inconclusive or inconsistent. Clearly, more research is needed.

16   Future research must be more systematic. Three directions especially warrant pursuit. First, although research to date has uncovered no personality correlates of salt passage compliance, this is probably due to the few numbers of personality traits that have been examined. There are still numerous personality traits left to investigate: Machiavellianism, authoritarianism, social desirability, tendency to embarrass easily, and so on. Possible interaction effects between source and receiver personality characteristics suggest that there are years of necessary research yet to be done in this area.

17   Second, future research needs to be concerned with the effects of demographic variables. The importance of race differences found by Hovland, *et al.* and Triandis cannot be overlooked. (The fact that the Triandis findings conflict with the findings of Hovland, *et al.* should not discourage us, but sensitize us to the complexity of the phenomenon under investigation.) Crucial demographic variables—like sex, age, preferred side of bed for arising in the morning, religion, and others—have yet to be examined.

18   Third, future research needs to be concerned with the effects of situational variables on salt passage. Kelley's "presence of steak" variable and Milgram's "high threat" variable are suggestive. Effects of information-rich environments, overcrowding, presence of armed conflict, and so on would seem to mediate the salt passage phenomenon.

19   Finally, given the complexity of salt passage, social scientists must be willing to abandon their traditional two-variables approach. More sophisticated methodologies are needed. Consideration must be given to using variables from all three research areas

to construct elaborated non-recursive path models permitting both correlated and uncorrelated error terms. Until our methods match the complexity of our phenomena, we are apt to be left with more questions than answers.

In summary, then, we find that at present social science has not   20
found firm evidence to support the validity of the folk belief that the utterance, "Please pass the salt," is causally linked to the movement of salt from one end of a table to another. Salt passage is a complex phenomenon and systematic research on the impact of personality traits, demographics, and situational variables must be assessed. The question of why the utterance, "Please pass the salt," should be associated with salt passage continues to be a source of puzzlement and intrigue for social scientists.

References

1. Asch, R. "Conformity as the Cause of Everything." *Journal of Unique Social Findings* 13, 1952, pp. 62–69.
2. Berm, R. *Beliefs, Attitudes, Values, Mores, Ethics, Existential Concerns, World Views, Notions of Reincarnation and Human Affairs.* Belmont, Cal.: Wadsworth, 1969.
3. Berkeley, R. *It's All in Your Head.* London: Oxford University Press, 1730.
4. Chaucer, R. "The Salt Merchant's Tale." In R. Chaucer (Ed.), *The Canterbury Tales.* London: Cambridge University Press, 1384.
5. Dickens, R. *David Saltmine.* London: Oxford University Press, 1857.
6. Festinger, R. "Let's Take the Salt out of the Salt Shaker and See What Happens." *Journal for Predictions Contrary to Common Sense* 10, 1956, pp. 1–20.
7. Festinger, R. "Let's Give Some Subjects $20 and Some Subjects $1 and See What Happens." *Journal for Predictions Contrary to Common Sense* 18, 1964, pp. 1–20.
8. Hovland, R., R. Lumsdaine, and R. Sheffield, "Praise the Lord and Pass the Salt." *Proceedings of the Academy of Wartime Chaplains* 5, 1949, pp. 13–23.
9. Hume, R. "A Refutation of Berkeley: An Empirical Approach to Salt Passing." *Philosophical Discourse* 278, 1770, pp. 284–296.
10. Janis, R. and R. Feshbach. "Vocal Utterances and Salt Passage: The Importance of the Phonemes in 'Salt'." *Linguistika* 18, 1954, pp. 112–118.
11. Kelley, R. "Attributions Based on Perceived Environmental Cues in Situations of Uncertainty: The Effects of Steak Presence on Salt Passage." *Journal of Pepper and Salt Psychology* 32, 1968, pp. 1–5.

12. McClelland, R. "Brown-nosing and Salt-passing." *Journal for Managerial and Applied Psychology* 18, 1961, pp. 353–362.
13. Milgram, R. "An Electrician's Wiring Guide to Social Science Experiments." *Popular Mechanics* 23, 1969, pp. 74–87.
14. Newcomb, R. "The ABS Model: When S Is Salt." *Journal for Emeritus Ideas* 12, 1958, pp. 10–18.
15. Orne, R. "Salt on Demand: Levels of Moral Reasoning in Salt Passing Behavior." Forthcoming unpublished manuscript.
16. Osgood, R. and R. Tannenbaum. "Taking Requests with a Grain of Salt: Effects of Source Credibility on Salt Passage." *Morton Salt Newsletter* 42, 1953, pp. 2–3.
17. Rokeach, R. *A Whole Earth Catalog of Personality Correlates for the Social Sciences.* New York: It's Academic Press, 1960.
18. Schramm, R. *Process and Effects of Mass Media Extend to Everything.* Frankfurt, Germany: Gutenburg Press, 1970.
19. Triandis, R. "Salt and Pepper: Racial Differences in Salt Passing Behavior." *Journal of Social Findings for Improved Social Relations* 110, 1973, pp. 16–61.
20. Whitehead, R. "A Refutation of Berkeley and Hume: The Need for a Process Perspective of Salt Passage." *Journal of Static Philosophy* 1, 1920, pp. 318–350.
21. Zimbardo, R. "Salt by Any Other Name Is Not Quite So Salty." *Reader's Digest* 38, 1964, pp. 86–114.

STUDY QUESTIONS

1. In paragraph 3, Pencil reports that the presence of other people at the table is a necessary condition for the utterance, "Pass the salt," to be effective. Which of Mill's Methods is used to prove this?

2. In paragraph 5, what method is used to support the hypothesis that the phonemes in "salt" are the causal mechanism? And what method is used in paragraph 6 to undermine that hypothesis?

3. For each of the "experiments" reported in paragraphs 7 through 14, determine what logical methods are being used.

4. The experiments Pencil reports are funny because they involve elaborate efforts to establish something obvious or because they involve testing hypotheses that are wildly off track. What does this tell us about the process by which scientists select actual hypotheses to test by experiment?

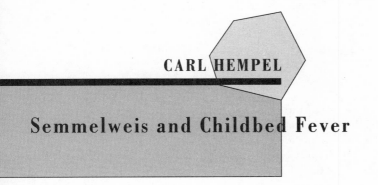

CARL HEMPEL

Semmelweis and Childbed Fever

Carl Hempel was Professor of Philosophy at the University of Pittsburgh, and taught previously at Yale, Harvard, and Princeton. In the following selection, Hempel recounts how in 1847, a physician, Dr. Ignaz Semmelweis, discovered the cause of "childbed fever," a disease that had killed many women who had recently given birth.

As a simple illustration of some important aspects of scientific inquiry let us consider Semmelweis' work on childbed fever. Ignaz Semmelweis, a physician of Hungarian birth, did this work during the years from 1844 to 1848 at the Vienna General Hospital. As a member of the medical staff of the First Maternity Division in the hospital, Semmelweis was distressed to find that a large proportion of the women who were delivered of their babies in that division contracted a serious and often fatal illness known as puerperal fever or childbed fever. In 1844, as many as 260 out of 3,157 mothers in the First Division, or 8.2 percent, died of the disease; for 1845, the death rate was 6.8 percent, and for 1846, it was 11.4 percent. These figures were all the more alarming because in the adjacent Second Maternity Division of the same hospital, which accommodated almost as many women as the First, the death toll from childbed fever was much lower: 2.3, 2.0, and 2.7 percent for the same years. In a book that he wrote later on the causation and the prevention

1

[Carl Hempel, excerpt from *Philosophy of Natural Science*. Prentice-Hall, 1966, pp. 3–6.]

of childbed fever, Semmelweis describes his efforts to resolve the dreadful puzzle.

2   He began by considering various explanations that were current at the time; some of these he rejected out of hand as incompatible with well-established facts; others he subjected to specific tests.

3   One widely accepted view attributed the ravages of puerperal fever to "epidemic influences," which were vaguely described as "atmospheric-cosmic-telluric changes" spreading over whole districts and causing childbed fever in women in confinement. But how, Semmelweis reasons, could such influences have plagued the First Division for years and yet spared the Second? And how could this view be reconciled with the fact that while the fever was raging in the hospital, hardly a case occurred in the city of Vienna or in its surroundings: a genuine epidemic, such as cholera, would not be so selective. Finally, Semmelweis notes that some of the women admitted to the First Division, living far from the hospital, had been overcome by labor on their way and had given birth in the street: yet despite these adverse conditions, the death rate from childbed fever among these cases of "street birth" was lower than the average for the First Division.

4   On another view, overcrowding was a cause of mortality in the First Division. But Semmelweis points out that in fact the crowding was heavier in the Second Division, partly as a result of the desperate efforts of patients to avoid assignment to the notorious First Division. He also rejects two similar conjectures that were current, by noting that there were no differences between the two Divisions in regard to diet or general care of the patients.

5   In 1846, a commission that had been appointed to investigate the matter attributed the prevalence of illness in the First Division to injuries resulting from rough examination by the medical students, all of whom received their obstetrical training in the First Division. Semmelweis notes in refutation of this view that (a) the injuries resulting naturally from the process of birth are much more extensive than those that might be caused by rough examination; (b) the midwives who received their training in the Second Division examined their patients in much the same manner but without the same ill effects; (c) when, in response to the commission's report, the number of medical students was halved and their examinations of the women were reduced to a minimum, the mortality, after a brief decline, rose to higher levels than ever before.

Various psychological explanations were attempted. One of them   6
noted that the First Division was so arranged that a priest bearing
the last sacrament to a dying woman had to pass through five wards
before reaching the sickroom beyond: the appearance of the priest,
preceded by an attendant ringing a bell, was held to have a terrifying and debilitating effect upon the patients in the wards and thus
to make them more likely victims of childbed fever. In the Second
Division, this adverse factor was absent, since the priest had direct
access to the sickroom. Semmelweis decided to test this conjecture.
He persuaded the priest to come by a roundabout route and without
ringing of the bell, in order to reach the sick chamber silently and
unobserved. But the mortality in the First Division did not decrease.

A new idea was suggested to Semmelweis by the observation that   7
in the First Division the women were delivered lying on their backs;
in the Second Division, on their sides. Though he thought it unlikely, he decided "like a drowning man clutching at a straw" to test
whether this difference in procedure was significant. He introduced
the use of the lateral position in the First Division, but again, the
mortality remained unaffected.

At last, early in 1847, an accident gave Semmelweis the decisive   8
clue for his solution of the problem. A colleague of his, Kolletschka,
received a puncture wound in the finger, from the scalpel of a
student with whom he was performing an autopsy, and died after
an agonizing illness during which he displayed the same symptoms
that Semmelweis had observed in the victims of childbed fever.
Although the role of micro-organisms in such infections had not yet
been recognized at the time, Semmelweis realized that "cadaveric
matter" which the student's scalpel had introduced into Kolletschka's blood stream had caused his colleague's fatal illness. And the
similarities between the course of Kolletschka's disease and that of
the women in his clinic led Semmelweis to the conclusion that his
patients had died of the same kind of blood poisoning: he, his
colleagues, and the medical students had been the carriers of the
infectious material, for he and his associates used to come to the
wards directly from performing dissections in the autopsy room, and
examine the women in labor after only superficially washing their
hands, which often retained a characteristic foul odor.

Again, Semmelweis put his idea to a test. He reasoned that if he   9
were right, then childbed fever could be prevented by chemically
destroying the infectious material adhering to the hands. He there-

fore issued an order requiring all medical students to wash their hands in a solution of chlorinated lime before making an examination. The mortality from childbed fever promptly began to decrease, and for the year 1848 it fell to 1.27 percent in the First Division, compared to 1.33 in the Second.

10   In further support of his idea, or of his hypothesis, as we will also say, Semmelweis notes that it accounts for the fact that the mortality in the Second Division consistently was so much lower: the patients there were attended by midwives, whose training did not include anatomical instruction by dissection of cadavers.

11   The hypothesis also explained the lower mortality among "street births": women who arrived with babies in arms were rarely examined after admission and thus had a better chance of escaping infection.

12   Similarly, the hypothesis accounted for the fact that the victims of childbed fever among the newborn babies were all among those whose mothers had contracted the disease during labor; for then the infection could be transmitted to the baby before birth, through the common bloodstream of mother and child, whereas this was impossible when the mother remained healthy.

13   Further clinical experiences soon led Semmelweis to broaden his hypothesis. On one occasion, for example, he and his associates, having carefully disinfected their hands, examined first a woman in labor who was suffering from a festering cervical cancer; then they proceeded to examine twelve other women in the same room, after only routine washing without renewed disinfection. Eleven of the twelve patients died of puerperal fever. Semmelweis concluded that childbed fever can be caused not only by cadaveric material, but also by "putrid matter derived from living organisms."

STUDY QUESTIONS

1. How many distinct hypotheses does Semmelweis consider to explain the different mortality rates in the First and Second Divisions?
2. For how many of those hypotheses does Semmelweis actually perform an experiment to test them?

3. The components of Semmelweis' reasoning in the case of the priest are as follows:

Hypothesis (H): The priest's presence in the First Division causes distress, which causes the higher mortality rates in Division 1.

Prediction (P): If the priest's presence is removed, the mortality rate in Division 1 will decline.

Experiment (E): The priest's presence is removed.

Result (R): The mortality rate in Division 1 does not decline.

Conclusion (C): H is false.

The pattern of his reasoning is as follows:

If H, then P.
Not P.
Therefore, not H.

Does Semmelweis use this same pattern of reasoning in rejecting the other failed hypotheses?

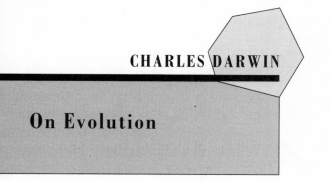

CHARLES DARWIN

On Evolution

Charles Darwin (1809–1882) is famous as the co-founder of the theory that evolution proceeds by natural selection. He was educated at Cambridge and Edinburgh, and early in his

[Charles Darwin. Excerpts from "Recapitulation." Chapter XIV of *On the Origin of Species.* A Facsimile of the First Edition. Harvard University Press, 1966, pp. 459, 466–469.]

career he took a job as naturalist on H.M.S. Beagle. *The* Beagle *spent five years circumnavigating the globe, giving Darwin the opportunity to study an incredible diversity of flora, fauna, and environments. In 1859 he published the highly controversial* On the Origin of Species, *an excerpt from which is republished here.*

1   As this whole volume is one long argument, it may be convenient to the reader to have the leading facts and inferences briefly recapitulated.

2   That many and grave objections may be advanced against the theory of descent with modification through natural selection, I do not deny. I have endeavored to give to them their full force. Nothing at first can appear more difficult to believe than that the more complex organs and instincts should have been perfected, not by means superior to, though analogous with, human reason, but by the accumulation of innumerable slight variations, each good for the individual possessor. Nevertheless, this difficulty, though appearing to our imagination insuperably great, cannot be considered real if we admit the following propositions, namely,—that gradations in the perfection of any organ or instinct, which we may consider, either do now exist or could have existed, each good of its kind,—that all organs and instincts are, in ever so slight a degree, variable,—and, lastly, that there is a struggle for existence leading to the preservation of each profitable deviation of structure or instinct. The truth of these propositions cannot, I think, be disputed.

3   It is, no doubt, extremely difficult even to conjecture by what gradations many structures have been perfected, more especially amongst broken and failing groups of organic beings; but we see so many strange gradations in nature, as is proclaimed by the canon, *"Natura non facit saltum,"*[1] that we ought to be extremely cautious in saying that any organ or instinct, or any whole being, could not have arrived at its present state by many graduated steps. . . .

4   Under domestication we see much variability. This seems to be mainly due to the reproductive system being eminently susceptible to changes in the conditions of life; so that this system, when not rendered impotent, fails to reproduce offspring exactly like the

1. "Nature does not make leaps"—Eds.

parent-form. Variability is governed by many complex laws—by correlation of growth, by use and disuse, and by the direct action of the physical conditions of life. There is much difficulty in ascertaining how much modification our domestic productions have undergone; but we may safely infer that the amount has been large, and that modifications can be inherited for long periods. As long as the conditions of life remain the same, we have reason to believe that a modification, which has already been inherited for many generations, may continue to be inherited for an almost infinite number of generations. On the other hand we have evidence that variability, when it has once come into play, does not wholly cease; for new varieties are still occasionally produced by our most anciently domesticated productions.

Man does not actually produce variability; he only unintentionally exposes organic beings to new conditions of life, and then nature acts on the organization, and causes variability. But man can and does select the variations given to him by nature, and thus accumulate them in any desired manner. He thus adapts animals and plants for his own benefit or pleasure. He may do this methodically, or he may do it unconsciously by preserving the individuals most useful to him at the time, without any thought of altering the breed. It is certain that he can largely influence the character of a breed by selecting, in each successive generation, individual differences so slight as to be quite inappreciable by an uneducated eye. This process of selection has been the great agency in the production of the most distinct and useful domestic breeds. That many of the breeds produced by man have to a large extent the character of natural species, is shown by the inextricable doubts whether very many of them are varieties or aboriginal species. 5

There is no obvious reason why the principles which have acted so efficiently under domestication should not have acted under nature. In the preservation of favored individuals and races, during the constantly recurrent Struggle for Existence, we see the most powerful and ever-acting means of selection. The struggle for existence inevitably follows from the high geometrical ratio of increase which is common to all organic beings. This high rate of increase is proved by calculation, by the effects of a succession of peculiar seasons, and by the results of naturalization, as explained in the third chapter. More individuals are born than can possibly 6 survive. A grain in the balance will determine which individual shall live and which shall die,—which variety or species shall increase in number, and which shall decrease, or finally become extinct. As the individuals of the same species come in all respects into the closest competition with each other, the struggle will generally be most severe between them; it will be almost equally severe between the varieties of the same species, and next in severity between the species of the same genus. But the struggle will often be very severe between beings most remote in the scale of nature. The slightest advantage in one being, at any age or during any season, over those with which it comes into competition, or better adaptation in however slight a degree to the surrounding physical conditions, will turn the balance.

7   With animals having separated sexes there will in most cases be a struggle between the males for possession of the females. The most vigorous individuals, or those which have most successfully struggled with their conditions of life, will generally leave most progeny. But success will often depend on having special weapons or means of defence, or on the charms of the males; and the slightest advantage will lead to victory.

8   As geology plainly proclaims that each land has undergone great physical chances, we might have expected that organic beings would have varied under nature, in the same way as they generally have varied under the changed conditions of domestication. And if there be any variability under nature, it would be an unaccountable fact if natural selection had not come into play. It has often been asserted, but the assertion is quite incapable of proof, that the amount of variation under nature is a strictly limited quantity. Man, though acting on external characters alone and often capriciously, can produce within a short period a great result by adding up mere individual differences in his domestic productions; and everyone admits that there are at least individual differences in species under nature. But, besides such differences, all naturalists have admitted the existence of varieties, which they think sufficiently distinct to be worthy of record in systematic works. No one can draw any clear distinction between individual differences and slight varieties; or between more plainly marked varieties and sub-species, and species. Let it be observed how naturalists differ in the rank which they assign to the many representative forms in Europe and North America.

If then we have under nature variability and a powerful agent   9
always ready to act and select, why should we doubt that variations
in any way useful to beings, under their excessively complex relations of life, would be preserved, accumulated, and inherited? Why,
if man can by patience select variations most useful to himself,
should nature fail in selecting variations useful, under changing
conditions of life, to her living products? What limit can be put to
this power, acting during long ages and rigidly scrutinizing the
whole constitution, structure, and habits of each creature,—favoring
the good and rejecting the bad? I can see no limit to this power, in
slowly and beautifully adapting each form to the most complex
relations of life. The theory of natural selection, even if we looked
no further than this, seems to me to be in itself probable. . . .

STUDY QUESTIONS

1. In his argument, Darwin relies on evidence from several
   different branches of science—for example, geology (paragraph 8) and comparative anatomy (paragraph 3). How many
   such categories of evidence does he rely upon?
2. In discussing comparing natural selection to domestic selection, Darwin makes the following points:
   (1)   Domestic animals exhibit slight variations.
   (2)   Humans prefer some features of domestic animals and
         not others.
   (3)   Humans select which domestic animals will breed.
   (4)   [Animals pass on their features via reproduction.]
   (5)   Therefore, over several generations, the features of domes-
         tic animals will exhibit the result of human selection.
   He then says, "There is no obvious reason why the principles
   which have acted so efficiently under domestication should
   not have acted under nature." What are the comparable
   factors in nature that Darwin is referring to?
3. Diagram the argument Darwin makes out of the following
   propositions. If necessary, supply any assumed premises:
   (1)   Organisms reproduce ever larger numbers of their own
         type (paragraph 6).

(2) [Resources are limited] (assumed).

(3) More organisms are born than can survive (paragraph 6).

(4) Each organism's organs and instincts are slightly different from those of other organisms (paragraph 2).

(5) Some variations in an organism's organs or instincts give it a better chance of surviving (paragraph 6).

(6) The struggle for existence leads to preservation of profitable deviations of structure or instinct (paragraph 9).

(7) The struggle for mates leads to higher rates of reproductive success for the most vigorous (paragraph 7).

(8) Geology shows that environments change greatly over time (paragraph 8).

(9) [Species evolve over time.]

4. In paragraph 2, Darwin indicates the there are "many and grave objections" to his theory. Given what you know, what might some of those objections be?

PART SIX

On Education

JEAN-JACQUES ROUSSEAU

Children Should Not Be Reasoned With

Jean-Jacques Rousseau (1712–1778) was a Swiss-born French intellectual. Through two widely read books, Emile, *from which the following passage is excerpted, and* The Social Contract *(both published 1762), Rousseau became an influential forerunner of Romanticism, a nineteenth-century intellectual and artistic movement. One of the major themes of Romanticism, which the following passage illustrates, is that feeling and instinct are much more important than reason as guides to human action.*

[J.-J. Rousseau, excerpt from *Emile*, transl. Eleanor Worthington. Boston: Ginn, Heath & Co., 1883, pp. 52–54.]

1   *Reasoning should not begin too soon*—Locke's[1] great maxim was that we ought to reason with children, and just now this maxim is much in fashion. I think, however, that its success does not warrant its reputation, and I find nothing more stupid than children who have been so much reasoned with. Reason, apparently a compound of all other faculties, the one latest developed, and with most difficulty, is the one proposed as agent in unfolding the faculties earliest used! The noblest work of education is to make a reasoning man, and we expect to train a young child by making him reason! This is beginning at the end; this is making an instrument of a result. If children understood how to reason they would not need to be educated. But by addressing them from their tenderest years in a language they cannot understand, you accustom them to be satisfied with words, to find fault with whatever is said to them, to think themselves as wise as their teachers, to wrangle and rebel. And what we mean they shall do from reasonable motives we are forced to obtain from them by adding the motive of avarice, or of fear, or of vanity.

2   Nature intends that children shall be children before they are men. If we insist on reversing this order we shall have fruit early indeed, but unripe and tasteless, and liable to early decay; we shall have young savants and old children. Childhood has its own methods of seeing, thinking, and feeling. Nothing shows less sense than to try to substitute our own methods for these. I would rather require a child ten years old to be five feet tall than to be judicious. Indeed, what use would he have at that age for the power to reason? It is a check upon physical strength, and the child needs none.

3   In attempting to persuade your pupils to obedience you add to this alleged persuasion force and threats, or worse still, flattery and promises. Bought over in this way by interest, or constrained by force, they pretend to be convinced by reason. They see plainly that as soon as you discover obedience or disobedience in their conduct, the former is an advantage and the latter a disadvantage to them. But you ask of them only what is distasteful to them; it is always irksome to carry out the wishes of another, so by stealth they carry out their own. They are sure that if their disobedience is not known they are doing well; but they are ready, for fear of greater evils, to

---

1. John Locke (1632–1704), English philosopher.—Eds.

acknowledge, if found out, that they are doing wrong. As the reason for the duty required is beyond their capacity, no one can make them really understand it. But the fear of punishment, the hope of forgiveness, your importunity, their difficulty in answering you, extort from them the confession required of them. You think you have convinced them, when you have only wearied them out or intimidated them.

What results from this? First of all that, by imposing upon them a duty they do not feel as such, you set them against your tyranny, and dissuade them from loving you; you teach them to be dissemblers, deceitful, wilfully untrue, for the sake of extorting rewards or of escaping punishments. Finally, by habituating them to cover a secret motive by an apparent motive, you give them the means of constantly misleading you, of concealing their true character from you, and of satisfying yourself and others with empty words when their occasion demands. You may say that the law, although binding on the conscience, uses constraint in dealing with grown men. I grant it; but what are these men but children spoiled by their education? This is precisely what ought to be prevented. With children use force, with men reason; such is the natural order of things. The wise man requires no laws.

4

STUDY QUESTIONS

1. Diagram the overall structure of Rousseau's argument.
2. What does Rousseau seem to mean by "reason" and "reasoning"?
3. In paragraphs 3 and 4, Rousseau argues that in attempting to teach children to reason, one ends up teaching them hypocrisy. What capacities does he assume children have that makes them capable of being hypocritical?
4. How many other bad consequences does Rousseau attribute to teaching children to reason?
5. What alternative method of dealing with children does Rousseau propose? Is this the only alternative?

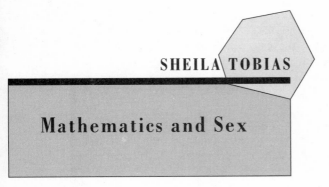

SHEILA TOBIAS

Mathematics and Sex

Sheila Tobias was Associate Provost at Wesleyan University. In this selection, taken from her book Overcoming Math Anxiety, *she evaluates various explanations for the disparity between boys' and girls' math skills.*

1   Men are not free to avoid math; women are.

2   In a major address to the American Academy of Arts and Sciences in 1976, Gerard Piel, publisher of *Scientific American,* cited some of the indicators of mathematics avoidance among girls and young women. "The SAT record plainly suggests that men begin to be separated from women in high school," he noted. "At Andover [an elite private high school] 60 percent of the boys take extra courses in both mathematics and science, but only 25 percent of the girls. . . . By the time the presently graduating high school classes are applying to graduate school," he concluded, "only a tenth as many young women as men will have retained the confidence and capacity to apply to graduate study in the sciences.

3   Some other measures of mathematics avoidance among females are these:

> Girls accounts for 49 percent of the secondary school students in the United States but comprise only 20 percent of those taking math beyond geometry.

[Sheila Tobias, excerpts from Chapter 3 of *Overcoming Math Anxiety.* New York: W. W. Norton, 1978, pp. 70–72, 74, 77–88, 91–96, some footnotes, illustrations, and cross-references deleted; second edition published 1994.]

The college and university population totals 45 percent women, yet only 15 percent of the majors in pure mathematics are women.

Women make up 47 percent of the labor force and 42 percent of those engaged in professional occupations. Yet they are only 12 percent of the scientific and technical personnel working in America today.

Are these data simply evidence of individual preference, or do they represent a pattern of math avoidance and even math anxiety among women? We know that there are differences in *interest* between the sexes. What we do not know is what causes such differences, that is whether these are differences in ability, differences in attitude, or both; and, even more important, whether such differences, if indeed they exist, are innate or learned.

Most learning psychologists doing research today are environmentalists; that is, they tend to be on the "nurture" side of the nature-nurture controversy. Most of them would therefore not subscribe to the man on the street's belief that mathematics ability is just one of those innate differences between men and women that can neither be ignored nor explained away. Yet even the most recent research on sex differences in intelligence accepts the fact that performance in math varies by gender. Because this is assumed to be natural and inevitable (if not genetic in origin) for a long time the causes of female underachievement in mathematics have not been considered a promising area for study and certainly not an urgent one.

But recently, as women began to aspire to positions in fields previously dominated by men, this attitude began to change. The women's movement and the accompanying feminist critique of social psychology can be credited, I believe, with the rise in interest in mathematics and sex and with the formulation of some important new questions. Do girls do poorly in math because they are afraid that people (especially boys) will think them abnormal if they do well, or is it because girls are not taught to believe that they will ever need mathematics? Are there certain kinds of math that girls do better? Which kinds? At what ages? Are there different ways to explain key concepts of math that would help some girls understand them better? . . .

In fact, math avoidance is not just a female phenomenon. Most people of both sexes stop taking math before their formal education is complete. Few people become mathematicians and many very smart people do not like math at all. Thus, "dropping out" of math is nearly universal, and is by no means restricted to girls and women. From this perspective, girls who avoid math and math-related subjects may simply be getting the message sooner than boys that math is unrewarding and irrelevant, but boys will also get that message in time.

8   A recent survey of attitudes toward math among ninth and twelfth graders demonstrated this point very well. Although ninth grade girls had a more negative attitude toward math than ninth grade boys, by the twelfth grade boys had caught up. The researcher concluded that by age 17 a majority of all students have developed an aversion to math, which is tragic but certainly not sex-related.

9   What then is gender-related? What can we say with certainty about mathematics and sex? . . .

10   Popular wisdom holds that females are better at computation and males at problem solving, females at "simple repetitive tasks" and males at restructuring complex ideas. However, since experts cannot even agree on what these categories are, still less on how to measure them, we have to be careful about accepting sex differences in "mathematical reasoning" or "analytic ability" as reported by the researchers in this field. It is fascinating to speculate that there are "innate capacities" to analyze or to reason mathematically, but these qualities have simply not been found.

11   What then do we know? As of 1978, are there any "facts" about male-female differences in mathematics performance that we can accept from the varied and not always consistent research findings? Possibly not, since the field is so very much in flux. But at least until recently, the "facts" were taken to be these:

12   Boys and girls may be born alike in math ability, but certain sex differences in performance emerge as early as such evidence can be gathered and remain through adulthood. They are:

1. Girls compute better than boys (elementary school and on).
2. Boys solve word problems better than girls (from age 13 on).
3. Boys take more math than girls (from age 16 on).
4. Girls learn to hate math sooner and possibly for different reasons.

13   One reason for the differences in performance, to be explored later in this chapter, is the amount of math learned and used at play.

Another may be the difference in male-female maturation.[1] If girls do better than boys at all elementary school tasks, then they may compute better only because arithmetic is part of the elementary school curriculum. As boys and girls grow older, girls are under pressure to become less competitive academically. Thus, the falling off of girls' math performance from age 10 to 15 may be the result of this kind of scenario:

1. Each year math gets harder and requires more work and commitment.
2. Both boys and girls are pressured, beginning at age 10, not to excel in areas designated by society as outside their sex-role domain.
3. Girls now have a good excuse to avoid the painful struggle with math; boys don't.

Such a model may explain girls' lower achievement in math 14 overall, but why should girls have difficulty in problem solving? In her 1964 review of the research on sex difference, Eleanor Maccoby also noted that girls are generally more conforming, more suggestible, and more dependent upon the opinion of others than boys (all learned, not innate behaviors).[2] Thus they may not be as willing to take risks or to think for themselves, two necessary behaviors for solving problems. Indeed, a test of third graders that cannot yet be cited found girls nowhere near as willing to estimate, to make judgments about "possible right answers," and to work with systems they had never seen before. Their very success at doing the expected seems very much to interfere with their doing something new.

If readiness to do word problems, to take one example, is as much 15 a function of readiness to take risks as it is of "reasoning ability," then there is more to mathematics performance than memory, computation, and reasoning. The differences between boys and girls—no matter how consistently they show up—cannot simply be attributed to differences in innate ability.

Still, if you were to ask the victims themselves, people who have 16

1. Girls are about two years ahead of boys on most indices of biological maturation throughout childhood.
2. This is confirmed by Susan Auslander of the Wesleyan Math Clinic, whose "Analysis of Changing Attitudes toward Mathematics" (1978, unpublished) found that females place more value on outside opinion of success in mathematics than males.

trouble doing math, they would probably not agree; they would say that it has to do with the way they are "wired." They feel that they somehow lack something—one ability or several—that other people have. Although women want to believe they are not mentally inferior to men, many fear that in math they really are. Thus, we must consider seriously whether there is any biological basis for mathematical ability, not only because some researchers believe there is, but because some victims agree with them.

The Arguments from Biology

17   The search for some biological basis for math ability or disability is fraught with logical and experimental difficulties. Since not all math underachievers are women and not all women avoid mathematics, it is not very likely on the face of it that poor performance in math can result from some genetic or hormonal difference between the sexes. Moreover, no amount of speculation so far has unearthed a "mathematical competency" in some tangible, measurable substance in the body. Since masculinity cannot be injected into women to see whether it improves their mathematics, the theories that attribute such ability to genes or hormones must depend on circumstantial evidence for their proof. To explain the percent of Ph.D.'s in mathematics earned by women, we would have to conclude either that these women have different genes, hormones, and brain organization than the rest of us; or that certain positive experiences in their lives have largely undone the negative influence of being female; or both. . . .

18   At the root of many of the assumptions about biology and intelligence is the undeniable fact that there have been fewer women "geniuses." The distribution of genius, however, is more a social than a biological phenomenon. An interesting aspect of the lives of geniuses is precisely their dependence on familial, social, and institutional supports. Without schools to accept them, men of wealth to commission their work, colleagues to talk to, and wives to do their domestic chores, they might have gone unrecognized—they might not even have been so smart. In a classic essay explaining why we have so few great women artists, Linda Nochlin Pommer tells us

that women were not allowed to attend classes in art schools because of the presence of nude (female) models. Nor were they given apprenticeships or mentors; and even when they could put together the materials they needed to paint or sculpt, they were not allowed to exhibit their work in galleries or museums.

Women in mathematics fared little better. Emmy Noether, who may be the only woman mathematician considered a genius, was honored (or perhaps mocked) during her lifetime by being called "Der Noether" ("Der" being the masculine form of "the"). Der Noether notwithstanding, the search for the genetic and hormonal origins of math ability goes on.   19

Genetically, the only difference between males and females (albeit a significant and pervasive one) is the presence of two chromosomes designated "X" in every female cell. Normal males have an "X-Y" combination. Since some kinds of mental retardation are associated with sex-chromosomal anomalies, a number of researchers have sought a link between specific abilities and the presence or absence of the second "X." But the link between genetics and mathematics is simply not supported by conclusive evidence.   20

Since intensified hormonal activity begins at adolescence and since, as we have noted, girls seem to lose interest in mathematics during adolescence, much more has been made of the unequal amounts of the sex-linked hormones, androgen and estrogen, in females and males. Estrogen is linked with "simple repetitive tasks" and androgen, with "complex restructuring tasks." The argument here is not only that such specific talents are biologically based (probably undemonstrable) but also that such talents are either-or; that one cannot be good at *both* repetitive and restructuring kinds of assignments.   21

Further, if the sex hormones were in any way responsible for our intellectual functioning, we should get dumber as we get older since our production of both kinds of sex hormones decreases with age.[3] But as far as we know, hormone production responds to mood,   22

3. Indeed, some people do claim that little original work is done by mathematicians once they reach age 30. But a counter explanation is that creative work is done not because of youth but because of "newness to the field." Mathematicians who originate ideas at 25, 20, and even 18 are benefiting not so much from hormonal vigor as from freshness of viewpoint and willingness to ask new questions. I am indebted to Stuart Gilmore, historian of science, for this idea.

activity level, and a number of other external and environmental conditions as well as to age. Thus, even if one day we were to find a sure correlation between the amount of hormone present and the degree of mathematical competence, we would not know whether it was the mathematical competence that caused the hormone level to increase or the hormone level that gave us the mathematical competence.

23   All this criticism of the biological arguments does not imply that what women do with their bodies has no effect on their mathematical skills. As we will see, toys, games, sports, training in certain cognitive areas, and exercise and experience may be the intervening variables we have previously mistaken for biological cause. But first we must look a little more closely at attitude.

Sex Roles and Mathematics Competence

24   The frequency with which girls tend to lose interest in math just at puberty (junior high school) suggests that puberty might in some sense cause girls to fall behind in math. Several explanations come to mind: the influence of hormones, more intensified sex-role socialization, or some extracurricular learning experience boys have at that age that girls do not have. Having set aside the argument that hormones operate by themselves, let us consider the other issues. Here we enter the world of attitudes, as formed by experience and expectation.

25   One group of seventh graders in a private school in New England gave a clue to what children themselves think about this. When visitors to their math class asked why girls do as well as boys in math until sixth grade but after sixth grade boys do better, the girls responded: "Oh, that's easy. After sixth grade, we have to do real math." The reason why "real math" should be considered accessible to boys and not to girls cannot be found in biology, but only in the ideology of sex differences.

26   Parents, peers, and teachers forgive a girl when she does badly in math at school, encouraging her to do well in other subjects instead.

"'There, there,' my mother used to say when I failed at math," one woman remembers. "But I got a talking-to when I did badly in French." "Mother couldn't figure out a 15 percent tip and Daddy seemed to love her more for her incompetence," remembers another. Lynn Fox, who has worked intensively in a program for mathematically gifted teenagers who are brought to the campus of Johns Hopkins University for special instruction, finds it difficult to recruit girls and to keep them in her program. Their parents sometimes prevent them from participating altogether for fear it will make their daughters too different, and the girls themselves often find it difficult to continue with mathematics, she reports, because they experience social ostracism. The math anxious girl we met in Chapter Two, who would have lost her social life if she had asked an interesting question in math class, was anticipating just that.

Where do these attitudes come from?   27

A study of the images of males and females in children's text-   28
books by sociologist Lenore Weitzman of the University of California at Davis, provides one clue to why math is associated with men
and boys in the minds of little children. "Two out of every three
pictures in the math books surveyed were of males, and the examples given of females doing math were insulting and designed to
reinforce the worst of the stereotypes," she reports.

Weitzman comments: "It seems ironic that housewives who use   29
so much math in balancing their accounts and in managing household budgets are shown as baffled by simple addition."

"Another feature of the mathematics textbooks," says   30
Weitzman, "is the frequent use of sex as a category for dividing
people, especially for explaining set theory."

"When sex is used as a category, girls are told that they can be   31
classified as different," Weitzman believes, "as typically emotional
or domestic . . . There is also strong sex typing in the examples used
and in the math problems."

"We found math problems," Weitzman writes, "in which girls   32
were paid less than boys for the same work. It would be hard to
imagine a textbook publisher allowing this example if a black boy
were being paid less than a white boy. Yet it seems legitimate to
underpay girls."

In another survey of math textbooks published in 1969, not one   33 picture of a girl was found and the arithmetic problems used as examples in the book showed adult women having to ask even their children for help with math, or avoiding the task entirely by saying, "Wait until your father comes home."

34   Adults remember their junior high school experiences in math as full of clues that math was a male domain. No so long ago, one junior high school regional math competition offered a tie clasp for first prize. A math teacher in another school, commenting unfavorably on the performance at the blackboard of a male student, said to him, "You think like a girl." If poor math thinkers think like girls, who are good math thinkers supposed to be? . . .

Street Mathematics: Things, Motion, and Scores

35   If a ballplayer is batting .233 going into a game and gets three hits in four times at bat (which means he has batted .750 for the day), someone watching the game might assume that the day's performance will make a terrific improvement in his batting average. But it turns out that the three-for-four day only raises the .233 to .252. Disappointing, but a very good personal lesson in fractions, ratios, and percents.

36   Scores, performances like this one, lengths, speeds of sprints or downhill slaloms are expressed in numbers, in ratios, and in other comparisons. The attention given to such matters surely contributes to a boy's familiarity with simple arithmetic functions, and must convince him, at least on some subliminal level, of the utility of mathematics. This does not imply that every boy who handles runs batted in and batting averages well during the game on Sunday will see the application of these procedures to his Monday morning school assignment. But handling figures as people do in sports probably lays the groundwork for using figures later on.

37   Not all the skills necessary for mathematics are learned in school. Measuring, computing, and manipulating objects that have dimensions and dynamic properties of their own are part of everyday life for some children. Other children who miss these experiences may not be well primed for math in school.

Feminists have complained for a long time that playing with   38
dolls is one way to convince impressionable little girls that they may
only be mothers or housewives, or, in emulation of the Barbie doll,
pinup girls when they grow up. But doll playing may have even
more serious consequences. Have you ever watched a little girl play
with a doll? Most of the time she is talking and not doing, and even
when she is doing (dressing, undressing, packing the doll away) she
is not learning very much about the world. Imagine her taking a
Barbie doll apart to study its talking mechanism. That's not the sort
of thing she is encouraged to do. Do girls find out about gravity and
distance and shapes and sizes playing with dolls? Probably not!

A college text written for inadequately prepared science students   39
begins with a series of supposedly simple problems dealing with
marbles, cylinders, poles made of different substances, levels, balances, and an inclined plane. Even the least talented male science
student will probably be able to see these items as objects, each
having a particular shape, size, and style of movement. He has
balanced himself or some other object on a teeter-totter; he has
watched marbles spin and even fly. He has probably tried to fit one
pole of a certain diameter inside another, or used a stick to pull up
another stick, learning leverage. Those trucks little boys clamor for
and get are moving objects. Things in little boys' lives drop and spin
and collide and even explode sometimes.

The more curious boy will have taken apart a number of house-   40
hold and play objects by the time he is ten; if his parents are lucky,
he may even have put them back together again. In all this he is
learning things that will be useful in physics and math. Taking out
parts that have to go back in requires some examination of form.
Building something that stays up or at least stays put for some time
involves working with structure. Perhaps the absence of things that
move in little girls' childhoods (especially if they are urban little
girls) quite as much as the presence of dolls makes the quantities
and relationships of math so alien to them.

In sports played, as well as sports watched, boys learn more   41
math-related concepts than girls do. Getting to first base on a not
very well hit grounder is a lesson in time, speed, and distance.
Intercepting a football in the air requires some rapid intuitive eye
calculations based on the ball's direction, speed, and trajectory. Since
physics is partly concerned with velocities, trajectories, and colli-
sions of objects, much of the math taught to prepare a student for

physics deals with relationships and formulas that can be used to express motion and acceleration. A young woman who has not closely observed objects travel and collide cannot appreciate the power of mathematics. . . .

Conclusion

42   After surveying the summaries of research in this area and interviewing people who claim to be incompetent at mathematics, I have reached a conclusion. Apart from general intelligence, which is probably equally distributed among males and females, the most important elements in predicting success at learning math are motivation, temperament, attitude, and interest. These are at least as salient as genes and hormones (about which we really know very little in relation to math), "innate reasoning ability" (about which there is much difference of opinion), or number sense. This does not, however, mean that there are no sex differences at all.

43   What is ironic (and unexpected) is that as far as I can judge sex differences seem to be lodged in *acquired skills;* not in computation, visualization, and reasoning *per se*, but in ability to take a math problem apart, in willingness to tolerate certain kinds of ambiguity, and in careful attention to mathematical detail. Such temperamental characteristics as persistence and willingness to take risks may be as important in doing math as pure memory or logic. And attitude and self-image, particularly during adolescence when the pressures to conform are at their greatest, may be even more important than temperament. Negative attitudes, as we all know from personal experience, can powerfully inhibit intellect and curiosity and can keep us from learning what is well within our power to understand. . . .

STUDY QUESTIONS

1. Early in the essay, Tobias cites the results of a number of studies showing that girls do less well at mathematics than

boys. Are the studies diverse and numerous enough to support such a generalization?

2. How many explanations does Tobias consider to account for the studies showing that girls perform less well than boys at math?

3. On what grounds does Tobias reject the view that biological differences account for the differences in performance? Does she consider any evidence in favor of the biological explanation?

4. Toward the end of the essay, how does Tobias link activities such as playing with dolls to poorer performances in mathematics? What skills does playing with dolls develop? Are any of them related to the skills needed for mathematics?

5. Do you suffer from "math anxiety"? If so, has Tobias convinced you that you can, in principle, do well at mathematics? Why or why not?

CAROLINE BIRD

College Is a Waste of Time and Money

Caroline Bird was born in New York in 1915. She was educated at Vassar College and the University of Toledo, and is the author of The Crowding Syndrome *and* The Case Against College, *from which the following selection is ex-*

[Caroline Bird, excerpt from *The Case Against College*. New York: David McKay Co., 1975, pp. 281–289.]

*cerpted. As the title of the essay indicates, Bird argues that col-
lege is not the good investment it is usually thought to be.*

1   A great majority of our nine million college students are not in
school because they want to be or because they want to learn. They
are there because it has become the thing to do or because college
is a pleasant place to be; because it's the only way they can get
parents or taxpayers to support them without working at a job they
don't like; because Mother wanted them to go, or some other reason
entirely irrelevant to the course of studies for which college is
supposedly organized.

2   As I crisscross the United States lecturing on college campuses, I
am dismayed to find that professors and administrators, when
pressed for a candid opinion, estimate that no more than 25 percent
of their students are turned on by classwork. For the rest, college is
at best a social center or aging vat, and at worst a young folks' home
or even a prison that keeps them out of the mainstream of economic
life for a few more years.

3   The premise—which I no longer accept—that college is the best
place for all high-school graduates grew out of a noble American
ideal. Just as the United States was the first nation to aspire to teach
every small child to read and write, so, during the 1950s, we became
the first and only great nation to aspire to higher education for all.
During the '60s we damned the expense and built great state
university systems as fast as we could. And adults—parents, employers, high-school counselors—began to push, shove and cajole
youngsters to "get an education."

4   It became a mammoth industry, with taxpayers footing more
than half the bill. By 1970, colleges and universities were spending
more than 30 billion dollars annually. But still only half our high-
school graduates were going on. According to estimates made by the
economist Fritz Machlup, if we had been educating every young
person until age 22 in that year of 1970, the bill for higher education
would have reached 47.5 billion dollars, 12.5 billion more than the
total corporate profits for the year.

5   Figures such as these have begun to make higher education for
all look financially prohibitive, particularly now when colleges are
squeezed by the pressures of inflation and a drop-off in the growth
of their traditional market.

Predictable demography has caught up with the university em-   6
pire builders. Now that the record crop of postwar babies has
graduated from college, the rate of growth of the student population
has begun to decline. To keep their mammoth plants financially
solvent, many institutions have begun to use hard-sell, Madison-
Avenue techniques to attract students. They sell college like soap,
promoting features they think students want: innovative programs,
an environment conducive to meaningful personal relationships,
and a curriculum so free that it doesn't sound like college at all.

Pleasing the customers is something new for college administra-   7
tors. Colleges have always known that most students don't like to
study, and that at least part of the time they are ambivalent about
college, but before the student riots of the 1960s educators never
thought it either right or necessary to pay any attention to student
feelings. But when students rebelling against the Vietnam war and
the draft discovered they could disrupt a campus completely, administrators had to act on some student complaints. Few understood
that the protests had tapped the basic discontent with college itself,
a discontent that did not go away when the riots subsided.

Today students protest individually rather than in concert. They   8
turn inward and withdraw from active participation. They drop out
to travel to India or to feed themselves on subsistence farms. Some
refuse to go to college at all. Most, of course, have neither the funds
nor the self-confidence for constructive articulation of their discontent. They simply hang around college unhappily and reluctantly.

All across the country, I have been overwhelmed by the prevail-   9
ing sadness on American campuses. Too many young people speak
little, and then only in drowned voices. Sometimes the mood surfaces as diffidence, wariness, or coolness, but whatever its form, it
looks like a defense mechanism, and that rings a bell. This is the
way it used to be with women, and just as society had systematically
damaged women by insisting that their proper place was in the
home, so we may be systematically damaging 18-year-olds by
insisting that their proper place is in college.

Campus watchers everywhere know what I mean when I say   10
students are sad, but they don't agree on the reason for it. During
the Vietnam war some ascribed the sadness to the draft; now others
blame affluence, or say it has something to do with permissive
upbringing.

11   Not satisfied with any of these explanations, I looked for some answers with the journalistic tools of my trade—scholarly studies, economic analyses, the historical record, the opinions of the especially knowledgeable, conversations with parents, professors, college administrators, and employers, all of whom spoke as alumni too. Mostly I learned from my interviews with hundreds of young people on and off campuses all over the country.

12   My unnerving conclusion is that students are sad because they are not needed. Somewhere between the nursery and the employment office, they become unwanted adults. No one has anything in particular against them. But no one knows what to do with them either. We already have too many people in the world of the 1970s, and there is no room for so many newly minted 18-year-olds. So we temporarily get them out of the way by sending them to college where in fact only a few belong.

13   To make it more palatable, we fool ourselves into believing that we are sending them there for their own best interests, and that it's good for them, like spinach. Some, of course, learn to like it, but most wind up preferring green peas.

14   Educators admit as much. Nevitt Sanford, distinguished student of higher education, says students feel they are "capitulating to a kind of voluntary servitude." Some of them talk about their time in college as if it were a sentence to be served. I listened to a 1970 Mount Holyoke graduate: "For two years I was really interested in science, but in my junior and senior years I just kept saying, 'I've done two years; I'm going to finish.' When I got out I made up my mind that I wasn't going to school anymore because so many of my courses had been bullshit."

15   But bad as it is, college is often preferable to a far worse fate. It is better than the drudgery of an uninspiring nine-to-five job, and better than doing nothing when no jobs are available. For some young people, it is a graceful way to get away from home and become independent without losing the financial support of their parents. And sometimes it is the only alternative to an intolerable home situation.

16   It is difficult to assess how many students are in college reluctantly. The conservative Carnegie Commission estimates from 5 to 30 percent. Sol Linowitz, who was once chairman of a special committee on campus tension of the American Council on Educa-

tion, found that "a significant number were not happy with their college experience because they felt they were there only in order to get the 'ticket to the big show' rather than to spend the years as productively as they otherwise could."

Older alumni will identify with Richard Baloga, a policeman's son, who stayed in school even though he "hated it" because he thought it would do him some good. But fewer students each year feel this way. Daniel Yankelovich has surveyed undergraduate attitudes for a number of years, and reported in 1971 that 74 percent thought education was "very important." But just two years earlier, 80 percent thought so.   17

The doubters don't mind speaking up. Leon Lefkowitz, chairman of the department of social studies at Central High School in Valley Stream, New York, interviewed 300 college students at random, and reports that 200 of them didn't think that the education they were getting was worth the effort. "In two years I'll pick up a diploma," said one student, "and I can honestly say it was a waste of my father's bread."   18

Nowadays, says one sociologist, you don't have to have a reason for going to college; it's an institution. His definition of an institution is an arrangement everyone accepts without question; the burden of proof is not on why you go, but why anyone thinks there might be a reason for not going. The implication is that an 18-year-old is too young and confused to know what he wants to do, and that he should listen to those who know best and go to college.   19

I don't agree. I believe that college has to be judged not on what other people think is good for students, but on how good it feels to the students themselves.   20

I believe that people have an inside view of what's good for them. If a child doesn't want to go to school some morning, better let him stay at home, at least until you find out why. Maybe he knows something you don't. It's the same with college. If high-school graduates don't want to go, or if they don't want to go right away, they may perceive more clearly than their elders that college is not for them. It is no longer obvious that adolescents are best off studying a core curriculum that was constructed when all educated men could agree on what made them educated, or that professors, advisors, or parents can be of any particular help to young people in choosing a major or a career. High-school graduates see college   21 graduates driving cabs, and decide it's not worth going. College students find no intellectual stimulation in their studies and drop out.

22   If students believe that college isn't necessarily good for them, you can't expect them to stay on for the general good of mankind. They don't go to school to beat the Russians to Jupiter, improve the national defense, increase the GNP, or create a new market for the arts—to mention some of the benefits taxpayers are supposed to get for supporting higher education.

23   Nor should we expect to bring about social equality by putting all young people through four years of academic rigor. At best, it's a roundabout and expensive way to narrow the gap between the highest and lowest in our society anyway. At worst, it is unconsciously elitist. Equalizing opportunity through universal higher education subjects the whole population to the intellectual mode natural only to a few. It violates the fundamental egalitarian principle of respect for the differences between people.

24   Of course, most parents aren't thinking of the "higher" good at all. They send their children to college because they are convinced young people benefit financially from those four years of higher education. But if money is the only goal, college is the dumbest investment you can make. I say this because a young banker in Poughkeepsie, New York, Stephen G. Necel, used a computer to compare college as an investment with other investments available in 1974 and college did not come out on top.

25   For the sake of argument, the two of us invented a young man whose rich uncle gave him, in cold cash, the cost of a four-year education at any college he chose, but the young man didn't have to spend the money on college. After bales of computer paper, we had our mythical student write to his uncle: "Since you said I could spend the money foolishly if I wished, I am going to blow it all on Princeton."

26   The much respected financial columnist Sylvia Porter echoed the common assumption when she said last year, "A college education is among the very best investments you can make in your entire life." But the truth is not quite so rosy, even if we assume that the Census Bureau is correct when it says that as of 1972, a man who completed four years of college would expect to earn $199,000 more between the ages of 22 and 64 than a man who had only a high-school diploma.

If a 1972 Princeton-bound high-school graduate had put the 27
$34,181 that his four years of college would have cost him into a
savings bank at 7.5 percent interest compounded daily, he would
have had at age 64 a total of $1,129,200, or $528,200 more than the
earnings of a male college graduate, and more than five times as
much as the $199,000 extra the more educated man could expect to
earn between 22 and 64.

The big advantage of getting your college money in cash now is 28
that you can invest it in something that has a higher return than a
diploma. For instance, a Princeton-bound high-school graduate of
1972 who liked fooling around with cars could have banked his
$34,181, and gone to work at the local garage at close to $1,000 more
per year than the average high-school graduate. Meanwhile, as he
was learning to be an expert auto mechanic, his money would be
ticking away in the bank. When he became 28, he would have
earned $7,199 less on his job from age 22 to 28 than his college-edu-
cated friend, but he would have had $73,113 in his passbook—
enough to buy out his boss, go into the used-car business, or acquire
his own new-car dealership. If successful in business, he could
expect to make more than the average college graduate. And if he
had the brains to get into Princeton, he would be just as likely to
make money without the four years spent on campus. Unfortunately, few college-bound high-school graduates get the opportunity to bank such a large sum of money, and then wait for it to make
them rich. And few parents are sophisticated enough to understand
that in financial returns alone, their children would be better off
with the money than with the education.

Rates of return and dollar signs on education are fascinating brain 29
teasers, but obviously there is a certain unreality to the game. Quite
aside from the noneconomic benefits of college, and these should
loom larger once the dollars are cleared away, there are grave
difficulties in assigning a dollar value to college at all.

In fact there is no real evidence that the higher income of college 30
graduates is due to college. College may simply attract people who
are slated to earn more money anyway; those with higher IQs, better
family backgrounds, a more enterprising temperament. No one who
has wrestled with the problem is prepared to attribute all of the
higher income to the impact of college itself.

Christopher Jencks, author of *Inequality*, a book that assesses the 31 effect of family and schooling in America, believes that education in general accounts for less than half of the difference in income in the American population. "The biggest single source of income differences," writes Jencks, "seems to be the fact that men from high-status families have higher incomes than men from low-status families even when they enter the same occupations, have the same amount of education, and have the same test scores."

32   Jacob Mincer of the National Bureau of Economic Research and Columbia University states flatly that of "20 to 30 percent of students at any level, the additional schooling has been a waste, at least in terms of earnings." College fails to work its income-raising magic for almost a third of those who go. More than half of those people in 1972 who earned $15,000 or more reached that comfortable bracket without the benefit of a college diploma. Jencks says that financial success in the U.S. depends a good deal on luck, and the most sophisticated regression analyses have yet to demonstrate otherwise.

33   But most of today's students don't go to college to earn more money anyway. In 1968, when jobs were easy to get, Daniel Yankelovich made his first nationwide survey of students. Sixty-five percent of them said they "would welcome less emphasis on money." By 1973, when jobs were scarce, that figure jumped to 80 percent.

34   The young are not alone. Americans today are all looking less to the pay of a job than to the work itself. They want "interesting" work that permits them "to make a contribution," express themselves" and "use their special abilities," and they think college will help them find it.

35   Jerry Darring of Indianapolis knows what it is to make a dollar. He worked with his father in the family plumbing business, on the line at Chevrolet, and in the Chrysler foundry. He quit these jobs to enter Wright State University in Dayton, Ohio, because "in a job like that a person only has time to work, and after that he's so tired that he can't do anything else but come home and go to sleep."

36   Jerry came to college to find work "helping people." And he is perfectly willing to spend the dollars he earns at dull, well-paid work to prepare for lower-paid work that offers the reward of service to others.

37   Jerry's case is not unusual. No one works for money alone. In

order to deal with the nonmonetary rewards of work, economists have coined the concept of "psychic income" which according to one economic dictionary means "income that is reckoned in terms of pleasure, satisfaction, or general feelings of euphoria."

Psychic income is primarily what college students mean when they talk about getting a good job. During the most affluent years of the late 1960s and early 1970s college students told their placement officers that they wanted to be researchers, college professors, artists, city planners, social workers, poets, book publishers, archeologists, ballet dancers, or authors. 38

The psychic income of these and other occupations popular with students is so high that these jobs can be filled without offering high salaries. According to one study, 93 percent of urban university professors would choose the same vocation again if they had the chance, compared with only 16 percent of unskilled auto workers. Even though the monetary gap between college professor and auto worker is now surprisingly small, the difference in psychic income is enormous. 39

But colleges fail to warn students that jobs of these kinds are hard to come by, even for qualified applicants, and they rarely accept the responsibility of helping students choose a career that will lead to a job. When a young person says he is interested in helping people, his counselor tells him to become a psychologist. But jobs in psychology are scarce. The Department of Labor, for instance, estimates there will be 4,300 new jobs for psychologists in 1975 while colleges are expected to turn out 58,430 B.A.s in psychology that year. 40

Of 30 psych majors who reported back to Vassar what they were doing a year after graduation in 1972, only five had jobs in which they could possibly use their courses in psychology, and two of these were working for Vassar. 41

The outlook isn't much better for students majoring in other psychic-pay disciplines: sociology, English, journalism, anthropology, forestry, education. Whatever college graduates want to do, most of them are going to wind up doing what there is to do. 42

John Shingleton, director of placement at Michigan State University, accuses the academic community of outright hypocrisy. "Educators have never said, 'Go to college and get a good job,' but this has been implied, and now students expect it. . . . If we care 43 what happens to students after college, then let's get involved with what should be one of the basic purposes of education: career preparation."

44   In the 1970s, some of the more practical professors began to see that jobs for graduates meant jobs for professors too. Meanwhile, students themselves reacted to the shrinking job market, and a "new vocationalism" exploded on campus. The press welcomed the change as a return to the ethic of achievement and service. Students were still idealistic, the reporters wrote, but they now saw that they could best make the world better by healing the sick as physicians or righting individual wrongs as lawyers.

45   But there are no guarantees in these professions either. The American Enterprise Institute estimated in 1971 that there would be more than the target ratio of 100 doctors for every 100,000 people in the population by 1980. And the odds are little better for would-be lawyers. Law schools are already graduating twice as many new lawyers every year as the Department of Labor thinks will be needed, and the oversupply is growing every year.

46   And it's not at all apparent that what is actually learned in a "professional" education is necessary for success. Teachers, engineers and others I talked to said they find that on the job they rarely use what they learned in school. In order to see how well college prepared engineers and scientists for actual paid work in their fields, The Carnegie Commission queried all the employees with degrees in these fields in two large firms. Only one in five said the work they were doing bore a "very close relationship" to their college studies, while almost a third saw "very little relationship at all." An overwhelming majority could think of many people who were doing their same work, but had majored in different fields.

47   Majors in nontechnical fields report even less relationship between their studies and their jobs. Charles Lawrence, a communications major in college and now the producer of "Kennedy & Co.," the Chicago morning television show, says, "You have to learn all that stuff and you never use it again. I learned my job doing it." Others employed as architects, nurses, teachers and other members of the so-called learned professions report the same thing.

48   Most college administrators admit that they don't prepare their graduates for the job market. "I just wish I had the guts to tell parents that when you get out of this place you aren't prepared to

do anything," the academic head of a famous liberal-arts college told us. Fortunately, for him, most people believe that you don't have to defend a liberal-arts education on those grounds. A liberal-arts education is supposed to provide you with a value system, a standard, a set of ideas, not a job. "Like Christianity, the liberal arts are seldom practiced and would probably be hated by the majority of the populace if they were," said one defender.

The analogy is apt. The fact is, of course, that the liberal arts are 49
a religion in every sense of that term. When people talk about them, their language becomes elevated, metaphorical, extravagant, theoretical and reverent. And faith in personal salvation by the liberal arts is professed in a creed intoned on ceremonial occasions such as commencements.

If the liberal arts are a religious faith, the professors are its priests. 50
But disseminating ideas in a four-year college curriculum is slow and most expensive. If you want to learn about Milton, Camus, or even Margaret Mead, you can find them in paperback books, the public library, and even on television.

And when most people talk about the value of a college educa- 51
tion, they are not talking about great books. When at Harvard commencement, the president welcomes the new graduates into "the fellowship of educated men and women," what he could be saying is, "Here is a piece of paper that is a passport to jobs, power and instant prestige." As Glenn Bassett, a personnel specialist at G.E., says, "In some parts of G.E., a college degree appears completely irrelevant to selection to, say, a manager's job. In most, however, it is a ticket of admission."

But now that we have doubled the number of young people 52
attending college, a diploma cannot guarantee even that. The most charitable conclusion we can reach is that college probably has very little, if any, effect on people and things at all. Today, the false premises are easy to see:

First, college doesn't make people intelligent, ambitious, happy, 53
or liberal. It's the other way around. Intelligent, ambitious, happy, liberal people are attracted to higher education in the first place.

Second, college can't claim much credit for the learning experi- 54
ences that really change students while they are there. Jobs, friends, history, and most of all the sheer passage of time, have as big an impact as anything even indirectly related to the campus.

55   Third, colleges have changed so radically that a freshman entering in the fall of 1974 can't be sure to gain even the limited value research studies assigned to colleges in the '60s. The sheer size of undergraduate campuses of the 1970s makes college even less stimulating now than it was 10 years ago. Today even motivated students are disappointed with their college courses and professors.

56   Finally, a college diploma no longer opens as many vocational doors. Employers are beginning to realize that when they pay extra for someone with a diploma, they are paying only for an empty credential. The fact is that most of the work for which employers now expect college training is now or has been capably done in the past by people without higher educations.

57   College, then, may be a good place for those few young people who are really drawn to academic work, who would rather read than eat, but it has become too expensive, in money, time, and intellectual effort to serve as a holding pen for large numbers of our young. We ought to make it possible for those reluctant, unhappy students to find alternative ways of growing up, and more realistic preparation for the years ahead.

STUDY QUESTIONS

1. Judging from your own experience, do you agree with Bird's claim that there is a "prevailing sadness" among college students? If you agree, do you think the sadness is for the reasons Bird suggests?

2. How many good reasons can you think of for going to college? Of these reasons, how many does Bird consider and reject as making college worthwhile? Does it make any difference to her argument if one has a specific career goal in mind?

3. How should one go about deciding whether a college degree is a good financial investment? What are all of the relevant factors? How does one factor in "psychic income"? (See paragraph 37 for a definition of "psychic income.")

4. In paragraphs 25–33, Bird presents her argument that a college degree is not a good financial investment. Has Bird taken into account all of the relevant factors?

5. What skills are necessary to succeed at most jobs? Why, according to paragraphs 46–56, does Bird think that students do not acquire the necessary skills at college?

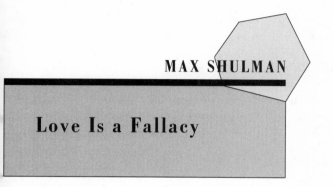

MAX SHULMAN

Love Is a Fallacy

Mr. Shulman, 1919–1988, was an American humorist. A graduate of the University of Minnesota in 1942, he served in the military in World War II. After the war, his writing career included several collections of short stories and a Broadway play, "The Tender Trap," which was later made into a movie. In this short story, a logic student with romantic ambitions finds that mixing love and logic doesn't always lead to success.

Cool was I and logical. Keen, calculating, perspicacious, acute and astute—I was all of these. My brain was as powerful as a dynamo, as precise as a chemist's scales, as penetrating as a scalpel. And— think of it!—I was only eighteen.

It is not often that one so young has such a giant intellect. Take, for example, Petey Bellows, my roommate at the university. Same age, same background, but dumb as an ox. A nice enough fellow, you understand, but nothing upstairs. Emotional type. Unstable. Impressionable. Worst of all, a faddist. Fads, I submit, are the very

[Max Shulman. "Love Is a Fallacy," from *The Many Loves of Dobie Gillis.* Doubleday, 1951.]

1

negation of reason. To be swept up in every new craze that comes along, to surrender yourself to idiocy just because everybody else is doing it—this, to me, is the acme of mindlessness. Not, however, to Petey.

One afternoon I found Petey lying on his bed with an expression of such distress on his face that I immediately diagnosed appendicitis. "Don't move," I said. "Don't take a laxative. I'll get a doctor."

"Raccoon," he mumbled thickly.

5 "Raccoon?" I said, pausing in my flight.

"I want a raccoon coat," he wailed.

I perceived that his trouble was not physical, but mental. "Why do you want a raccoon coat?"

"I should have known it," he cried, pounding his temples. "I should have known they'd come back when the Charleston came back. Like a fool I spent all my money for textbooks, and now I can't get a raccoon coat."

"Can you mean," I said incredulously, "that people are actually wearing raccoon coats again?"

10 "All the Big Men on Campus are wearing them. Where've you been?"

"In the library," I said, naming a place not frequented by Big Men on Campus.

He leaped from the bed and paced the room. "I've got to have a raccoon coat," he said passionately. "I've got to!"

"Petey, why? Look at it rationally. Raccoon coats are unsanitary. They shed. They smell bad. They weigh too much. They're unsightly. They—"

"You don't understand," he interrupted impatiently. "It's the thing to do. Don't you want to be in the swim?"

15 "No," I said truthfully.

"Well, I do," he declared. "I'd give anything for a raccoon coat. Anything!"

My brain, that precision instrument, slipped into high gear. "Anything?" I asked, looking at him narrowly.

"Anything," he affirmed in ringing tones.

I stroked my chin thoughtfully. It so happened that I knew where to get my hands on a raccoon coat. My father had had one in his undergraduate days; it lay now in a trunk in the attic back home. It also happened that Petey had something I wanted. He didn't *have* it exactly, but at least he had first rights on it. I refer to his girl, Polly Espy.

I had long coveted Polly Espy. Let me emphasize that my desire   20
for this young woman was not emotional in nature. She was, to be sure, a girl who excited the emotions, but I was not one to let my heart rule my head. I wanted Polly for a shrewdly calculated, entirely cerebral reason.

I was a freshman in law school. In a few years I would be out in practice. I was well aware of the importance of the right kind of wife in furthering a lawyer's career. The successful lawyers I had observed were, almost without exception, married to beautiful, gracious, intelligent women. With one omission, Polly fitted these specifications perfectly.

Beautiful she was. She was not yet of pin-up proportions, but I felt sure that time would supply the lack. She already had the makings.

Gracious she was. By gracious I mean full of graces. She had an erectness of carriage, an ease of bearing, a poise that clearly indicated the best of breeding. At table her manners were exquisite. I had seen her at the Kozy Kampus Korner eating the specialty of the house—a sandwich that contained scraps of pot roast, gravy, chopped nuts, and a dipper of sauerkraut—without even getting her fingers moist.

Intelligent she was not. In fact, she veered in the opposite direction. But I believed that under my guidance she would smarten up. At any rate, it was worth a try. It is, after all, easier to make a beautiful dumb girl smart than to make an ugly smart girl beautiful.

"Petey," I said, "are you in love with Polly Espy?"   25

"I think she's a keen kid," he replied, "but I don't know if you'd call it love. Why?"

"Do you," I asked, "have any kind of formal arrangement with her? I mean are you going steady or anything like that?"

"No. We see each other quite a bit, but we both have other dates. Why?"

"Is there," I asked, "any other man for whom she has a particular fondness?"

"Not that I know of. Why?"   30

I nodded with satisfaction. "In other words, if you were out of the picture, the field would be open. Is that right?"

"I guess so. What are you getting at?"

"Nothing, nothing," I said innocently, and took my suitcase out of the closet.

"Where you going?" asked Petey.

35   "Home for the week end." I threw a few things into the bag.

"Listen," he said, clutching my arm eagerly, "while you're home, you couldn't get some money from your old man, could you, and lend it to me so I can buy a raccoon coat?"

"I may do better than that," I said with a mysterious wink and closed my bag and left.

"Look," I said to Petey when I got back Monday morning. I threw open the suitcase and revealed the huge, hairy, gamy object that my father had worn in his Stutz Bearcat in 1925.

"Holy Toledo!" said Petey reverently. He plunged his hands into the raccoon coat and then his face. "Holy Toledo!" he repeated fifteen or twenty times.

40   "Would you like it?" I asked.

"Oh yes!" he cried, clutching the greasy pelt to him. Then a canny look came into his eyes. "What do you want for it?"

"Your girl," I said, mincing no words.

"Polly?" he said in a horrified whisper. "You want Polly?"

"That's right."

45   He flung the coat from him. "Never," he said stoutly.

I shrugged. "Okay. If you don't want to be in the swim, I guess it's your business."

I sat down in a chair and pretended to read a book, but out of the corner of my eye I kept watching Petey. He was a torn man. First he looked at the coat with the expression of a waif at a bakery window. Then he turned away and set his jaw resolutely. Then he looked back at the coat, with even more longing in his face. Then he turned away, but with not so much resolution this time. Back and forth his head swiveled, desire waxing, resolution waning. Finally he didn't turn away at all; he just stood and stared with mad lust at the coat.

"It isn't as though I was in love with Polly," he said thickly. "Or going steady or anything like that."

"That's right," I murmured.

50   "What's Polly to me, or me to Polly?"

"Not a thing," said I.

"It's just been a casual kick—just a few laughs, that's all."

"Try on the coat," said I.

He complied. The coat bunched high over his ears and dropped all the way down to his shoe tops. He looked like a mound of dead raccoons. "Fits fine," he said happily.

I rose from my chair. "Is it a deal?" I asked, extending my hand.   55
He swallowed. "It's a deal," he said and shook my hand.

I had my first date with Polly the following evening. This was in the nature of a survey; I wanted to find out just how much work I had to do to get her mind up to the standard I required. I took her first to dinner. "Gee, that was a delish dinner," she said as left the restaurant. Then I took her to a movie. "Gee, that was a marvy movie," she said as we left the theater. And then I took her home. "Gee, I had a sensaysh time," she said as she bade me good night.

I went back to my room with a heavy heart. I had gravely underestimated the size of my task. This girl's lack of information was terrifying. Nor would it be enough merely to supply her with information. First she had to be taught to *think*. This loomed as a project of no small dimensions, and at first I was tempted to give her back to Petey. But then I got to thinking about her abundant physical charms and about the way she entered a room and the way she handled a knife and fork, and I decided to make an effort.

I went about it, as in all things, systematically. I gave her a course in logic. It happened that I, as a law student, was taking a course in logic myself, so I had all the facts at my finger tips. "Polly," I said to her when I picked her up on our next date, "tonight we are going over to the Knoll and talk."

"Oo, terrif," she replied. One thing I will say for this girl: you   60
would go far to find another so agreeable.

We went to the Knoll, the campus trysting place, and we sat down under an old oak, and she looked at me expectantly. "What are we going to talk about?" she asked.

"Logic."

She thought this over for a minute and decided she liked it. "Magnif," she said.

"Logic," I said, clearing my throat, "is the science of thinking. Before we can think correctly, we must first learn to recognize the common fallacies of logic. These we will take up tonight."

"Wow-dow!" she cried, clapping her hands delightedly.   65

I winced, but went bravely on. "First let us examine the fallacy called Dicto Simpliciter."

"By all means," she urged, batting her lashes eagerly.

"Dicto Simpliciter means an argument based on an unqualified generalization. For example: Exercise is good. Therefore everybody should exercise."

"I agree," said Polly earnestly. "I mean exercise is wonderful. I mean it builds the body and everything."

70 "Polly," I said gently, "the argument is a fallacy. *Exercise is good* is an unqualified generalization. For instance, if you have heart disease, exercise is bad, not good. Many people are ordered by their doctors *not* to exercise. You must *qualify* the generalization. You must say exercise is *usually* good, or exercise is good *for most people.* Otherwise you have committed a Dicto Simpliciter. Do you see?"

"No," she confessed. "But this is marvy. Do more! Do more!"

"It will be better if you stop tugging at my sleeve," I told her, and when she desisted, I continued. "Next we take up a fallacy called Hasty Generalization. Listen carefully: You can't speak French. I can't speak French. Petey Bellows can't speak French. I must therefore conclude that nobody at the University of Minnesota can speak French."

"Really?" said Polly, amazed. *"Nobody?"*

I hid my exasperation. "Polly, it's a fallacy. The generalization is reached too hastily. There are too few instances to support such a conclusion."

75 "Know any more fallacies?" she asked breathlessly. "This is more fun than dancing even."

I fought off a wave of despair. I was getting nowhere with this girl, absolutely nowhere. Still, I am nothing if not persistent. I continued. "Next comes Post Hoc. Listen to this: Let's not take Bill on our picnic. Every time we take him out with us, it rains."

"I know somebody just like that," she exclaimed. "A girl back home—Eula Becker, her name is. It never fails. Every single time we take her on a picnic—"

"Polly," I said sharply, "it's a fallacy. Eula Becker doesn't *cause* the rain. She has no connection with the rain. You are guilty of Post Hoc if you blame Eula Becker."

"I'll never do it again," she promised contritely. "Are you mad at me?"

I sighed. "No, Polly, I'm not mad." 80
"Then tell me some more fallacies."
"All right. Let's try Contradictory Premises."
"Yes, let's," she chirped, blinking her eyes happily.
I frowned, but plunged ahead. "Here's an example of Contradictory Premises: If God can do anything, can He make a stone so heavy that He won't be able to lift it?"
"Of course," she replied promptly. 85
"But if He can do anything. He can lift the stone," I pointed out.
"Yeah," she said thoughtfully. "Well, then I guess He can't make the stone."
"But He can do anything," I reminded her.
She scratched her pretty, empty head. "I'm all confused," she admitted.
"Of course you are. Because when the premises of an argument 90 contradict each other, there can be no argument. If there is an irresistible force, there can be no immovable object. If there is an immovable object, there can be no irresistible force. Get it?"
"Tell me some more of this keen stuff," she said eagerly.
I consulted my watch. "I think we'd better call it a night. I'll take you home now, and you go over all the things you've learned. We'll have another session tomorrow night."
I deposited her at the girls' dormitory, where she assured me that she had had a perfectly terrif evening, and I went glumly home to my room. Petey lay snoring in his bed, the raccoon coat huddled like a great hairy beast at his feet. For a moment I considered waking him and telling him that he could have his girl back. It seemed clear that my project was doomed to failure. The girl simply had a logic-proof head.
But then I reconsidered. I had wasted one evening; I might as well waste another. Who knew? Maybe somewhere in the extinct crater of her mind a few embers still smoldered. Maybe somehow I could fan them into flame. Admittedly it was not a prospect fraught with hope, but I decided to give it one more try.
Seated under the oak the next evening I said, "Our first fallacy 95 tonight is called Ad Misericordiam."
She quivered with delight.
"Listen closely," I said. "A man applies for a job. When the boss asks him what his qualifications are, he replies that he has a wife

and six children at home, the wife is a helpless cripple, the children have nothing to eat, no clothes to wear, no shoes on their feet, there are no beds in the house, no coal in the cellar, and winter is coming."

A tear rolled down each of Polly's pink cheeks. "Oh, this is awful, awful," she sobbed.

"Yes, it's awful," I agreed, "but it's no argument. The man never answered the boss's question about his qualifications. Instead he appealed to the boss's sympathy. He committed the fallacy of Ad Misericordiam. Do you understand?"

100   "Have you got a handkerchief?" she blubbered.

I handed her a handkerchief and tried to keep from screaming while she wiped her eyes. "Next," I said in a carefully controlled tone, "we will discuss False Analogy. Here is an example: Students should be allowed to look at their textbooks during examinations. After all, surgeons have X rays to guide them during an operation, lawyers have briefs to guide them during a trial, carpenters have blueprints to guide them when they are building a house. Why, then, shouldn't students be allowed to look at their textbooks during an examination?"

"There now," she said enthusiastically, "is the most marvy idea I've heard in years."

"Polly," I said testily, "the argument is all wrong. Doctors, lawyers, and carpenters aren't taking a test to see how much they have learned, but students are. The situations are altogether different, and you can't make an analogy between them."

"I still think it's a good idea," said Polly.

105   "Nuts," I muttered. Doggedly I pressed on. "Next we'll try Hypothesis Contrary to Fact."

"Sounds yummy," was Polly's reaction.

"Listen: If Madame Curie had not happened to leave a photographic plate in a drawer with a chunk of pitchblende, the world today would not know about radium."

"True, true," said Polly, nodding her head. "Did you see the movie? Oh, it just knocked me out. That Walter Pidgeon is so dreamy. I mean he fractures me."

"If you can forget Mr. Pidgeon for a moment," I said coldly, "I would like to point out that the statement is a fallacy. Maybe Madame Curie would have discovered radium at some later date. Maybe somebody else would have discovered it. Maybe any number of things would have happened. You can't start with a hypothesis that is not true and then draw any supportable conclusions from it."

"They ought to put Walter Pidgeon in more pictures," said Polly. "I hardly ever see him any more."

One more chance, I decided. But just one more. There is a limit to what flesh and blood can bear. "The next fallacy is called Poisoning the Well."

"How cute!" she gurgled.

"Two men are having a debate. The first one gets up and says, 'My opponent is a notorious liar. You can't believe a word that he is going to say.'... Now, Polly, think. Think hard. What's wrong?"

I watched her closely as she knit her creamy brow in concentration. Suddenly a glimmer of intelligence—the first I had seen— came into her eyes. "It's not fair," she said with indignation. "It's not a bit fair. What chance has the second man got if the first man calls him a liar before he even begins talking?"

"Right!" I cried exultantly. "One hundred per cent right. It's not fair. The first man has *poisoned the well* before anybody could drink from it. He has hamstrung his opponent before he could even start.... Polly, I'm proud of you."

"Pshaw," she murmured, blushing with pleasure.

"You see, my dear, these things aren't so hard. All you have to do is concentrate. Think—examine—evaluate. Come now, let's review everything we have learned."

"Fire away," she said with an airy wave of her hand.

Heartened by the knowledge that Polly was not altogether a cretin, I began a long, patient review of all I had told her. Over and over and over again I cited instances, pointed out flaws, kept hammering away without letup. It was like digging a tunnel. At first everything was work, sweat, and darkness. I had no idea when I would reach the light, or even *if* I would. But I persisted. I pounded and clawed and scraped, and finally I was rewarded. I saw a chink of light. And then the chink got bigger and the sun came pouring in and all was bright.

Five grueling nights this took, but it was worth it. I had made a logician out of Polly; I had taught her to think. My job was done. She was worthy of me at last. She was a fit wife for me, a proper hostess for my many mansions, a suitable mother for my well-heeled children.

It must not be thought that I was without love for this girl. Quite the contrary. Just as Pygmalion loved the perfect woman he had fashioned, so I loved mine. I decided to acquaint her with my feelings at our very next meeting. The time had come to change our relationship from academic to romantic.

"Polly," I said when next we sat beneath our oak, "tonight we will not discuss fallacies."

"Aw, gee," she said, disappointed.

"My dear," I said, favoring her with a smile. "we have now spent five evenings together. We have gotten along splendidly. It is clear that we are well matched."

125   "Hasty Generalization," said Polly brightly.

"I beg your pardon," said I.

"Hasty Generalization," she repeated. "How can you say that we are well matched on the basis of only five dates?"

I chuckled with amusement. The dear child had learned her lessons well. "My dear," I said, patting her hand in a tolerant manner, "five dates is plenty. After all, you don't have to eat a whole cake to know that it's good."

"False Analogy," said Polly promptly. "I'm not a cake. I'm a girl."

130   I chuckled with somewhat less amusement. The dear child had learned her lessons perhaps too well. I decided to change tactics. Obviously the best approach was a simple, strong, direct declaration of love. I paused for a moment while my massive brain chose the proper words. Then I began:

"Polly, I love you. You are the whole world to me, and the moon and the stars and the constellations of outer space. Please, my darling, say that you will go steady with me, for if you will not, life will be meaningless. I will languish. I will refuse my meals. I will wander the face of the earth, a shambling, hollow-eyed hulk."

There, I thought, folding my arms, that ought to do it.

"Ad Misericordiam," said Polly.

I ground my teeth. I was not Pygmalion; I was Frankenstein, and my monster had me by the throat. Frantically I fought back the tide of panic surging through me. At all costs I had to keep cool.

135   "Well, Polly," I said, forcing a smile, "you certainly have learned your fallacies."

"You're darn right," she said with a vigorous nod.

"And who taught them to you, Polly?"

"You did."

"That's right. So you do owe me something, don't you, my dear? If I hadn't come along you never would have learned about fallacies."

"Hypothesis Contrary to Fact," she said instantly.   140

I dashed perspiration from my brow. "Polly," I croaked, "you mustn't take all these things so literally. I mean this is just classroom stuff. You know that the things you learn in school don't have anything to do with life."

"Dicto Simpliciter," she said, wagging her finger at me playfully.

That did it. I leaped to my feet, bellowing like a bull. "Will you or will you not go steady with me?"

"I will not," she replied.

"Why not?" I demanded.   145

"Because this afternoon I promised Petey Bellows that I would go steady with him."

I reeled back, overcome with the infamy of it. After he promised, after he made a deal, after he shook my hand! "The rat!" I shrieked, kicking up great chunks of turf. "You can't go with him, Polly. He's a liar. He's a cheat. He's a rat."

"Poisoning the Well," said Polly, "and stop shouting. I think shouting must be a fallacy too."

With an immense effort of will, I modulated my voice. "All right," I said. "You're a logician. Let's look at this thing logically. How could you choose Petey Bellows over me? Look at me—a brilliant student, a tremendous intellectual, a man with an assured future. Look at Petey—a knothead, a jitterbug, a guy who'll never know where his next meal is coming from. Can you give me one logical reason why you should go steady with Petey Bellows?"

"I certainly can," declared Polly. "He's got a raccoon coat."   150

PART SEVEN

On Justice and Rights

NICCOLÒ MACHIAVELLI

On Cruelty and Clemency: Whether It Is Better to Be Loved or Feared

> *Niccolò Machiavelli (1469–1527) was a Florentine statesman and author of* Il Principe *(The Prince, 1513), from which the following selection is excerpted.* Il Principe *has become a famous and influential work in political theory for its argument that politicians may use dishonesty and other treacherous methods to maintain and increase their power.*

Continuing now with our list of qualities, let me say that every   1
prince should prefer to be considered merciful rather than cruel, yet

[Niccolò Machiavelli, "On Cruelty and Clemency: Whether It Is Better to be Loved or Feared," Section XVII of *The Prince*, transl. Robert M. Adams. New York: W. W. Norton, 1977, pp. 47–49, some footnotes deleted.]

he should be careful not to mismanage this clemency of his. People thought Cesare Borgia was cruel, but that cruelty of his reorganized the Romagna, united it, and established it in peace and loyalty. Anyone who views the matter realistically will see that this prince was much more merciful than the people of Florence, who, to avoid the reputation of cruelty, allowed Pistoia to be destroyed. Thus, no prince should mind being called cruel for what he does to keep his subjects united and loyal; he may make examples of a very few, but he will be more merciful in reality than those who, in their tender-heartedness, allow disorders to occur, with their attendant murders and lootings. Such turbulence brings harm to an entire community, while the executions ordered by a prince affect only one individual at a time. A new prince, above all others, cannot possibly avoid a name for cruelty, since new states are always in danger. And Virgil, speaking through the mouth of Dido, says:

> Res dura et regni novitas me talia cogunt
> Moliri, et late fines custode tueri.[1]

Yet a prince should be slow to believe rumors and to commit himself to action on the basis of them. He should not be afraid of his own thoughts; he ought to proceed cautiously, moderating his conduct with prudence and humanity, allowing neither overconfidence to make him careless, nor overtimidity to make him intolerable.

2   Here the question arises: is it better to be loved than feared, or vice versa? I don't doubt that every prince would like to be both; but since it is hard to accommodate these qualities, if you have to make a choice, to be feared is much safer than to be loved. For it is a good general rule about men, that they are ungrateful, fickle, liars and deceivers, fearful of danger and greedy for gain. While you serve their welfare, they are all yours, offering their blood, their belong-ings, their lives, and their children's lives, as we noted above—so long as the danger is remote. But when the danger is close at hand, they turn against you. Then, any prince who has relied on their words and has made no other preparations will come to grief; because friendships that are bought at a price, and not with great-ness and nobility of soul, may be paid for but they are not acquired,

---

1. "Harsh pressures and the newness of my reign / Compel me to these steps; I must maintain / My borders against foreign foes. . . ." (*Aeneid,* II, 563–4).

and they cannot be used in time of need. People are less concerned with offending a man who makes himself loved than one who makes himself feared: the reason is that love is a link of obligation which men, because they are rotten, will break any time they think doing so serves their advantage; but fear involves dread of punishment, from which they can never escape.

Still, a prince should make himself feared in such a way that,   3
even if he gets no love, he gets no hate either; because it is perfectly possible to be feared and not hated, and this will be the result if only the prince will keep his hands off the property of his subjects or citizens, and off their women. When he does have to shed blood, he should be sure to have a strong justification and manifest cause; but above all, he should not confiscate people's property, because men are quicker to forget the death of a father than the loss of a patrimony. Besides, pretexts for confiscation are always plentiful; it never fails that a prince who starts living by plunder can find reasons to rob someone else. Excuses for proceeding against someone's life are much rarer and more quickly exhausted.

But a prince at the head of his armies and commanding a   4
multitude of soldiers should not care a bit if he is considered cruel; without such a reputation, he could never hold his army together and ready for action. Among the marvelous deeds of Hannibal, this was prime: that, having an immense army, which included men of many different races and nations, and which he led to battle in distant countries, he never allowed them to fight among themselves or to rise against him, whether his fortune was good or bad. The reason for this could only be his inhuman cruelty, which, along with his countless other talents [*virtù*], made him an object of awe and terror to his soldiers; and without the cruelty, his other qualities [*le altre sua virtù*] would never have sufficed. The historians who pass snap judgments on these matters admire his accomplishments and at the same time condemn the cruelty which was their main cause.

When I say, "His other qualities would never have sufficed," we   5
can see that this is true from the example of Scipio, an outstanding man not only among those of his own time, but in all recorded history; yet his armies revolted in Spain, for no other reason than his excessive leniency in allowing his soldiers more freedom than military discipline permits. Fabius Maximus rebuked him in the senate for this failing, calling him the corrupter of the Roman

armies. When a lieutenant of Scipio's plundered the Locrians, he took no action in behalf of the people, and did nothing to discipline that insolent lieutenant; again, this was the result of his easygoing nature. Indeed, when someone in the senate wanted to excuse him on this occasion, he said there are many men who knew better how to avoid error themselves than how to correct error in others. Such a soft temper would in time have tarnished the fame and glory of Scipio, had he brought it to the office of emperor; but as he lived under the control of the senate, this harmful quality of his not only remained hidden but was considered creditable.

6   Returning to the question of being feared or loved, I conclude that since men love at their own inclination but can be made to fear at the inclination of the prince, a shrewd prince will lay his foundations on what is under his own control, not on what is controlled by others. He should simply take pains not to be hated, as I said.

STUDY QUESTIONS

1. In paragraph 1, Machiavelli argues that since new states are always in danger, a new prince "cannot possibly avoid a name for cruelty." What premises are assumed in this argument?

2. What assumptions about human nature does Machiavelli make in advising the prince?

3. Why does Machiavelli think it is dangerous for a prince to rely on the love of the citizens? What account of love does his argument depend upon?

4. How many historical examples does Machiavelli use to justify the use of cruelty over love? Can you think of any counterexamples from history? For example, did George Washington succeed by following Machiavelli's advice?

5. Is the argument in paragraph 6 the same as the argument in paragraph 2?

6. Machiavelli argues that a prince can strive to be obeyed out of love or out of fear. Are these the only options? If not, has Machiavelli presented us with a false alternative?

THOMAS JEFFERSON

The Declaration of Independence

Thomas Jefferson (1743–1826) was governor of Virginia, a lawyer, writer, architect, founder of the University of Virginia, and the third President of the United States.

When in the course of human events, it becomes necessary for one people to dissolve the political bands which have connected them with another, and to assume among the Powers of the earth, the separate and equal station to which the Laws of Nature and of Nature's God entitle them, a decent respect to the opinions of mankind requires that they should declare the causes which impel them to the separation.

We hold these truths to be self-evident, that all men are created equal, that they are endowed by their Creator with certain unalienable Rights, that among these are Life, Liberty and the pursuit of Happiness. That to secure these rights, Governments are instituted among Men deriving their just powers from the consent of the governed. That whenever any Form of Government becomes destructive of these ends, it is the Right of the People to alter or to abolish it, and to institute new Government, laying its foundation on such principles and organizing its powers in such form, as to them shall seem most likely to effect their Safety and Happiness. Prudence, indeed, will dictate that Governments long established should not be changed for light and transient causes; and accordingly all experience hath shown, that mankind are more disposed to suffer, while evils are sufferable, than to right themselves by abolishing the forms to which they are accustomed. But when a long train of abuses and usurpations pursuing invariably the same Object evinces a design to reduce them under absolute Despotism, it is their right, it is their duty, to throw off such government, and to provide new Guards for their future security. Such has been the patient sufferance of these Colonies; and such is now the necessity which constrains them to alter their former Systems of Government. The history of the present King of Great Britain is a history of repeated injuries and usurpations, all having in direct object the establishment of an absolute Tyranny over these States. To prove this, let Facts be submitted to a candid world.

3   He has refused his Assent to Laws, the most wholesome and necessary for the public good.

4   He has forbidden his Governors to pass Laws of immediate and pressing importance, unless suspended in their operation till his Assent should be obtained; and when so suspended, he has utterly neglected to attend to them.

5   He has refused to pass other Laws for the accommodation of large districts of people, unless those people would relinquish the right of Representation in the Legislature, a right inestimable to them and formidable to tyrants only.

6   He has called together legislative bodies at places unusual, uncomfortable, and distant from the depository of their Public Records, for the sole purpose of fatiguing them into compliance with his measures.

7   He has dissolved Representative Houses repeatedly, for opposing with manly firmness his invasions on the rights of the people.

8   He has refused for a long time, after such dissolutions, to cause others to be elected; whereby the Legislative Powers, incapable of Annihilation, have returned to the People at large for their exercise; the State remaining in the mean time exposed to all the dangers of invasion from without, and convulsions within.

9   He has endeavoured to prevent the population of these States; for that purpose obstructing the Laws of Naturalization of Foreigners; refusing to pass others to encourage their migration hither, and raising the conditions of new Appropriations of Lands.

10   He has obstructed the Administration of Justice, by refusing his Assent to Laws for establishing Judiciary Powers.

11   He has made Judges dependent on his Will alone, for the tenure of their offices, and the amount and payment of their salaries.

He has erected a multitude of New Offices, and sent hither   12
swarms of Officers to harass our People, and eat out their substance.

He has kept among us, in time of peace, Standing Armies without   13
the Consent of our Legislature.

He has affected to render the Military independent of and supe-   14
rior to the Civil Power.

He has combined with others to subject us to jurisdictions foreign   15
to our constitution, and unacknowledged by our laws; giving his
Assent to their acts of pretended Legislation:

For quartering large bodies of armed troops among us: 16

For protecting them, by a mock Trial, from Punishment for any   17
Murders which they should commit on the Inhabitants of these
States:

For cutting off our Trade with all parts of the world: 18

For imposing Taxes on us without our Consent: 19

For depriving us in many cases, of the benefits of Trial by Jury: 20

For transporting us beyond Seas to be tried for pretended of-   21
fenses:

For abolishing the free System of English Laws in a Neighbour-   22
ing Province, establishing therein an Arbitrary government, and
enlarging its boundaries so as to render it at once an example and
fit instrument for introducing the same absolute rule into these
Colonies:

For taking away our Charters, abolishing our most valuable   23
Laws, and altering fundamentally the Forms of our Governments:

For suspending our own Legislatures, and declaring themselves   24
invested with Power to legislate for us in all cases whatsoever.

He has abdicated Government here, by declaring us out of his   25
Protection and waging War against us.

He has plundered our seas, ravaged our Coasts, burnt our towns   26
and destroyed the Lives of our people.

He is at this time transporting large Armies of foreign Mercenar-   27
ies to compleat works of death, desolation and tyranny, already
begun with circumstances of Cruelty and perfidy scarcely paralleled
in the most barbarous ages, and totally unworthy the Head of a
civilized nation.

He has constrained our fellow Citizens taken Captive on the high   28
Seas to bear Arms against their Country, to become the executioners
of their friends and Brethren, or to fall themselves by their Hands.

29 He has excited domestic insurrections amongst us, and has endeavoured to bring on the inhabitants of our frontiers, the merciless Indian Savages, whose known rule of warfare, is an undistinguished destruction of all ages, sexes and conditions.

30 In every stage of these Oppressions We Have Petitioned for Redress in the most humble terms: Our repeated petitions have been answered only by repeated injury. A Prince, whose character is thus marked by every act which may define a Tyrant, is unfit to be the ruler of a free People.

31 Nor have We been wanting in attention to our British brethren. We have warned them from time to time of attempts by their legislature to extend an unwarrantable jurisdiction over us. We have reminded them of the circumstances of our emigration and settlement here. We have appealed to their native justice and magnanimity and we have conjured them by the ties of our common kindred to disavow these usurpations, which would inevitably interrupt our connections and correspondence. They too have been deaf to the voice of justice and of consanguinity. We must, therefore acquiesce in the necessity, which denounces our Separation, and hold them, as we hold the rest of mankind, Enemies in War, in Peace Friends.

32 We, therefore, the Representatives of the United States of America, in General Congress, Assembled, appealing to the Supreme Judge of the world for the rectitude of our intentions, do, in the Name, and by Authority of the good People of these Colonies, solemnly publish and declare, That these United Colonies are, and of Right ought to be Free and Independent States; that they are Absolved from all Allegiance to the British Crown, and that all political connection between them and the State of Great Britain, is and ought to be totally dissolved; and that as Free and Independent States, they have full power to levy War, conclude Peace, contract Alliances, establish Commerce, and to do all other Acts and Things which Independent States may of right do. And for the support of this Declaration, with a firm reliance on the protection of Divine Providence, we mutually pledge to each other our lives, our Fortunes and our sacred Honor.

STUDY QUESTIONS

1. The core of Jefferson's argument is in paragraph 2. Diagram the argument.
2. In paragraphs 3 through 31, Jefferson lists over two dozen complaints against the king's governance. Which of the complaints support Jefferson's claim, in paragraph 2, that the king's goal is "to reduce them under an absolute Despotism"?
3. In paragraph 2, what does Jefferson consider to be the proper ends of government? Of the complaints he lists, which support that claim that the king's governance has been "destructive of these ends"?
4. Notice Jefferson's use of emotionally charged language. Does it supplement or replace argument?
5. How does Jefferson anticipate and respond to the following objection: "Perhaps the King has not protected rights as well as he should. Even so, isn't rebellion too extreme a response? Wouldn't calls for reform be more appropriate?"
6. In what way does Jefferson think "that all men are created equal"? What account of *equality* does the rest of his argument seem to require?

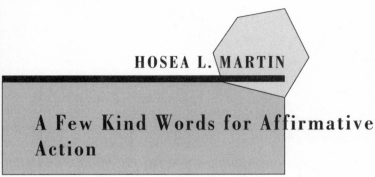

HOSEA L. MARTIN

A Few Kind Words for Affirmative Action

Hosea L. Martin is vice-president of the United Way San Francisco office. In the following selection, originally publish-ed in The Wall Street Journal, *Martin defends the practice of using race as a criterion for hiring in some cases.*

1   What with all the debate about the current versions of the Civil Rights bill, I feel it's time for me to raise my voice. I'm for affirm-ative action. I can make the argument on economic grounds—the disproportionate number of blacks out of work in this country should be enough evidence that the policy isn't taking jobs away from whites.

2   But there's a second reason for my bias. Except for a sweaty warehousing job that I was forced to take when laid off in 1984, all the jobs I've had since graduating from college in 1960 were because of affirmative action. In most cases, I was one of only a handful of black managers or professionals in an organization, and a few times I found myself to be the only one in a department. I never got around to feeling lonely, because I was too busy being grateful for being on the payroll.

3   Nor did I have gnawing doubts about my qualifications for the jobs I held. I know that it's currently popular to believe that I always sat silently in the darkest corner of the conference room, ashamed that I was hired for "political reasons," but that wasn't the way it was for me.

[Hosea L. Martin, "A Few Kind Words for Affirmative Action." *The Wall Street Journal,* April 25, 1991, op-ed page.]

The truth is, I sat as close to the boss as possible and pontificated   4
as much as anyone else at the table. I realized that somewhere there
was someone who could do my job better than I could, but I also
knew that every person in the room would have to say the same
thing if he or she were strictly honest. Every single one of us—black
and white, male and female—had been hired for reasons beyond
our being able to do the job.

That's the case with just about every job in this country. There's   5
a lot of hoopla about the U.S. being a meritocracy, but even a casual
examination of performances tells us that this is a myth.

I know that this is hard to accept. Quite often the reaction to   6
hearing it is similar to that of a swaggering gunfighter of the Old
West. "Somebody's faster 'n me? You're loco!" But somewhere there
was someone quicker on the draw. Ask any ghost from Boot Hill.

It's the same in today's job market. Every person wants to believe   7
that he or she was selected over hundreds of other applicants because
he or she was the "fastest gun." 'Tain't so. There probably were
dozens of faster guns in that stack of resumes on the personnel
director's desk, but you, if you were the lucky person who got the
job, were judged to be the "best fit."

Being the best fit for a job entails more than having the best set   8
of credentials (e.g., good grades, high test scores, impressive record).
Usually, the people who apply for a particular job have met all the
criteria—education, experience, career expectations, etc.—that the
ad asked for, and you can be sure that a low-level clerk has been
instructed to screen out those applications that fail to clear this
initial barrier. What winds up on the personnel director's desk is a
stack of resumes that are astonishingly uniform. A black Stanford
MBA may have survived the cut, but you can bet that a black
high-school dropout didn't.

The task of the personnel director (or whoever does the hiring)   9
would be easy if all he or she had to do was pick the person who
could "do the job"—chances are, anyone in the stack could—but
there are other considerations that have to be made, and these
considerations aren't always limited to race and sex. Satisfying these
considerations means responding to pressures outside as well as
inside the organization.

If that Stanford MBA is selected, and finds himself the only black   10
person in his department, he shouldn't feel deflated when he learns
that he owes his good fortune to affirmative action. Eventually he'll

find out that just about everybody he's working with got special consideration for one reason or another. Some had connections who were able to get them interviewed and hired; others had attended the "right" schools; still others had been hired because they were from a particular part of the country, or were members of a particular class, religion, nationality or fraternity. (I'll never forget when, as an Army clerk, I had to type dozens of application letters for a white officer who was being discharged; he never brought up his college academic record—which I knew was horrible—but in every single letter he mentioned that he was a member of Phi-something fraternity. He got a great job.)

11   Seldom will you find a person who got a job because he was the very best at doing it. No? Come on, are you trying to tell me that Dan Quayle was the best that George Bush could find?

12   Sure, there are some exceptionally capable people, and I've observed that they don't gripe about affirmative action; they know that, sooner or later, talent will out. The run-of-the-mill plodders are the ones who complain that affirmative action is blocking their career path; take away this excuse and they'd probably blame their lack of progress on sunspots. For them, it's always something.

13   Affirmative action is needed in education as well as in the workplace. Those who criticize affirmative action in their campaign against "political correctness" are wrong. Without the policy there would be a sharp drop in the already-small number of black professionals that colleges produce to serve inner-city communities and small towns. The affirmative action programs that raised the share of minorities in medical school to 10% in 1980 from about 5% in the 1960s produced tremendous benefits to society.

14   As for me, each morning I go to work with pride and confidence. I know I can do the job. I also know that I'm a beneficiary of a law—good ol' affirmative action—that does not require an organization to hire a person who clearly doesn't have the education, credentials or skills that a job demands. Any organization that has done this is guilty of ignoring qualified minority people, and of cynically setting someone up for failure. Such an organization began with the premise that no minority person could do the job, and set out to prove it.

15   One final question: If it's true that affirmative action is cramming the offices and board rooms of corporate America with blacks, why

do I see so few of them when I'm walking around San Francisco's financial district on my lunch hour?

STUDY QUESTIONS

1. What things count as job qualifications, according to Martin?
2. Other than qualifications, what are the factors Martin says are used to judge whether someone is the "best fit" for a job?
3. Martin rejects the idea that the United States is a "meritocracy," that is, that hiring is based on qualifications. Do you think it follows from this that hiring *ought* not to be done on grounds of qualifications?
4. How many different benefits does Martin argue that affirmative action programs lead to?
5. In paragraph 12, Martin responds to the objection that affirmative action programs unfairly harm some people. On what grounds does he set aside this objection?
6. Identify the generalizations Martin uses. What role do they play in the case he is making? What is the strength of the evidence he offers for them?

LISA H. NEWTON

Bakke and Davis: Justice, American Style

Lisa H. Newton was born in New Jersey in 1939. She received her Ph.D. in Philosophy from Columbia University, and is a professor of philosophy at Fairfield University in Connecticut. In the following essay, Newton discusses the famous Bakke v. Regents of the University of California *(1978) case, in which Bakke, a white male, sued the University of California for reverse discrimination on the grounds that he had been denied admission to its medical school at Davis even though his grades and test scores were significantly higher than those of several minority students who were admitted.*

1   The use of the special minority quota or "goal" to achieve a desirable racial mix in certain professions might appear to be an attractive solution to the problem of justice posed by generations of racial discrimination. Ultimately, however, the quota solution fails. It puts an intolerable burden of injustice on a system strained by too much of that in the past, and prolongs the terrible stereotypes of inferiority into the indefinite future. It is a serious error to urge this course on the American people.

2   The quota system, as employed by the University of California's medical school at Davis or any similar institution, is unjust, for all the same reasons that the discrimination it attempts to reverse is

[Lisa H. Newton, "Bakke and Davis: Justice, American Style." *National Forum (The Phi Beta Kappa Journal)* LVIII, no. 1 (Winter 1978), pp. 22–23, legal references omitted.]

unjust. It diminishes the opportunities of some candidates for a social purpose that has nothing to do with them, to make "reparation" for acts they never committed. And "they" are no homogeneous "majority": as Swedish-Americans, Irish-Americans, Americans of Polish or Jewish or Italian descent, they can claim a past history of the same irrational discrimination, poverty and cultural deprivation that now plagues Blacks and Spanish-speaking individuals. In simple justice, all applicants (except, of course, the minority of WASPs!) should have access to a "track" specially constructed for their group, if any do. And none should. The salvation of every minority in America has been strict justice, the merit system strictly applied; the Davis quota system is nothing but a suspension of justice in favor of the most recent minorities, and is flatly unfair to all the others.

The quota system is generally defended by suggesting that a little   3
bit of injustice is far outweighted by the great social good which will follow from it; the argument envisions a fully integrated society where all discrimination will be abolished. Such a result hardly seems likely. Much more likely, if ethnic quotas are legitimated by the Court in the Bakke Case, all the other ethnic minorities will promptly organize to secure special tracks of their own, including minorities which have never previously organized at all. In these days, the advantage of a medical education is sufficiently attractive to make the effort worthwhile. As elsewhere, grave political penalties will be inflicted on legislatures and institutions that attempt to ignore these interest groups. I give Davis, and every other desirable school in the country, one decade from a Supreme Court decision favorable to quotas, to collapse under the sheer administrative weight of the hundreds of special admissions tracks and quotas it will have to maintain.

But the worst effect of the quota system is on the minorities   4
supposedly favored by it. In the past, Blacks were socially stereotyped as less intelligent than whites because disproportionately few Blacks could get into medical school; the stereotype was the result of the very racial discrimination that it attempted to justify. Under any minority quota system, ironically, that stereotype would be tragically reinforced. From the day the Court blesses the two-track system of admissions at Davis, the word is out that Black physicians, or those of Spanish or Asian derivation, are less qualified, just a little

less qualified, than their "White-Anglo" counterparts, for they did not have to meet as strict a test for admission to medical school. And that judgment will apply, as the quota applies, on the basis of race alone, for we will have no way of knowing which Blacks, Spanish or Asians were admitted in a medical school's regular competition and which were admitted on the "special minority" track. The opportunity to bury their unfavorable ethnic stereotypes by clean and public success in strictly fair competition, an opportunity that our older ethnic groups seized enthusiastically, will be denied to these "special minorities" for yet another century.

5   In short, there are no gains, for American society or for groups previously disadvantaged by it, in quota systems that attempt reparation by reverse discrimination. The larger moral question of whether we should set aside strict justice for some larger social gain, does not have to be taken up in a case like this one, where procedural injustice produces only substantive harm for all concerned. Blacks, Hispanic and other minority groups which are presently economically disadvantaged will see real progress when, and only when, the American economy expands to make room for more higher status employment for all groups. The economy is not improved in the least by special tracks and quotas for special groups; on the contrary, it is burdened by the enormous weight of the nonproductive administrative procedure required to implement them. No social purpose will be served, and no justice done, by the establishment of such procedural monsters; we should hope that the Supreme Court will see its way clear to abolishing them once and for all.

STUDY QUESTIONS

1. In paragraph 2, Newton argues that minority quotas are unjust. In paragraph 4, she argues that quotas reinforce racial stereotypes. How many distinct arguments does she raise against quotas?

2. "Justice" is a key concept in paragraphs 1 and 2 of Newton's argument. What does she mean by justice? For instance, what is "the problem of justice posed by generations of racial discrimination"? And what is the "strict justice" that has been "the salvation of every minority in America"?

3. In paragraph 3, what does Newton state to be the position of those in favor of a quota system?
4. How do you think Newton would respond to the following statement: "Perhaps the use of quota systems will reinforce negative stereotypes of minorities. But perhaps the affected minorities would prefer the benefits of preferential policies even with that problem"?

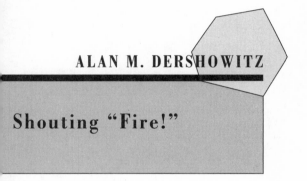

ALAN M. DERSHOWITZ

Shouting "Fire!"

Alan M. Dershowitz is an attorney, professor of law at Harvard University, and author of a weekly syndicated column as well as several books. He was also a member of O. J. Simpson's defense team, and wrote a book about the trial, entitled Reasonable Doubts *(1996).*

When the Reverend Jerry Falwell learned that the Supreme Court   1
had reversed his $200,000 judgment against *Hustler* magazine for the emotional distress that he had suffered from an outrageous parody, his response was typical of those who seek to censor speech: "Just as no person may scream 'Fire!' in a crowded theater when there is no fire, and find cover under the First Amendment, likewise, no sleazy merchant like Larry Flynt should be able to use the First Amendment as an excuse for maliciously and dishonestly attacking public figures, as he has so often done."

Justice Oliver Wendell Holmes's classic example of unprotected   2
speech—falsely shouting "Fire!" in a crowded theater—has been

Alan M. Dershowitz, "Shouting 'Fire!'" *Atlantic Monthly* (January 1989), pp. 72–74.

invoked so often, by so many people, in such diverse contexts, that it has become part of our national folk language. It has even appeared—most appropriately—in the theater: in Tom Stoppard's play *Rosencrantz and Guildenstern Are Dead* a character shouts at the audience, "Fire!" He then quickly explains: "It's all right—I'm demonstrating the misuse of free speech." Shouting "Fire!" in the theater may well be the only jurisprudential analogy that has assumed the status of a folk argument. A prominent historian recently characterized it as "the most brilliantly persuasive expression that ever came from Holmes' pen." But in spite of its hallowed position in both the jurisprudence of the First Amendment and the arsenal of political discourse, it is and was an inapt analogy, even in the context in which it was originally offered. It has lately become—despite, perhaps even because of, the frequency and promiscuousness of its invocation—little more than a caricature of logical argumentation.

3   The case that gave rise to the "Fire!"-in-a-crowded-theater analogy—*Schenck* v. *United States*—involved the prosecution of Charles Schenck, who was the general secretary of the Socialist Party in Philadelphia, and Elizabeth Baer, who was its recording secretary. In 1917 a jury found Schenck and Baer guilty of attempting to cause insubordination among soldiers who had been drafted to fight in the First World War. They and other party members had circulated leaflets urging draftees not to "submit to intimidation" by fighting in a war being conducted on behalf of "Wall Street's chosen few."

4   Schenck admitted, and the Court found, that the intent of the pamphlets' "impassioned language" was to "influence" draftees to resist the draft. Interestingly, however, Justice Holmes noted that nothing in the pamphlet suggested that the draftees should use unlawful or violent means to oppose conscription: "In form at least [the pamphlet] confined itself to peaceful measures, such as a petition for the repeal of the act" and an exhortation to exercise "your right to assert your opposition to the draft." Many of its most impassioned words were quoted directly from the Constitution.

5   Justice Holmes acknowledged that "in many places and in ordinary times the defendants, in saying all that was said in the circular, would have been within their constitutional rights." "But," he added, "the character of every act depends upon the circumstances in which it is done." And to illustrate that truism he went on to say,

> The most stringent protection of free speech would not protect a man in falsely shouting fire in a theater, and causing a panic. It does not even protect a man from an injunction against uttering words that may have all the effect of force.

Justice Holmes then upheld the convictions in the context of a wartime draft, holding that the pamphlet created "a clear and present danger" of hindering the war effort while our soldiers were fighting for their lives and our liberty.   6

The example of shouting "Fire!" obviously bore little relationship to the facts of the Schenck case. The Schenck pamphlet contained a substantive political message. It urged its draftee readers to *think* about the message and then—if they so chose—to act on it in a lawful and nonviolent way. The man who shouts "Fire!" in a crowded theater is neither sending a political message nor inviting his listener to think about what he has said and decide what to do in a rational, calculated manner. On the contrary, the message is designed to force action *without* contemplation. The message "Fire!" is directed not to the mind and the conscience of the listener but, rather, to his adrenaline and his feet. It is a stimulus to immediate *action*, not thoughtful reflection. It is—as Justice Holmes recognized in his follow-up sentence—the functional equivalent of "uttering words that may have all the effect of force."   7

Indeed, in that respect the shout of "Fire!" is not even speech, in any meaningful sense of that term. It is a *clang* sound—the equivalent of setting off a nonverbal alarm. Had Justice Holmes been more honest about his example, he would have said that freedom of speech does not protect a kid who pulls a fire alarm in the absence of a fire. But that obviously would have been irrelevant to the case at hand. The proposition that pulling an alarm is not protected speech certainly leads to the conclusion that shouting the word *fire* is also not protected. But the core analogy is the nonverbal alarm, and the derivative example is the verbal shout. By cleverly substituting the derivative shout for the core alarm, Holmes made it possible to analogize one set of words to another—as he could not have done if he had begun with the self-evident proposition that setting off an alarm bell is not free speech.   8

The analogy is thus not only inapt but also insulting. Most Americans do not respond to political rhetoric with the same kind   9 of automatic acceptance expected of schoolchildren responding to a fire drill. Not a single recipient of the Schenck pamphlet is known to have changed his mind after reading it. Indeed, one draftee, who appeared as a prosecution witness, was asked whether reading a pamphlet asserting that the draft law was unjust would make him "immediately decide that you must erase that law." Not surprisingly, he replied, "I do my own thinking." A theatergoer would probably not respond similarly if asked how he would react to a shout of "Fire!"

10   Another important reason why the analogy is inapt is that Holmes emphasizes the factual falsity of the shout "Fire!" The Schenck pamphlet, however, was not factually false. It contained political opinions and ideas about the causes of the war and about appropriate and lawful responses to the draft. As the Supreme Court recently reaffirmed (in *Falwell* v. *Hustler*), "The First Amendment recognizes no such thing as a 'false' idea." Nor does it recognize false opinions about the causes of or cures for war.

11   A closer analogy to the facts of the Schenck case might have been provided by a person's standing outside a theater, offering the patrons a leaflet advising them that in his opinion the theater was structurally unsafe, and urging them not to enter but to complain to the building inspectors. That analogy, however, would not have served Holmes's argument for punishing Schenck. Holmes needed an analogy that would appear relevant to Schenck's political speech but that would invite the conclusion that censorship was appropriate.

12   Unsurprisingly, a war-weary nation—in the throes of a know-nothing hysteria over immigrant anarchists and socialists—welcomed the comparison between what was regarded as a seditious political pamphlet and a malicious shout of "Fire!" Ironically, the "Fire!" analogy is nearly all that survives from the Schenck case; the ruling itself is almost certainly not good law. Pamphlets of the kind that resulted in Schenck's imprisonment have been circulated with impunity during subsequent wars.

13   Over the past several years I have assembled a collection of instances—cases, speeches, arguments—in which proponents of censorship have maintained that the expression at issue is "just like" or "equivalent to" falsely shouting "Fire!" in a crowded theater and ought to be banned, "just as" shouting "Fire!" ought to be banned.

The analogy is generally invoked, often with self-satisfaction, as an absolute argument-stopper. It does, after all, claim the high authority of the great Justice Oliver Wendell Holmes. I have rarely heard it invoked in a convincing, or even particularly relevant, way. But that, too, can claim lineage from the great Holmes.

Not unlike Falwell, with his silly comparison between shouting 14 "Fire!" and publishing an offensive parody, courts and commentators have frequently invoked "Fire!" as an analogy to expression that is not an automatic stimulus to panic. A state supreme court held that "Holmes' aphorism . . . applies with equal force to pornography"—in particular to the exhibition of the movie *Carmen Baby* in a drive-in theater in close proximity to highways and homes. Another court analogized "picketing . . . in support of a secondary boycott" to shouting "Fire!" because in both instances "speech and conduct are brigaded." In the famous Skokie case one of the judges argued that allowing Nazis to march through a city where a large number of Holocaust survivors live "just might fall into the same category as one's 'right' to cry fire in a crowded theater."

Outside court the analogies become even more badly stretched. 15 A spokesperson for the New Jersey Sports and Exposition Authority complained that newspaper reports to the effect that a large number of football players had contracted cancer after playing in the Meadowlands—a stadium atop a landfill—were the "journalistic equivalent of shouting fire in a crowded theater." An insect researcher acknowledged that his prediction that a certain amusement park might become roach-infested "may be tantamount to shouting fire in a crowded theater." The philosopher Sidney Hook, in a letter to the *New York Times* bemoaning a Supreme Court decision that required a plaintiff in a defamation action to prove that the offending statement was actually false, argued that the First Amendment does not give the press carte blanche to accuse innocent persons "any more than the First Amendment protects the right of someone falsely to shout fire in a crowded theater."

Some close analogies to shouting "Fire!" or setting off an alarm 16 are, of course, available: calling in a false bomb threat; dialing 911 and falsely describing an emergency; making a loud, gunlike sound in the presence of the President; setting off a voice-activated sprinkler system by falsely shouting "Fire!" In one case in which the "Fire!" analogy was directly to the point, a creative defendant tried to get around it. The case involved a man who calmly advised an airline clerk that he was "only here to hijack the plane." He was charged, in effect, with shouting "Fire!" in a crowded theater, and his rejected defense—as quoted by the court—was as follows: "If we built fireproof theaters and let people know about this, then the shouting of 'Fire!' would not cause panic."

17   Here are some more-distant but still related examples: the recent incident of the police slaying in which some members of an onlooking crowd urged a mentally ill vagrant who had taken an officer's gun to shoot the officer; the screaming of racial epithets during a tense confrontation; shouting down a speaker and preventing him from continuing his speech.

18   Analogies are, by their nature, matters of degree. Some are closer to the core example than others. But any attempt to analogize political ideas in a pamphlet, ugly parody in a magazine, offensive movies in a theater, controversial newspaper articles, or any of the other expressions and actions catalogued above to the very different act of shouting "Fire!" in a crowded theater is either self-deceptive or self-serving.

19   The government does, of course, have some arguably legitimate bases for suppressing speech which bear no relationship to shouting "Fire!" It may ban the publication of nuclear-weapon codes, of information about troop movements, and of the identity of undercover agents. It may criminalize extortion threats and conspiratorial agreements. These expressions may lead directly to serious harm, but the mechanisms of causation are very different from that at work when an alarm is sounded. One may also argue—less persuasively, in my view—against protecting certain forms of public obscenity and defamatory statements. Here, too, the mechanisms of causation are very different. None of these exceptions to the First Amendment's exhortation that the government "shall make no law ... abridging the freedom of speech, or of the press" is anything like falsely shouting "Fire!" in a crowded theater; they all must be justified on other grounds.

20   A comedian once told his audience, during a stand-up routine, about the time he was standing around a fire with a crowd of people and got in trouble for yelling "Theater, theater!" That, I think, is about as clever and productive a use as anyone has ever made of Holmes's flawed analogy.

STUDY QUESTIONS

1. The key propositions in Holmes's argument are as follows:
   (1) Shouting "Fire!" in a theater creates a "clear and present danger."
   (2) Creating a "clear and present danger" is not protected by the First Amendment.
   (3) Shouting "Fire!" in a theater is not protected by the First Amendment.
   (4) Schenck's distributing the leaflet to draftees is similar to shouting "Fire!" in a theater.
   (5) Schenck's distributing the leaflet to draftees is not protected by the First Amendment.
   Diagram the argument.
2. In an analogical argument, the first thing to check is the premise that makes the similarity claim—in this case, proposition (4). What similarities are there between Schenck's distributing the leaflet and shouting "Fire!" in a crowded theater?
3. In paragraphs 5 and 6, Dershowitz quotes Holmes as stating that the First Amendment does not protect words that cause a panic, "words that may have all the effect of force," or words that create a "clear and present danger." Given what you know about Schenck's case, does it seem that his distributing the leaflet falls under any of these categories? If so, why? If not, what characteristic of Schenck's action prevents it from doing so?
4. Dershowitz thinks Holmes made a bad analogy, and he states what he thinks are two important disanalogies in paragraphs 7 and 10. What are they? How do they fit with your answers to question 3?
5. In paragraph 8, Dershowitz offers what he thinks is a better analogy for shouting "Fire!" in a theater; and in paragraph 11, he offers what he thinks is a better analogy for Schenck's handing out leaflets. Are they in fact better analogies?

On Economic Freedom and Government Regulation

JUSTICE LOUIS BRANDEIS

New State Ice Co. v. *Liebmann* [The Government May Prohibit Competition]

Louis D. Brandeis (1856–1941) was born in Louisville, Kentucky, attended Harvard Law School, and eventually became a U.S. Supreme Court Justice. The following case deals with the issue of whether the State can legitimately prohibit competition among private enterprises. The majority of the Court agreed with the argument for the defendant, Mr. Liebmann, that since Mr. Liebmann's ice company was a private business, the State could not legitimately prohibit him from competing with New State Ice Company. This decision was based on the Fourteenth Amendment to the Federal Constitution:

[Justice Brandeis, dissenting opinion, *New State Ice Co.* v. *Liebmann*, 463 U.S. 262 (1931), pp. 262–311, all references omitted.]

> *No State shall make or enforce any law which shall abridge the privileges or immunities of citizens of the United States; nor shall any State deprive any person of life, liberty, or property, without due process of law; nor deny to any person within its jurisdiction the equal protection of the laws.*

The reasons for the majority's decision are summarized first; Justice Brandeis's dissenting opinion follows.

1   Argued February 19, 1932.—Decided March 21, 1932.

1. The business of manufacturing ice and selling it is essentially a private business and not so affected with a public interest that a legislature may constitutionally limit the number of those who may engage in it, in order to control competition.
2. An Oklahoma statute, declaring that the manufacture, sale and distribution of ice is a public business, forbids anyone to engage in it without first having procured a license from a state commission; no license is to issue without proof of necessity for the manufacture, sale or distribution of ice in the community or place to which the application relates, and if the facilities already existing and licensed at such place are sufficient to meet the public needs therein, the commission may deny the application. *Held* repugnant to the due process clause of the Fourteenth Amendment.
3. A state law infringing the liberty guaranteed to individuals by the Constitution can not be upheld upon the ground that the State is conducting a legislative experiment.

Affirmed.

Mr. Justice Brandeis, dissenting.

2   Chapter 147 of the Session Laws of Oklahoma, 1925, declares that the manufacture of ice for sale and distribution is "a public business"; confers upon the Corporation Commission in respect to it the powers of regulation customarily exercised over public utilities; and provides specifically for securing adequate service. The statute

makes it a misdemeanor to engage in the business without a license from the Commission; directs that the license shall not issue except pursuant to a prescribed written application, after a formal hearing upon adequate notice both to the community to be served and to the general public, and a showing upon competent evidence, of the necessity "at the place desired;" and it provides that the application may be denied, among other grounds, if "the facts proved at said hearing disclose that the facilities for the manufacture, sale and distribution of ice by some person, firm or corporation already licensed by said Commission at said point, community or place are sufficient to meet the public needs therein."

Under a license, so granted, the New State Ice Company is, and for some years has been, engaged in the manufacture, sale and distribution of ice at Oklahoma City, and has invested in that business $500,000. While it was so engaged, Liebmann, without having obtained or applied for a license, purchased a parcel of land in that city and commenced the construction thereon of an ice plant for the purpose of entering the business in competition with the plaintiff. To enjoin him from doing so this suit was brought by the Ice Company. Compare *Frost* v. *Corporation Commission.* Liebmann contends that the manufacture of ice for sale and distribution is not a public business; that it is a private business and, indeed, a common calling; that the right to engage in a common calling is one of the fundamental liberties guaranteed by the due process clause; and that to make his right to engage in that calling dependent upon a finding of public necessity deprives him of liberty and property in violation of the Fourteenth Amendment. Upon full hearing the District Court sustained that contention and dismissed the bill. Its decree was affirmed by the Circuit Court of Appeals. The case is here on appeal. In my opinion, the judgment should be reversed.

First. The Oklahoma statute makes entry into the business of manufacturing ice for sale and distribution dependent, in effect, upon a certificate of public convenience and necessity. Such a certificate was unknown to the common law. It is a creature of the machine age, in which plants have displaced tools and businesses are substituted for trades. The purpose of requiring it is to promote the public interest by preventing waste. Particularly in those businesses in which interest and depreciation charges on plant constitute a large element in the cost of production, experience has taught that the financial burdens incident to unnecessary duplication of facilities are likely to bring high rates and poor service. There, cost is usually dependent, among other things, upon volume; and division of possible patronage among competing concerns may so raise the unit cost of operation as to make it impossible to provide adequate service at reasonable rates. The introduction in the United States of the certificate of public convenience and necessity marked the growing conviction that under certain circumstances free competition might be harmful to the community and that, when it was so, absolute freedom to enter the business of one's choice should be denied.

5   Long before the enactment of the Oklahoma statute here challenged a like requirement had become common in the United States in some lines of business. The certificate was required first for railroads; then for street railways; then for other public utilities whose operation is dependent upon the grant of some special privilege.

Latterly, the requirement has been widely extended to common carriers by motor vehicle which use the highways, but which, unlike street railways and electric light companies, are not dependent upon the grant of any special privilege. In Oklahoma the certificate was required, as early as 1915, for cotton gins—a business then declared a public one, and, like the business of manufacturing ice, conducted wholly upon private property. See *Frost* v. *Corporation Commission.* As applied to public utilities, the validity under the Fourteenth Amendment of the requirement of the certificate has never been successfully questioned.

6   *Second.* Oklahoma declared the business of manufacturing ice for sale and distribution a "public business"; that is, a public utility. So far as appears, it was the first State to do so. Of course, a legislature cannot by mere legislative fiat convert a business into a public utility. *Producers Transportation Co.* v. *Railroad Commission.* But the conception of a public utility is not static. The welfare of the community may require that the business of supplying ice be made a public utility, as well as the business of supplying water or any other necessary commodity or service. If the business is, or can be made, a public utility, it must be possible to make the issue of a certificate a prerequisite to engaging in it.

7   Whether the local conditions are such as to justify converting a

private business into a public one is a matter primarily for the determination of the state legislature. Its determination is subject to judicial review; but the usual presumption of validity attends the enactment. The action of the State must be held valid unless clearly arbitrary, capricious or unreasonable. "The legislature being familiar with local conditions is, primarily, the judge of the necessity of such enactments. The mere fact that a court may differ with the legislature in its views of public policy, or that judges may hold views inconsistent with the propriety of the legislation in question, affords no ground for judicial interference. . . ." *McLean* v. *Arkansas.* Whether the grievances are real or fancied, whether the remedies are wise or foolish, are not matters about which the Court may concern itself. "Our present duty is to pass upon the statute before us, and if it has been enacted upon a belief of evils that is not arbitrary we cannot measure their extent against the estimate of the legislature." *Tanner* v. *Little.* A decision that the legislature's belief of evils was arbitrary, capricious and unreasonable may not be made without enquiry into the facts with reference to which it acted.

Third. Liebmann challenges the statute—not an order of the Corporation Commission. If he had applied for a license and been denied one, we should have been obliged to enquire whether the evidence introduced before the Commission justified it in refusing permission to establish an additional ice plant in Oklahoma City. As he did not apply but challenges the statute itself, our enquiry is of an entirely different nature. Liebmann rests his defense upon the broad claim that the Federal Constitution gives him the right to enter the business of manufacturing ice for sale even if his doing so be found by the properly constituted authority to be inconsistent with the public welfare. He claims that, whatever the local conditions may demand, to confer upon the Commission power to deny that right is an unreasonable, arbitrary and capricious restraint upon his liberty. 8

The function of the Court is primarily to determine whether the conditions in Oklahoma are such that the legislature could not reasonably conclude (1) that the public welfare required treating the manufacture of ice for sale and distribution as a "public business"; and (2) that in order to ensure to the inhabitants of some communities an adequate supply of ice at reasonable rates it was necessary to give the Commission power to exclude the estab- 9 lishment of an additional ice plant in places where the community was already well served. Unless the Court can say that the Federal Constitution confers an absolute right to engage anywhere in the business of manufacturing ice for sale, it cannot properly decide that the legislators acted unreasonably without first ascertaining what was the experience of Oklahoma in respect to the ice business. The relevant facts appear, in part, of record. Others are matters of common knowledge to those familiar with the ice business. Compare *Muller* v. *Oregon.* They show the actual conditions, or the beliefs, on which the legislators acted. In considering these matters we do not, in a strict sense, take judicial notice of them as embodying statements of uncontrovertible facts. Our function is only to determine the reasonableness of the legislature's belief in the existence of evils and in the effectiveness of the remedy provided. In performing this function we have no occasion to consider whether all the statements of fact which may be the basis of the prevailing belief are well-founded; and we have, of course, no right to weigh conflicting evidence.

10 (A) In Oklahoma a regular supply of ice may reasonably be considered a necessary of life, comparable to that of water, gas and electricity. The climate, which heightens the need of ice for comfortable and wholesome living, precludes resort to the natural product. There, as elsewhere, the development of the manufactured ice industry in recent years has been attended by deep-seated alterations in the economic structure and by radical changes in habits of popular thought and living. Ice has come to be regarded as a household necessity, indispensable to the preservation of food and so to economical household management and the maintenance of health. Its commercial uses are extensive. In urban communities, they absorb a large proportion of the total amount of ice manufactured for sale. The transportation, storage and distribution of a great part of the nation's food supply is dependent upon a continuous, and dependable supply of ice. It appears from the record that in certain parts of Oklahoma a large trade in dairy and other products has been built up as a result of rulings of the Corporation Commission under the Act of 1925, compelling licensed manufacturers to serve agricultural communities; and that this trade would be destroyed if the supply of ice were withdrawn. We cannot say that the legislature of Oklahoma acted arbitrarily in declaring that ice is an article of

primary necessity, in industry and agriculture as well as in the household, partaking of the fundamental character of electricity, gas, water, transportation and communication.

Nor can the Court properly take judicial notice that, in Oklahoma, the means of manufacturing ice for private use are within the reach of all persons who are dependent upon it. Certainly it has not been so. In 1925 domestic mechanical refrigeration had scarcely emerged from the experimental stage. Since that time, the production and consumption of ice manufactured for sale, far from diminishing, has steadily increased. In Oklahoma the mechanical household refrigerator is still an article of relative luxury. Legislation essential to the protection of individuals of limited or no means is not invalidated by the circumstance that other individuals are financially able to protect themselves. The businesses of power companies and of common carriers by street railway, steam railroad or motor vehicle fall within the field of public control, although it is possible, for a relatively modest outlay, to install individual power plants, or to purchase motor vehicles for private carriage of passengers or goods. The question whether in Oklahoma the means of securing refrigeration otherwise than by ice manufactured for sale and distribution has become so general as to destroy popular dependence upon ice plants is one peculiarly appropriate for the determination of its legislature and peculiarly inappropriate for determination by this Court, which cannot have knowledge of all the relevant facts.

The business of supplying ice is not only a necessity, like that of supplying food or clothing or shelter, but the legislature could also consider that it is one which lends itself peculiarly to monopoly. Characteristically the business is conducted in local plants with a market narrowly limited in area, and this for the reason that ice manufactured at a distance cannot effectively compete with a plant on the ground. In small towns and rural communities the duplication of plants, and in larger communities the duplication of delivery service, is wasteful and ultimately burdensome to consumers. At the same time the relative ease and cheapness with which an ice plant may be constructed exposes the industry to destructive and frequently ruinous competition. Competition in the industry tends to be destructive because ice plants have a determinate capacity, and inflexible fixed charges and operating costs, and because in a market

11

12

of limited area the volume of sales is not readily expanded. Thus, the erection of a new plant in a locality already adequately served often causes managers to go to extremes in cutting prices in order to secure business. Trade journals and reports of association meetings of ice manufacturers bear ample witness to the hostility of the industry to such competition, and to its unremitting efforts, through trade associations, informal agreements, combination of delivery systems, and in particular through the consolidation of plants, to protect markets and prices against competition of any character.

13   That these forces were operative in Oklahoma prior to the passage of the Act under review, is apparent from the record. Thus, it was testified that in only six or seven localities in the State containing, in the aggregate, not more than 235,000 of the total population of approximately 2,000,000, was there "a semblance of competition"; and that even in those localities the prices of ice were ordinarily uniform. The balance of the population was, and still is, served by companies enjoying complete monopoly. Compare *Munn* v. *Illinois; Sinking Fund Cases; Wabash, St. L. & P. Ry. Co.* v. *Illinois; Spring Valley Water Works* v. *Schottler; Budd* v. *New York; Wolff Co.* v. *Industrial Court.* Where there was competition, it often resulted to the disadvantage rather than the advantage of the public, both in respect to prices and to service. Some communities were without ice altogether, and the State was without means of assuring their supply. There is abundant evidence of widespread dissatisfaction with ice service prior to the Act of 1925, and of material improvement in the situation subsequently. It is stipulated in the record that the ice industry as a whole in Oklahoma has acquiesced in and accepted the Act and the status which it creates.

14   (B) The statute under review rests not only upon the facts just detailed but upon a long period of experience in more limited regulation dating back to the first year of Oklahoma's statehood. For 17 years prior to the passage of the Act of 1925, the Corporation Commission under §13 of the Act of June 10, 1908, had exercised jurisdiction over the rates, practices and service of ice plants, its action in each case, however, being predicated upon a finding that the company complained of enjoyed a "virtual monopoly" of the ice business in the community which it served. The jurisdiction thus exercised was upheld by the Supreme Court of the State in *Oklahoma Light & Power Co.* v. *Corporation Commission.* The court said,

at p. 24: "The manufacture, sale, and distribution of ice in many respects closely resemble the sale and distribution of gas as fuel, or electric current, and in many communities the same company that manufactures, sells, and distributes electric current is the only concern that manufactures, sells, and distributes ice, and by reason of the nature and extent of the ice business it is impracticable in that community to interest any other concern in such business. In this situation, the distributor of such a necessity as ice should not be permitted by reason of the impracticability of any one else engaging in the business to charge unreasonable prices, and if such an abuse is persisted in, the regulatory power of the State should be invoked to protect the public." See also *Consumers Light & Power Co.* v. *Phipps.*

By formal orders, the Commission repeatedly fixed or approved   15
prices to be charged in particular communities; required ice to be sold without discrimination and to be distributed as equitably as possible to the extent of the capacity of the plant; forbade short weights and ordered scales to be carried on delivery wagons and ice to be weighed upon the customer's request; and undertook to compel sanitary practices in the manufacture of ice and courteous service of patrons. Many of these regulations, other than those fixing prices, were embodied in a general order to all ice companies, issued July 15, 1921, and are still in effect. Informally, the Commission adjusted a much greater volume of complaints of a similar nature. It appears from the record that for some years prior to the Act of 1925 one day of each week was reserved by the Commission to hear complaints relative to the ice business.

As early as 1911, the Commission in its annual report to the   16
Governor, had recommended legislation more clearly delineating its powers in this field:

> There should be a law passed putting the regulation of ice plants   17
> under the jurisdiction of the Commission. The Commission is now
> assuming this jurisdiction under an Act passed by the Legislature
> known as the anti-trust law. A specific law upon this subject would
> obviate any question of jurisdiction.

This recommendation was several times repeated, in terms revealing the extent and character of public complaint against the practices of ice companies.

18   The enactment of the so-called Ice Act in 1925 enlarged the
existing jurisdiction of the Corporation Commission by removing
the requirement of a finding of virtual monopoly in each particular
case, compare *Budd* v. *New York* with *Brass* v. *Stoeser;* by conferring
the same authority to compel adequate service as in the case of other
public utilities; and by committing to the Commission the function
of issuing licenses equivalent to a certificate of public convenience
and necessity. With the exception of the granting and denying of
such licenses and the exertion of wider control over service, the
regulatory activity of the Commission in respect to ice plants has
not changed in character since 1925. It appears to have diminished
somewhat in volume.

19   In 1916, the Commission urged, in its report to the Governor, that
all public utilities under its jurisdiction be required to secure from
the Commission "what is known as a 'certificate of public convenience and necessity' before the duplication of facilities.

20   "This would prevent ruinous competition resulting in the driving out of business of small though competent public service utilities
by more powerful corporations, and often consequent demoraliza-
tion of service, or the requiring of the public to patronize two
utilities in a community where one would be adequate."

21   Up to that time a certificate of public convenience and necessity
to engage in the business had been applied only to cotton gins. In
1917 a certificate from the Commission was declared prerequisite
to the construction of new telephone or telegraph lines. In 1923 it
was required for the operation of motor carriers. In 1925, the year
in which the Ice Act was passed, the requirement was extended also
to power, heat, light, gas, electric or water companies proposing to
do business in any locality already possessing one such utility.

22   *Fourth.* Can it be said in the light of these facts that it was not an
appropriate exercise of legislative discretion to authorize the Commission to deny a license to enter the business in localities where
necessity for another plant did not exist? The need of some remedy
for the evil of destructive competition, where competition existed,
had been and was widely felt. Where competition did not exist, the
propriety of public regulation had been proven. Many communities
were not supplied with ice at all. The particular remedy adopted
was not enacted hastily. The statute was based upon a long-estab-
lished state policy recognizing the public importance of the ice

business, and upon 17 years' legislative and administrative experience in the regulation of it. The advisability of treating the ice business as a public utility and of applying to it the certificate of convenience and necessity had been under consideration for many years. Similar legislation had been enacted in Oklahoma under similar circumstances with respect to other public services. The measure bore a substantial relation to the evils found to exist. Under these circumstances, to hold the Act void as being unreasonable, would, in my opinion involve the exercise not of the function of judicial review, but the function of a super-legislature. If the Act is to be stricken down, it must be on the ground that the Federal Constitution guarantees to the individual the absolute right to enter the ice business, however detrimental the exercise of that right may be to the public welfare. Such, indeed, appears to be the contention made

Fifth. The claim is that manufacturing ice for sale and distribution is a business inherently private, and, in effect, that no state of facts can justify denial of the right to engage in it. To supply one's self with water, electricity, gas, ice or any other article, is inherently a matter of private concern. So also may be the business of supplying the same articles to others for compensation. But the business of supplying to others, for compensation, any article or service whatsoever may become a matter of public concern. Whether it is, or is not, depends upon the conditions existing in the community affected. If it is a matter of public concern, it may be regulated, whatever the business. The public's concern may be limited to a single feature of the business, so that the needed protection can be secured by a relatively slight degree of regulation. Such is the concern over possible incompetence, which dictates the licensing of dentists, *Dent* v. *West Virginia, Douglas* v. *Noble,* or the concern over possible dishonesty, which led to the licensing of auctioneers or hawkers, *Baccus* v. *Louisiana.* On the other hand, the public's concern about a particular business may be so pervasive and varied as to require constant detailed supervision and a very high degree of regulation. Where this is true, it is common to speak of the business as being a "public" one, although it is privately owned. It is to such businesses that the designation "public utility" is commonly applied; or they are spoken of as "affected with a public interest." *German Alliance Ins. Co.* v. *Lewis.*

23

24   A regulation valid for one kind of business may, of course, be invalid for another; since the reasonableness of every regulation is dependent upon the relevant facts. But so far as concerns the power to regulate, there is no difference in essence, between a business called private and one called a public utility or said to be "affected with a public interest." Whatever the nature of the business, whatever the scope or character of the regulation applied, the source of the power invoked is the same. And likewise the constitutional limitation upon that power. The source is the police power. The limitation is that set by the due process clause, which, as construed, requires that the regulation shall be not unreasonable, arbitrary or capricious; and that the means of regulation selected shall have a real or substantial relation to the object sought to be obtained. The notion of a distinct category of business "affected with a public interest," employing property "devoted to a public use," rests upon historical error. The consequences which it is sought to draw from those phrases are belied by the meaning in which they were first used centuries ago, and by the decision of this Court, in *Munn* v. *Illinois*, which first introduced them into the law of the Constitution. In my opinion, the true principle is that the State's power extends to every regulation of any business reasonably required and appropriate for the public protection. I find in the due process clause no other limitation upon the character or the scope of regulation permissible.

25   *Sixth.* It is urged specifically that manufacturing ice for sale and distribution is a common calling; and that the right to engage in a common calling is one of the fundamental liberties guaranteed by the due process clause. To think of the ice-manufacturing business as a common calling is difficult; so recent is it in origin and so peculiar in character. Moreover, the Constitution does not require that every calling which has been common shall ever remain so. The liberty to engage in a common calling, like other liberties, may be limited in the exercise of the police power. The slaughtering of cattle had been a common calling in New Orleans before the monopoly sustained in *Slaughter-House Cases*, was created by the legislature. Prior to the Eighteenth Amendment selling liquor was a common calling, but this Court held it to be consistent with the due process clause for a State to abolish the calling, *Bartemeyer* v. *Iowa, Mugler* v. *Kansas,* or to establish a system limiting the number

of licenses, *Crowley* v. *Christensen*. Every citizen has the right to navigate a river or lake, and may even carry others thereon for hire. But the ferry privilege may be made exclusive in order that the patronage may be sufficient to justify maintaining the ferry service, *Conway* v. *Taylor's Executor*.

It is settled that the police power commonly invoked in aid of health, safety and morals, extends equally to the promotion of the public welfare. The cases just cited show that, while, ordinarily, free competition in the common callings has been encouraged, the public welfare may at other times demand that monopolies be created. Upon this principle is based our whole modern practice of public utility regulation. It is no objection to the validity of the statute here assailed that it fosters monopoly. That, indeed, is its design. The certificate of public convenience and invention is a device—a recent social-economic invention—through which the monopoly is kept under effective control by vesting in a commission the power to terminate it whenever that course is required in the public interest. To grant any monopoly to any person as a favor is forbidden even if terminable. But where, as here, there is reasonable ground for the legislative conclusion that in order to secure a necessary service at reasonable rates, it may be necessary to curtail the right to enter the calling, it is, in my opinion, consistent with the due process clause to do so, whatever the nature of the business. The existence of such power in the legislature seems indispensable in our ever-changing society.

It is settled by unanimous decisions of this Court, that the due process clause does not prevent a State or city from engaging in the business of supplying its inhabitants with articles in general use, when it is believed that they cannot be secured at reasonable prices from the private dealers. Thus, a city may, if the local law permits, buy and sell at retail coal and wood, *Jones* v. *Portland*, or gasoline, *Standard Oil Co.* v. *Lincoln*. And a State may, if permitted by its own Constitution, build and operate warehouses, elevators, packing-houses, flour mills or other factories, *Green* v. *Frazier*. As States may engage in a business, because it is a public purpose to assure to their inhabitants an adequate supply of necessary articles, may they not achieve this public purpose, as Oklahoma has done, by exercising the lesser power of preventing single individuals from wantonly engaging in the business and thereby making impossible a depend-

26

27

able private source of supply? As a State so entering upon a business may exert the taxing power all individual dealers may be driven from the calling by the unequal competition. If States are denied the power to prevent the harmful entry of a few individuals into a business, they may thus, in effect, close it altogether to private enterprise.

28   *Seventh.* The economic emergencies of the past were incidents of scarcity. In those days it was preëminently the common callings that were the subjects of regulation. The danger then threatening was excessive prices. To prevent what was deemed extortion, the English Parliament fixed the prices of commodities and of services from time to time during the four centuries preceding the Declaration of Independence. Like legislation was enacted in the Colonies; and in the States, after the Revolution. When the first due process clause was written into the Federal Constitution, the price of bread was being fixed by statute in at least two of the States, and this practice continued long thereafter. Dwelling houses when occupied by the owner are preëminently private property. From the foundation of our Government those who wished to lease residential property had been free to charge to tenants such rentals as they pleased. But for years after the World War had ended, the scarcity of dwellings in the City of New York was such that the State's legislative power was invoked to ensure reasonable rentals. The constitutionality of the statute was sustained by this Court. *Marcus Brown Holding Co.* v. *Feldman.* Similar legislation of Congress for the City of Washington was also upheld. *Block* v. *Hirsh.*

29   *Eighth.* The people of the United States are now confronted with an emergency more serious than war. Misery is wide-spread, in a time, not of scarcity, but of over-abundance. The long-continued depression has brought unprecedented unemployment, a catastrophic fall in commodity prices and a volume of economic losses which threatens our financial institutions. Some people believe that the existing conditions threaten even the stability of the capitalistic system. Economists are searching for the causes of this disorder and are reexamining the bases of our industrial structure. Business men are seeking possible remedies. Most of them realize that failure to distribute widely the profits of industry has been a prime cause of our present plight. But rightly or wrongly, many persons think that one of the major contributing causes has been unbridled competi-

tion. Increasingly, doubt is expressed whether it is economically wise, or morally right, that men should be permitted to add to the producing facilities of an industry which is already suffering from over-capacity. In justification of that doubt, men point to the excess-capacity of our productive facilities resulting from their vast expansion without corresponding increase in the consumptive capacity of the people. They assert that through improved methods of manufacture, made possible by advances in science and invention and vast accumulation of capital, our industries had become capable of producing from thirty to one hundred per cent. more than was consumed even in days of vaunted prosperity; and that the present capacity will, for a long time, exceed the needs of business. All agree that irregularity in employment—the greatest of our evils—cannot be overcome unless production and consumption are more nearly balanced. Many insist there must be some form of economic control. There are plans for proration. There are many proposals for stabilization. And some thoughtful men of wide business experience insist that all projects for stabilization and proration must prove futile unless, in some way, the equivalent of the certificate of public convenience and necessity is made a prerequisite to embarking new capital in an industry in which the capacity already exceeds the production schedules.

Whether that view is sound nobody knows. The objections to the proposal are obvious and grave. The remedy might bring evils worse than the present disease. The obstacles to success seem insuperable. The economic and social sciences are largely uncharted seas. We have been none too successful in the modest essays in economic control already entered upon. The new proposal involves a vast extension of the area of control. Merely to acquire the knowledge essential as a basis for the exercise of this multitude of judgments would be a formidable task; and each of the thousands of these judgments would call for some measure of prophecy. Even more serious are the obstacles to success inherent in the demands which execution of the project would make upon human intelligence and upon the character of men. Man is weak and his judgment is at best fallible. 30

Yet the advances in the exact sciences and the achievements in invention remind us that the seemingly impossible sometimes happens. There are many men now living who were in the habit of 31 using the age-old expression: "It is as impossible as flying." The discoveries in physical science, the triumphs in invention, attest the value of the process of trial and error. In large measure, these advances have been due to experimentation. In those fields experimentation has, for two centuries, been not only free but encouraged. Some people assert that our present plight is due, in part, to the limitations set by courts upon experimentation in the fields of social and economic science; and to the discouragement to which proposals for betterment there have been subjected otherwise. There must be power in the States and the Nation to remould, through experimentation, our economic practices and institutions to meet changing social and economic needs. I cannot believe that the framers of the Fourteenth Amendment, or the States which ratified it, intended to deprive us of the power to correct the evils of technological unemployment and excess productive capacity which have attended progress in the useful arts.

32   To stay experimentation in things social and economic is a grave responsibility. Denial of the right to experiment may be fraught with serious consequences to the Nation. It is one of the happy incidents of the federal system that a single courageous State may, if its citizens choose, serve as a laboratory; and try novel social and economic experiments without risk to the rest of the country. This Court has the power to prevent an experiment. We may strike down the statute which embodies it on the ground that, in our opinion, the measure is arbitrary, capricious or unreasonable. We have power to do this, because the due process clause has been held by the Court applicable to matters of substantive law as well as to matters of procedure. But in the exercise of this high power, we must be ever on our guard, lest we erect our prejudices into legal principles. If we would guide by the light of reason, we must let our minds be bold.

STUDY QUESTIONS

1. Brandeis's overall conclusion is that the State of Oklahoma was justified in not allowing Liebmann to manufacture ice for sale. To support this conclusion he argues three points:
   (i)   That prohibiting competition in this case was to the public's welfare;

(ii) That there are precedents for states' creating monopolies as public utilities;

(iii) That the State's action does not violate the Fourteenth Amendment.

Here is a reconstruction of his argument in support of (i):

> The State's function is to promote the public welfare.
> It is to the public's welfare not to have waste, expensive products, or poor service.
>
> So the State should not to allow waste, expensive products, or poor service.
> Sometimes competition leads to waste, expensive products, or poor service.
>
> So sometimes the State should not to allow competition.
> Competition in the ice business in Oklahoma led to waste and poor service.
>
> Therefore, it was legitimate for the State of Oklahoma not to allow competition in the ice business.

For each of the premises in this argument, determine whether Brandeis assumes its truth or provides an argument for it. And for those premises he argues for, diagram the arguments.

2. "The public welfare" is the key phrase in Brandeis's argument. Does he offer a definition of it, or list the criteria by which we can tell what is or is not to the public's welfare?

3. Brandeis discusses the Fourteenth Amendment to the Federal Constitution in paragraphs 3, 8, 9, and 22–27. He argues against interpreting the Fourteenth Amendment as giving an individual an "absolute" right to engage in business. Write a short paragraph summarizing how Brandeis interprets the Fourteenth Amendment. Under what circumstances does he argue that the right can be limited?

4. Has Brandeis argued successfully that the State of Oklahoma neither abridged Liebmann's privileges or immunities, nor deprived him of liberty or property, nor denied him equal protection of the laws?

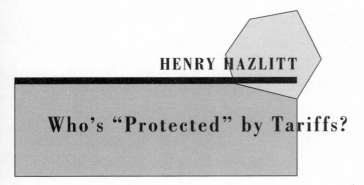

HENRY HAZLITT

Who's "Protected" by Tariffs?

*Henry Hazlitt (1894–1993) is best known for his clear and
graceful defenses of free market economic concepts. Drawing
on the work of economists Claude-Frédéric Bastiat, Philip
Wicksteed, and Ludwig von Mises, Hazlitt wrote the popular*
Economics in One Lesson, *from which the following excerpt
is taken. He also wrote a novel entitled* Time Will Run Back.

1   An American manufacturer of woolen sweaters goes to Congress or
to the State Department and tells the committee or officials concerned that it would be a national disaster for them to remove or
reduce the tariff on British sweaters. He now sells his sweaters for
$30 each, but English manufacturers could sell their sweaters of the
same quality for $25. A duty of $5, therefore, is needed to keep him
in business. He is not thinking of himself, of course, but of the
thousand men and women he employs, and of the people to whom
their spending in turn gives employment. Throw them out of work,
and you create unemployment and a fall in purchasing power,
which would spread in ever-widening circles. And if he can prove
that he really would be forced out of business if the tariff were
removed or reduced, his argument against that action is regarded
by Congress as conclusive.

2   But the fallacy comes from looking merely at this manufacturer
and his employees, or merely at the American sweater industry. It
comes from noticing only the results that are immediately seen, and

[Henry Hazlitt, excerpt from Chapter XI of *Economics in One Lesson.* Westport, Conn.: Arlington House, 1946; reprinted 1962, 1979; pp. 75–77.]

neglecting the results that are not seen because they are prevented from coming into existence.

The lobbyists for tariff protection are continually putting forward arguments that are not factually correct. But let us assume that the facts in this case are precisely as the sweater manufacturer has stated them. Let us assume that a tariff of $5 a sweater is necessary for him to stay in business and provide employment at sweater-making for his workers.

We have deliberately chosen the most unfavorable example of any for the removal of a tariff. We have not taken an argument for the imposition of a new tariff in order to bring a new industry into existence, but an argument for the retention of a tariff *that has already brought an industry into existence,* and cannot be repealed without hurting somebody.

The tariff is repealed; the manufacturer goes out of business; a thousand workers are laid off; the particular tradesmen whom they patronized are hurt. This is the immediate result that is seen. But there are also results which, while much more difficult to trace, are no less immediate and no less real. For now sweaters that formerly cost retail $30 apiece can be bought for $25. Consumers can now buy the same quality of sweater for less money, or a much better one for the same money. If they buy the same quality of sweater, they not only get the sweater, but they have $5 left over, which they would not have had under the previous conditions, to buy something else. With the $25 that they pay for the imported sweater they help employment—as the American manufacturer no doubt predicted—in the sweater industry in England. With the $5 left over they help employment in any number of other industries in the United States.

But the results do not end there. By buying English sweaters they furnish the English with dollars to buy American goods here. This, in fact (if I may here disregard such complications as fluctuating exchange rates, loans, credits, etc.), is the only way in which the British can eventually make use of these dollars. Because we have permitted the British to sell more to us, they are now able to buy more from us. They are, in fact, eventually *forced* to buy more from us if their dollar balances are not to remain perpetually unused. So as a result of letting in more British goods, we must export more American goods. And though fewer people are now employed in the American sweater industry, more people are employed—and much

3

4

5

6

more efficiently employed—in, say, the American washing-ma-
chine or aircraft-building business. American employment on net
balance has not gone down, but American and British production
on net balance has gone up. Labor in each country is more fully
employed in doing just those things that it does best, instead of being
forced to do things that it does inefficiently or badly. Consumers in
both countries are better off. They are able to buy what they want
where they can get it cheapest. American consumers are better
provided with sweaters, and British consumers are better provided
with washing machines and aircraft.

STUDY QUESTIONS

1. In the first paragraph, Hazlitt summarizes the pro-tariff
   argument he is attacking. The argument is a hypothetical
   one:

   > If the tariff of $5 is repealed, then the sweater manufacturer will
   > be forced out of business by English competitors.
   > If the sweater manufacturer is forced out of business, then a
   > thousand men and women will be put out of work.
   > If a thousand men and women are put out of work, then they
   > have less purchasing power.
   > If the thousand men and women have less purchasing power,
   > then this fact is felt in ever-widening circles (i.e., the U.S.
   > economy as a whole suffers).
   > [Therefore, if the tariff of $5 is repealed, the U.S. economy
   > suffers.]
   > [We don't want the U.S. economy to suffer.]
   > [Therefore, we should not repeal the tariff of $5.]

   Although the pro-tariff argument is valid, Hazlitt says it
   commits a fallacy. How, in general terms, does Hazlitt describe the fallacy he thinks is committed?

2. In paragraph 5, Hazlitt asks us to suppose that the tariff is
   repealed, and toward the end of paragraph 6 he reaches the
   conclusions that "American employment on net balance has
   not gone down" and that "Consumers in both countries are

better off." Reconstruct the chain of reasoning Hazlitt uses to reach those conclusions.

3. One of the premises in Hazlitt's argument is that "By buying English sweaters they [American consumers] furnish the English with dollars to buy American goods here." Why couldn't the English use those dollars to buy goods from other countries? Why does Hazlitt say they are *"forced"* to buy more U.S. goods?

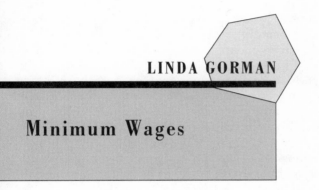

LINDA GORMAN

Minimum Wages

Formerly a professor of economics at the Naval Postgraduate School, Linda Gorman is a free-lance economic journalist living in Denver.

Minimum wage laws set legal minimums for the hourly wages paid   1
to certain groups of workers. Invented in Australia and New Zealand with the admirable purpose of guaranteeing a minimum standard of living for unskilled workers, they have been widely acclaimed as both the bulwark protecting workers from exploitation by employers and as a major weapon in the war on poverty. Minimum wage legislation in the United States has increased the federal minimum wage from $.25 per hour in 1938 to $4.25 as of April 1991, and expanded its coverage from 43.4 percent of all private, nonsu-

[Linda Gorman, "Minimum Wages," *The Fortune Encyclopedia of Economics,* ed. David Henderson. Warner 1993, pp. 499–503.]

pervisory, nonagricultural workers in 1938 to over 87 percent by 1990. As the steady legislative expansion indicates, the minimum wage has had widespread political support enjoyed by few other public policies.

2   Unfortunately, neither laudable intentions nor widespread support can alter one simple fact: although minimum wage laws can set wages, they cannot guarantee jobs. In reality, minimum wage laws place additional obstacles in the path of the most unskilled workers who are struggling to reach the lowest rungs of the economic ladder. According to a 1978 article in *American Economic Review,* the American Economic Association's main journal, fully 90 percent of the economists surveyed agreed that the minimum wage increases unemployment among low-skilled workers. It also reduces the on-the-job training offered by employers and shrinks the number of positions offering fringe benefits. To those who lose their jobs, their training opportunities, or their fringe benefits as a result of the minimum wage, the law is simply one more example of good intentions producing hellish results.

3   To understand why minimum wage policies have such pernicious effects, one must understand how wages are determined in the free market. Consider, for example, the owner-operator of a small diner. To stay in business, he has to make sufficient profits to provide adequate support for his family. The market dictates how much he can charge for his meals because people can choose to eat at other restaurants or prepare their meals at home. The market also dictates what he must pay for food, restaurant space, electricity, equipment, and other factors required to produce his meals. Although the restaurant owner has little control over either the prices he can charge for his meals or the prices that he must pay for the inputs needed to produce them, he can control his costs by changing the combinations of inputs that he uses. He can, for example, hire teenagers to wash and slice raw potatoes for french fries, or he can purchase ready-cut potatoes from a large company with an automated french-fry production process.

4   The combination of inputs used and the amount that the diner owner can afford to pay for each one depend both on the productivity of the input and on the price that customers will pay for the product. Suppose that a trainee french-fry cutter can peel, cut, and prepare ten orders of fries in an hour, and that the diner's customers

order about ten orders of french fries an hour at $1.00 each. If the minimum profit required to keep the owner in business plus all costs except the cutter's labor amounts to $.80 for each order, then the owner can afford a wage of up to $2.00 per hour for one trainee. Legislating a minimum wage of $4.50 per hour means that the diner owner loses $2.50 an hour on the trainee. The owner will respond by firing the trainee. The minimum wage prices the trainee out of the labor market. Similarly, other employers will respond to the increased minimum wage by substituting skilled labor (which does not cost as much more than unskilled labor as it did before the minimum wage) for unskilled labor, by substituting machines for people, by moving production abroad, and by abandoning some types of production entirely.

Australia provided one of the earliest practical demonstrations of   5
the harmful effects of minimum wages when, in 1921, the federal court institutionalized a real minimum wage for unskilled men. The court set the wage by estimating what employees needed, while ignoring what employers could afford to pay. As a result unskilled workers were priced out of the market. These laborers could find work only in occupations not covered by the law or with employers willing to break it. Aggressive reporting of violations by vigilant unions made evasion difficult, and the historical record shows that unemployment remained a particular problem for unskilled laborers throughout the rest of the decade.

The same type of thing happened in the United States when a   6
hospital fired a group of women after the Minimum Wage Board in the District of Columbia ordered their wages raised to the legal minimum. Ironically, the women sued to halt enforcement of the minimum wage law. In 1923 the U.S. Supreme Court, in *Adkins* v. *Children's Hospital,* ruled that the minimum wage law was simple price-fixing and an unreasonable infringement on individuals' freedom to determine the price at which they would sell their services. Although the peculiar logic of the last seventy years has seen this line of reasoning completely abrogated, the battle over allowing people to work at whatever wage they choose continues.

One recent skirmish occurred in 1990 when the U.S. Department   7
of Labor ordered the Salvation Army to pay the minimum wage to voluntary participants in its work therapy programs. The programs provide participants, many of them homeless alcoholics and drug

addicts, a small weekly stipend and up to ninety days of food, shelter, and counseling in exchange for processing donated goods. The Salvation Army said that the expense of complying with the minimum wage order would force it to close the programs. Ignoring both the fact that the beneficiaries of the program could leave to take a higher-paying job at any time and the cash value of the food, shelter, and supervision, the Labor Department insisted that it was protecting workers' rights by enforcing the minimum wage. By the peculiar logic of the minimum wage laws, workers have the right to remain unemployed but not the right to get a job by selling their labor for less than the minimum wage.

8   In addition to affecting how many people will be employed, minimum wage laws may also leave workers worse off by changing how they are compensated. For many low-wage employees fringe benefits such as paid vacation, free room and board, inexpensive insurance, subsidized child care, and on-the-job training (OJT) are an important part of the total compensation package. To avoid increasing total compensation, employers react to arbitrary boosts in money wages by cutting other benefits. In extreme cases, employers may convert low-wage full-time jobs with fringe benefits to high-wage part-time jobs with reduced benefits and fewer hours. Employees who prefer working full time with benefits are simply out of luck.

9   The reduction in benefits may be substantial. Masanori Hashimoto used data from the 1967–68 U.S. minimum wage hike to calculate its effect on the value of on-the-job training received by white men. Hashimoto estimated that the 28 percent increase in the minimum wage reduced the value of OJT by 2.7 to 15 percent. Because OJT is an important source of education, particularly for those with limited formal schooling, Hashimoto's findings have ominous implications. By reducing OJT, the minimum wage law increases the number of dead-end jobs and effectively consigns some of the unskilled to a lifetime of reduced opportunity.

10   Estimates of the overall effect of increases in the minimum wage on total U.S. employment often focus on teenagers, who, as a group, contain the highest proportion of unskilled workers. Most studies suggest that a 10 percent increase in the minimum wage decreases teenage employment by 1 to 3 percent. Using these estimates to

forecast small increases in unemployment from future minimum wage increases is risky because most of the estimates rely on data from the sixties and early seventies, when minimum wage legislation applied to fewer occupations.

Raising the minimum wage when it applies to a relatively small proportion of occupations will not necessarily increase unemployment. Some people will lose their jobs in covered occupations and withdraw from the labor market entirely. These people are not included in the unemployment statistics. Others who lose their jobs or are offered fewer hours of work will seek jobs at lower pay in uncovered occupations. This labor influx drives down wages in the uncovered sector, but people do find jobs and unemployment remains constant. As minimum wage legislation expands to cover more occupations, however, the shrinking uncovered sector may not be able to absorb all of the people thrown out of work, and unemployment may increase. In the United States the 1989 minimum wage legislation brought this possibility one step closer by extending coverage to all workers engaged in interstate commerce regardless of employer size. Small businesses previously exempt from the minimum wage faced an 11.8 percent increase in money wages. If the repeal of the exemption that affected more than 6 percent of the nation's hourly workers substantially reduces the number of uncovered jobs, then overt unemployment caused by the minimum wage could become a more serious problem.

Estimates of the overall effect of minimum wage increases also tend to blur the regional and sectoral shifts that average together to produce the national result. A federal minimum wage of $4.25 an hour may have little effect in a large city where almost everyone earns more. But it may cause greater unemployment in a rural area where it substantially exceeds the prevailing wage. Regional and sectoral studies leave little doubt that substantial increases in the minimum in areas with lower wages can cause industries to shrink and can inhibit job creation. The growth of the textile industry in the South, for example, was propelled by low wages. Had the federal minimum wage been set at the wage earned by northern workers, the expansion might never have occurred.

This explains why unions, whose members seldom hold minimum wage jobs, encourage minimum wage legislation and, as in the Australian case, assiduously help enforce its provisions by reporting suspected violations. Unions have historically represented skilled, highly productive workers. As has been demonstrated in the construction industry, employers facing excessive wage demands from union members may find it less expensive to hire unskilled workers at low wages and to train them on the job. Unskilled workers often benefit: accepting lower wages in return for training increases their expected future income. With high minimum wages like those specified for government construction by the Davis-Bacon Act, the wages plus the training cost may exceed the total compensation that employers can afford. In that case the employer would prefer the union member to his unskilled competitor, and passage of a minimum wage law reduces the competition faced by union members.

14   In spite of evidence indicating that minimum wage laws reduce the number of jobs and distort compensation packages, some people still argue that their benefits outweigh their costs because they increase the incomes of the poor. This argument implicitly assumes that minimum wage workers are the sole earner in a family. This assumption is false. In 1988, for example, the vast majority of minimum wage workers were members of households containing other wage earners. Moreover, only 8 percent of all minimum wage workers were men or women who maintained families, and not all of those families were poor. The simple fact is that most minimum wage workers are young and work part-time. In 1988, 60 percent of minimum wage workers were sixteen to twenty-four years old, and about 70 percent worked part-time.

15   In view of what minimum wage laws actually do, their often uncritical acceptance as a major weapon in the war on poverty stands as one of the supreme ironies of modern politics. If a minimum wage set $.50 above the prevailing wage helps the working poor with no ill effects, why not eliminate poverty completely by simply legislating a minimum wage of $10.00? The problem, of course, is that pricing people out of a job does not reduce poverty. Neither does skewing compensation packages toward money wages and away from training, or encouraging employers to substitute skilled workers for unskilled workers, part-time jobs for full-time jobs, foreign labor for domestic labor, and machines for people. Minimum wage laws do all of these things and, in the process, almost surely do the disadvantaged more harm than good.

STUDY QUESTIONS

1. Given Ms. Gorman's explanation of minimum wages in paragraph 1, construct a genus and differentia definition of "minimum wage."

2. Gorman's core argument is hypothetical. What conclusions are left unstated as propositions 4 and 6?

    (1) If the minimum wage is increased, then employers find it more expensive to hire workers (paragraph 4).

    (2) If employers find it more expensive to hire workers, they will hire fewer workers (paragraphs 4 and 5).

    (3) If employers hire fewer workers, unemployment is increased.

    (4) Therefore,

    (5) Those usually working for minimum wages are unskilled workers (paragraph 1).

    (6) Therefore,

    (7) The purpose of minimum wage laws is to help unskilled workers (paragraph 1).

    (8) Therefore, the consequence of minimum wage laws is the opposite of their purpose (paragraph 15).

3. In paragraph 13, Gorman argues that unions typically favor minimum wage increases.

    (1) Members of unions are typically skilled workers.

    (2) If union wages are increased, employers are more likely to hire unskilled workers instead of skilled workers.

    (3) If employers hire more unskilled workers instead of skilled workers, then the union workers lose jobs.

    (4) If minimum wages are increased, employers are less likely to want to hire unskilled workers.

    (5) Therefore, unions favor minimum wage increases.

    In this reconstruction, what premise is assumed between propositions 4 and 5?

4. In paragraph 2, Gorman offers the startling statistic that 90 percent of economists agree that raising the minimum wage increases unemployment among low-skilled workers. Does Gorman in her article offer an explanation for why, despite what economists believe, the minimum wage has remained in place and increased?

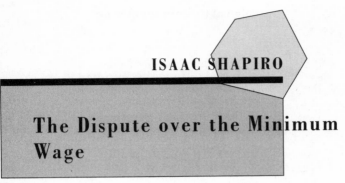

ISAAC SHAPIRO

The Dispute over the Minimum Wage

Isaac Shapiro is a senior research analyst at the Center on Budget and Policy Priorities. He is the co-author, with Sar Leviton, of Working But Poor: America's Contradiction. *In the following, Mr. Shapiro argues in favor of increasing the minimum wage.*

1   The case for an increase in the federal minimum wage has long been persuasive. The wage floor of $3.35 an hour has not been raised for eight years; adjusted for inflation, its purchasing power has fallen to its lowest level since 1955. As the wage floor has deteriorated, the number of people who work but live in poverty has risen, and there has been growing evidence of stagnating or declining standards of living among many of the near poor and the middle class.

2   The old argument [against the minimum wage] is, that by artificially raising the cost of labor, a minimum-wage increase would price many workers out of jobs. Let us see if [this] argument is valid.

The Fall of the Minimum Wage

3   The period since January 1981 represents the longest spell without an increase in the wage floor since the federal minimum wage was established in 1938. Prices rose 37 percent between January

[Isaac Shapiro, The Dispute over the Minimum Wage, *Dissent* 1989, pp. 18–20.]

1981 and August 1988, and the value of the minimum wage fell to a historically low level.

In 1988, a person working full-time year-round at the minimum wage earns $2,500 less than the estimated poverty line for a family of three. In sharp contrast, during the 1960s and 1970s full-time year-round minimum wage earnings averaged slightly above the three-person poverty threshold. *Full-time year-round minimum wage earnings now equal only 74 percent of the estimated three-person poverty threshold.*

The minimum wage now equals only 36 percent of the average private, nonsupervisory wage, compared to the historical goal of 50 percent that was usually achieved in the 1960s and nearly attained in parts of the 1970s.

In 1987 some 6.3 million hourly and salaried workers earned the minimum wage or less. An additional 10.8 million such workers earned between $3.35 and $4.50 an hour.

Most workers earning the minimum wage or less do not fit the stereotype of teenagers in their first job. Half are twenty-five years or older; 20 percent are aged twenty to twenty-four; only 30 percent are teenagers. (Among workers who earned $3.36 to $4.49 an hour in 1987, more than half—53 percent—were twenty-five years or older and only 24 percent were teenagers.)

Benefits of a Minimum Wage

The minimum-wage standard assists workers who generally lack political clout, are not unionized, and are in little position to bargain for themselves. Freezing the minimum wage at $3.35 an hour for an indefinite period of time, while prices continue to rise, would suggest that this society is willing to accept the standard's gradual erosion to the point where it may cease to have meaning.

While a primary barrier to more work effort among poor individuals is the unavailability of employment, it is also important to consider the impact on work of the wages and benefits provided by available jobs.

With a low minimum wage, the benefits from working may be less, or only minimally more, than the benefits from government assistance. This is because the rewards from working are small, not because government assistance is especially generous. In fact, the support provided by government programs has diminished in recent years and, for the most part, leaves recipients well below the poverty line. Between 1977 and 1987 the maximum value of Aid to Families with Dependent Children benefits for a three person family with no other income dropped by 24 percent in the typical state.

10   The current debate concerning work incentives and the poor has focused largely on whether significant disincentives arise from welfare assistance, while often neglecting the disincentives when working is not sufficiently rewarded. A higher minimum wage might lead some individuals—including youths, young men, and mothers on public assistance—to increase their work activity.

11   The minimum-wage erosion is of particular importance because of the increase in the number of working poor in the 1980s. In 1987 nearly 1.9 million people worked full-time year-round yet remained in poverty, 43 percent more than in 1979. An additional 6.6 million who were poor worked on less than a full-time year-round basis, up 28 percent since 1979.

12   Now it is true that most minimum-wage workers are not poor. An estimated seven out of ten workers paid by the hour and earning the minimum wage or less live in households with incomes more than 150 percent of the poverty line.

13   This does not mean, however, that the minimum wage has little connection to poverty. On the contrary, more than half—about 60 percent—of all workers who are paid by the hour and are in poverty have earnings at or near the minimum wage. For many of these workers, the serious deterioration of the minimum wage has compounded their income problems. An increase in the wage standard would help lessen their poverty.

14   Moreover, the needs of minimum wage workers who live in non-poor households should not be dismissed. Some of these families are struggling to get by even though they are two-earner families, because one or both workers may be employed at or near the minimum wage.

Partial Job Losses

15   The chief argument raised against a minimum wage increase is that it would decrease the demand for labor. Young workers in

particular, it is argued, would have fewer opportunities because they are the least productive employees.

Although minimum-wage increases probably would cause some employment loss, it is likely to be far smaller than the figures cited by opponents. Virtually all of their estimates are based on outdated studies of pre-1980 labor markets.

16

The best of these pre-1980 studies was conducted by economists of the Minimum Wage Study Commission, established by Congress in 1977. They reviewed all previous studies and conducted an updated study of their own. They found that a 10 percent increase in the minimum wage is associated with a 1 percent decrease in teenage employment and a decrease of one-quarter of 1 percent in the employment of young adults (twenty to twenty-four years old). The economists did not find compelling evidence of any job loss for adults twenty-five and over. Nonetheless, many of the jobs loss projections now cited use estimates based on the high range of the pre-1980 studies reviewed by the commission, without noting that this range is substantially higher than that of the commission staff's estimates.

17

Moreover, even the job loss estimates of the commission staff are now out of date. They are based on labor market data through 1979 and do not reflect the important differences between today's low-wage labor market and that of the 1960s and 1970s.

18

Fortunately, a new study—conducted by Alison Wellington of the University of Michigan under the supervision of one of the commission's senior economists—has replicated the work of the commission staff, but with labor market data through 1986. *It finds that a minimum-wage increase of 10 percent is associated with a 0.56 percent decrease in employment opportunities and that there is no effect on the employment of young adults.*

19

Several factors support estimates that a minimum-wage boost would cause only modest job losses. Higher wages may enhance job stability and commitment among workers, not minor factors in low-wage labor markets often characterized by quick job turnover. Employers, in turn, may respond to a minimum wage hike by reorganizing production processes to make better use of existing employees. As a result of increased productivity, the actual cost of labor may not rise as much as the increase in the minimum wage.

20

Moreover, now is a particularly auspicious time to raise the minimum wage. First, since the current minimum wage is sub-

21

stantially lower than in the past, relatively fewer workers now work at or near the minimum wage. An increase in the minimum wage is thus likely to have a smaller effect on the economy than in the past.

22   Second, a shortage in the supply of teenage workers may be emerging. The number of sixteen to nineteen year olds rose in all but one of the twenty-five years preceding 1978, but has fallen sharply in the 1980s. The disemployment estimates cited above, as well as those noted by some opponents of a minimum wage increase, are based primarily on years when the youth population was rising and thus may be overstated.

23   Finally, eleven states and the District of Columbia have boosted their minimum-wage levels above the federal level, including California, which has raised its minimum wage to $4.25 an hour. In these areas, the economic effects of restoring the federal minimum wage have been partially preempted, thus dampening any possible negative employment effects due to changes in federal law.

STUDY QUESTIONS

1. In paragraphs 9 and 10, Mr. Shapiro makes the following argument. Is it valid?
   (1) If the minimum wage is low, then individuals have a higher incentive not to work.
   (2) If those individuals choose not to work, then they will likely turn to government assistance programs.
   (3) Therefore, if the minimum wage is raised, it is likely that fewer individuals will turn to government assistance programs.
2. Linda Gorman argued in her essay that raising the minimum wage would lower the demand for unskilled, younger workers. In paragraphs 15 through 23, Shapiro responds to that argument. His argument is outlined below, but each argument has been left incomplete. Supply the missing premise(s) or conclusion(s) to make each argument complete.

Older studies were based on outdated data (16)

Raising the minimum wage may boost productivity (20)

There are now relatively fewer workers working near minmum wage (21)

There may be a shortage of teenage workers emerging (22)

Several states have already raised their minimum wages (23)

Raising the minimum wage wouldn't cause the loss of too many jobs

3. Shapiro's argument relies heavily on statistical evidence. Of the many statistics he cites, identify the two or three that are, in your judgment, most significant for his argument.

LIBERTY NETWORK ASSOCIATION

The New World Order

*The following anonymously written essay is a classic example
of a conspiracy theory, arguing that the best explanation for a
wide range of historical facts is a conspiracy by international
bankers and others to form a world dictatorship.*

Dear Fellow Americans:

1   Enclosed is a brief summary about The New World Order, a secret
plan to establish a world-wide dictatorship, possibly within the next
few years. As more information about this conspiracy comes to
light, freedom-loving citizens are becoming angered and
aroused. If we act quickly, before martial law is declared and our
Constitution suspended, we can defeat this menace by lawful,
peaceful means.

2   The key to our success is to pool our information, to make the
public aware of what is going on behind the scenes, and to prosecute
those who would destroy our liberty by force and violence.

3   The selected references are a sampling of the research which has
been gathered on this subject so far. If you have or know of any
additional sources of information, please share them with us. In
particular, we would like facts about the Council on Foreign Relations, the Trilateral Commission, the Federal Reserve System, the

[Liberty Network Association, "The New World Order." Mailing from Liberty
Network Association, c/o 13223 Black Mountain Road, 1–311, San Diego, California 92129.]

International Monetary Fund, the Central Intelligence Agency, the Federal Emergency Management Agency, the Multi-Jurisdictional Task Force, and the Financial Crime Enforcement Network, especially as it relates to their clandestine operations. We, of course, will be glad to share with you what we know.

Your input and your suggestions on how we can inform the public will be appreciated.   4

Liberty Network Association

The New World Order

Evidence is accumulating about a highly secret plan to set up a   5
world-wide dictatorship during the next few years, and to dissolve the present nations of the world. This, of course, would mean the end of the United States of America as we know it, including the U.S. Constitution and the Bill of Rights. In its place would be a despotic regime under the control of the international bankers.

This sounds pretty incredible, doesn't it? We didn't believe it   6
ourselves at first. But as the facts come in, they tend to reinforce each other and to make sense out of many puzzling current events.

The history of this conspiracy begins more than 200 years ago.   7
The Order of the Illuminati (The Enlightened Ones) was formed in May 1776. It was a small, secret group of powerful men who planned to gradually take control of the world by taking control of each country's monetary system. Its symbol was the all-seeing eye, which became part of the Great Seal of the United States of America, and which appears on our present $1 Federal Reserve Notes. Interestingly, this group was formed only two months before our Declaration of Independence was sent to King George III.

In the 1870s John Ruskin was teaching at Oxford University. He   8
advocated dictatorship as a form of government, with state control of the means of production. One of his students was Cecil Rhodes, who applied Ruskin's teachings in Africa with the blessing of the British government. Rhodes made a fortune in gold and diamond

mining. The Rhodes Scholarships spring from this source. President
Bill Clinton was one of the Rhodes Scholars at Oxford.

9   In 1891 Cecil Rhodes formed a secret order called the Circle of
Initiates, which was the core of a larger group called the Circle of
Helpers. Their objective was to gain control of the world economy
by means of control of the monetary systems of all countries.
Rhodes' associate, Lord Alfred Milner, organized Round Table
groups in each of the English-speaking nations to further this cause.

10   In 1910, a group of American bankers and their wealthy friends
met at the Millionaire's Club on Jekyll Island, Georgia, to plan what
became the Federal Reserve System. This is really the same debt
money system which originated in Babylon 5,000 years ago. The
scam is basically fairly simple—a group of private bankers get
together to form a central banking system which appears to be a
government agency but which is actually privately owned. The
national Treasury borrows money—at interest—from the central
bank. The central bank creates money out of thin air by making
bookkeeping entries, and sells the government debt instruments to
the public.

11   Getting this scheme enacted was the hard part. In the 1912
elections, President William Taft was heavily favored to defeat the
Democratic Party candidate sponsored and controlled by the bankers, Woodrow Wilson. So the bankers also sponsored former President Teddy Roosevelt to run on the Bull Moose ticket, thereby
drawing votes away from Taft and allowing Wilson to win.

12   In December, 1913, Congress passed the Federal Reserve Act,
thereby giving the international banking conspiracy total control of
our nation's money. In that same year, the Sixteenth (Income Tax)
Amendment was supposedly approved. Recent research indicates
that there were irregularities in the approval process in every state,
so the Income Tax has actually been illegal from the outset. A third
major blunder of Wilson's administration was getting the United
States involved in World War I.

13   In 1918, Col. Edward House (who was Woodrow Wilson's political mentor) and a group of wealthy New York bankers and others
organized what is now called the Council on Foreign Relations

(CFR). This secret group has as its goal the complete political and economic control of the world in the hands of wealthy capitalists and international bankers. Today there are some 1,400 members, mostly graduates of the liberal Ivy League colleges, consisting of leading bankers, lawyers, government officials, educators, and news media executives. Collectively, they are the behind-the-scenes government of the United States. President Clinton and former President Bush are members.

The CFR strives to maintain a very low visibility. It is not even mentioned in the *Encyclopedia Britannica* or the *Encyclopedia Americana*. There are several books about it, including *The Imperial Brain Trust*, by Laurence H. Shoup and William Minter, written in 1977. They state that the CFR was formed to equip the U.S. for an imperial role on the world scene. Their comment on page 279 is very revealing: "U.S. Imperialism is characterized by the Vietnam War, assassination of foreign leaders, support of reactionary regimes, bribes and corruption, domestic repression, political trials of dissenters, FBI-CIA harassment of radicals, and wiretaps." Not a very pretty picture, but all too true. More recent events include the invasion of Panama, the Iran Contra affair, and the war in Kuwait.

In 1954, the Bilderberger Group was formed. The name came from the Bilderberger Hotel in the Netherlands, where the first meeting took place. The central players in this secret group were David Rockefeller of Chase Manhattan Bank and Prince Bernhard of the Netherlands.

In 1963, President John F. Kennedy issued an executive order authorizing the U.S. Treasury to issue U.S. notes directly, thereby bypassing the Federal Reserve System and depriving the international bankers of potential interest income. Shortly thereafter, he was assassinated in Dallas, the home state of then Vice President Lyndon Johnson. The accused assassin, Lee Harvey Oswald, was killed in jail by Jack Ruby. Lyndon Johnson, a CFR member, became the President. One of his first official acts was to rescind the executive order which had authorized the U.S. notes.

A similar fate befell President Abraham Lincoln when he authorized the Treasury to issue greenback notes, rather than borrow money at 19% interest from the international bankers, to finance the Civil War. As you know, President Lincoln was assassinated by John Wilkes Booth. Coincidence or conspiracy? You be the judge.

18   In 1973, another secret organization was formed—the Trilateral Commission. This group consisted of approximately 180 wealthy and influential people in the United States, Western Europe, and Japan, including David Rockefeller and George Bush. The purpose of this organization was to promote economic and political control of the world by the leading capitalists and international bankers. President Clinton is a member of this group. The upcoming Group of Seven economic summit talks in Tokyo should be interesting, especially in light of Prime Minister Miyazawa's recent ouster due to the widespread corruption of the Social Democratic Party, which had been in power for some forty years.

19   Recent events in the United States are extremely disturbing. The Multi-Jurisdictional Task Force (MJTF) was organized by then-President George Bush in 1989. This is a national police force comprised of state, federal and local forces, such as National Guard units and local police and sheriff departments, under Federal control. Its mission will be to conduct search and seizure raids on private homes and businesses, to capture dissidents, and to run the system of 43 detention camps now authorized by the Federal Emergency Management Agency.

20   MJTF operates on the medieval principle of pillage—steal what you want under the color of law. This is the same concept as the Drug Enforcement Agency uses to confiscate property from drug dealers. It's as illegal as hell, but it's done anyway.

21   The MJTF has entered into a contract with the Cryps and the Bloods street gangs in Los Angeles, and are negotiating similar contracts elsewhere. The plan is to use gang members as the shock troops, similar to Hitler's SA Brown Shirts. They will enter homes and businesses wearing their ski masks as a terror tactic, and take the brunt of the resistance, thereby sparing the more highly trained police officers.

22   Another secret group is the so-called Financial Crime Enforcement Network (FINCEN). These are mostly highly trained military personnel from many foreign nations operating under United Na-

tions control. Like the MJTF, these foreign mercenaries will be used primarily for search and seizure missions. Elements of these forces are reportedly training in Montana right now. Former U.S.S.R. bombers now reportedly fly training missions into the United States from bases in Canada.

The main concern of these national and international police forces is the guns and ammunition in the possession of free citizens. If this firepower can be removed from the citizens, they will no longer have the means to resist tyrannical aggression. The Founding Fathers recognized this threat, of course, which is why we have the Second Amendment to our Constitution. It explains the real reason for the raid on the Branch Davidian complex in Waco, Texas by the Bureau of Alcohol, Tobacco, and Firearms, and the F.B.I. 23

The government's fear of an armed citizenry is also the rationale for the Gun Control Act of 1968 (which was taken directly from Nazi Germany's 1938 law on that subject) and the proposed Brady Bill. If all honest citizens register their guns, the government knows where to go to confiscate them. 24

As you may know, the Federal Emergency Management Act gives the President the power to declare a national emergency and declare martial law, taking control of all aspects of our lives. The country would be divided into ten districts, each with a governor appointed by the President. What might trigger such a national emergency? 25

In his book, *Bankruptcy 1995*, Harry Figgie concludes that the Federal debt will become so large by 1995 that the government will be forced to default on its obligations. This could cause bank closures, bankruptcies of private businesses, loss of many jobs, hyperinflation, and a major depression. 26

Tying all these facts together, is it possible that the international bankers and capitalists are plotting the collapse of our economy in the next few years so that they can grasp total political and economic control of the world? If so, what can we do about it? 27

Our main defense is the education of the American public. Most Americans are very patriotic and loyal to this country. The conspirators are aware of this fact, which accounts for their passion for 28 secrecy. Thus exposure of the conspiracy will force it to retreat. A key question here is whether the news media will prove to be more loyal to the American public or to the government and the CFR, which largely control them.

29   A second major factor is the element of big government on which the conspiracy depends to achieve its objectives. More and more people are becoming aware that big government is more likely to be the *cause* of problems, rather than to be the solution to problems. We are witnessing the demise of socialism nearly everywhere in the world except the United States, and it is questionable how long we Americans will put up with that nonsense. The answer is more individual and business freedom to lead our lives without Big Brother trying to micromanage us.

30   The third major factor is the control of the monetary system by the international bankers, under the guise of the Federal Reserve System. Simply disbanding the Fed and transferring the monetary functions to the U.S. Treasury would not accomplish much, because the same individuals would still be in control of the system. We need to return to the gold and silver standards to prevent human meddling with the system. As you may recall, when we had the gold standard, an ounce of gold was the exchange rate for $35. Gold is now selling for about $375 an ounce. This is another way of saying that the present dollar is worth 9.34 cents today, compared to what it was worth when we abandoned the gold standard in 1934. Did you ever wonder why you feel less well off now than you did in the past? Did you ever wonder whether the government and the bankers may have something to do with this?

31   Are you willing to help restore this country to its proper status as a Constitutional Republic? We can stop these conspirators by exposing them, and by trying the leaders for treason. But we'll need to pull together on this and work pretty fast. We don't have much time.

Liberty Network Association
July 4, 1993

STUDY QUESTIONS

1. In paragraph 6, the author says that the purpose of his conspiracy theory is to *explain* several "puzzling current events." What are the four or five most significant current events that the author has in mind?

2. In paragraph 8, the author spans 120 years to connect President Bill Clinton to Professor John Ruskin.

   (1)   John Ruskin advocated dictatorship at Oxford.
   (2)   John Ruskin taught Cecil Rhodes.
   (3)   Cecil Rhodes applied dictatorial ideas in Africa.
   (4)   The British government approved of Cecil Rhodes's application of dictatorial ideas in Africa.
   (5)   Cecil Rhodes funded the Rhodes Scholars.
   (6)   Bill Clinton was a Rhodes Scholar at Oxford.

   The conclusion as well as many premises are left unstated. What is the unstated conclusion, and what premises are needed to make the argument complete?

3. One of the hallmark arguments of conspiracy theorists is to claim that the absence of evidence for the proposed conspiracy just shows how diabolically powerful and clever the conspirators are. In paragraph 14, for example, the author points out that the Council on Foreign Relations is not mentioned in two major encyclopedias, and suggests that this is because of the CFR's efforts not to let its plans be known. Take the following version of the argument as your starting point:

   (1)   If a powerful, clever conspiracy exists, it will succeed in suppressing evidence of its existence.
   (2)   There is no evidence proving the existence of this proposed conspiracy.
   (3)   Therefore, this proposed powerful, clever conspiracy really exists.

   What, if anything, is wrong with this argument?

4. At several places in the essay (e.g., paragraphs 1 and 31), the author suggests that we do not have much time before the conspiracy takes over. What evidence does the author offer that time is short?

PART NINE

On Abortion

RONALD REAGAN

Abortion and the Conscience of the Nation

Ronald Reagan, born in 1911 in Tampico, Illinois, was a radio sports announcer, an actor in such films as Knute Rockne, All-American, *and* The Hasty Heart, *governor of California, and, from 1981 to 1989, the President of the United States. In the following essay, Reagan offers his grounds for opposing the practice of abortion.*

The tenth anniversary of the Supreme Court decision in *Roe* v. *Wade* is a good time for us to pause and reflect. Our nationwide

1

[Ronald Reagan, excerpt from *Abortion and the Conscience of the Nation.* Nashville, Tenn.: Thomas Nelson Publishers, 1984, pp. 15–16, 18–19, 21–25, 27–36, 38.]

policy of abortion-on-demand through all nine months of pregnancy was neither voted for by our people nor enacted by our legislators—not a single state had such unrestricted abortion before the Supreme Court decreed it to be national policy in 1973. But the consequences of this judicial decision are now obvious: since 1973, more than 15 million unborn children have had their lives snuffed out by legalized abortions. That is over ten times the number of Americans lost in all our nation's wars.

2   Make no mistake, abortion-on-demand is not a right granted by the Constitution. No serious scholar, including one disposed to agree with the Court's result, has argued that the framers of the Constitution intended to create such a right. Shortly after the *Roe* v. *Wade* decision, Professor John Hart Ely, now Dean of Stanford Law School, wrote that the opinion "is not constitutional law and gives almost no sense of an obligation to try to be." Nowhere do the plain words of the Constitution even hint at a "right" so sweeping as to permit abortion up to the time the child is ready to be born. Yet that is what the Court ruled.

3   As an act of "raw judicial power" (to use Justice White's biting phrase), the decision by the seven-man majority in *Roe* v. *Wade* has so far been made to stick. But the Court's decision has by no means settled the debate. Instead, *Roe* v. *Wade* has become a continuing prod to the conscience of the nation.

4   Abortion concerns not just the unborn child, it concerns every one of us. The English poet, John Donne, wrote: " . . . any man's death diminishes me, because I am involved in mankind; and therefore never send to know for whom the bell tolls; it tolls for thee."

5   We cannot diminish the value of one category of human life— the unborn—without diminishing the value of all human life. We saw tragic proof of this truism last year[1] when the Indiana courts allowed the starvation death of "Baby Doe" in Bloomington because the child had Down's Syndrome.

6   Many of our fellow citizens grieve over the loss of life that has followed *Roe* v. *Wade*. Margaret Heckler, soon after being nominated to head the largest department of our government, Health and Human Services, told an audience that she believed abortion to be the greatest moral crisis facing our country today. And the

1. I.e., 1983.—Eds.

revered Mother Teresa, who works in the streets of Calcutta minis-
tering to dying people in her world-famous mission of mercy, has
said that "the greatest misery of our time is the generalized abortion
of children."

Over the first two years of my administration I have closely   7
followed and assisted efforts in Congress to reverse the tide of
abortion—efforts of congressmen, senators and citizens responding
to an urgent moral crisis. Regrettably, I have also seen the massive
efforts of those who, under the banner of "freedom of choice," have
so far blocked every effort to reverse nationwide abortion-on-demand.

Despite the formidable obstacles before us, we must not lose   8
heart. This is not the first time our country has been divided by a
Supreme Court decision that denied the value of certain human
lives. The *Dred Scott* decision of 1857 was not overturned in a day,
or a year, or even a decade. At first, only a minority of Americans
recognized and deplored the moral crisis brought about by denying
the full humanity of our black brothers and sisters; but that minority
persisted in their vision and finally prevailed. They did it by appealing to the hearts and minds of their countrymen, to the truth of
human dignity under God. From their example, we know that
respect for the sacred value of human life is too deeply engrained
in the hearts of our people to remain forever suppressed. But the
great majority of the American people have not yet made their
voices heard, and we cannot expect them to—any more than the
public voice arose against slavery—*until* the issue is clearly framed
and presented.

What, then, is the real issue? I have often said that when we talk   9
about abortion, we are talking about two lives—the life of the
mother and the life of the unborn child. Why else do we call a
pregnant woman a mother? I have also said that anyone who doesn't
feel sure whether we are talking about a second human life should
clearly give life the benefit of the doubt. If you don't know whether
a body is alive or dead, you would never bury it. I think this
consideration itself should be enough for all of us to insist on
protecting the unborn.

The case against abortion does not rest here, however, for medical   10
practice confirms at every step the correctness of these moral sensi-
bilities. Modern medicine treats the unborn child as a patient.

Medical pioneers have made great breakthroughs in treating the unborn—for genetic problems, vitamin deficiencies, irregular heart rhythms, and other medical conditions. Who can forget George Will's moving account of the little boy who underwent brain surgery six times during the nine weeks before he was born? Who is the *patient* if not that tiny unborn human being who can feel pain when he or she is approached by doctors who come to kill rather than to cure?

11   The real question today is not when human life begins, but, *What is the value of human life?* The abortionist who reassembles the arms and legs of a tiny baby to make sure all its parts have been torn from its mother's body can hardly doubt whether it is a human being. The real question for him and for all of us is whether that tiny human life has a God-given right to be protected by the law—the same right we have.

12   What more dramatic confirmation could we have of the real issue than the Baby Doe case in Bloomington, Indiana? The death of that tiny infant tore at the hearts of all Americans because the child was undeniably a live human being—one lying helpless before the eyes of the doctors and the eyes of the nation. The real issue for the courts was *not* whether Baby Doe was a human being. The real issue was whether to protect the life of a human being who had Down's Syndrome, who would probably be mentally handicapped, but who needed a routine surgical procedure to unblock his esophagus and allow him to eat. A doctor testified to the presiding judge that, even with his physical problem corrected, Baby Doe would have a "nonexistent" possibility for "a minimally adequate quality of life"—in other words, that retardation was the equivalent of a crime deserving the death penalty. The judge let Baby Doe starve and die, and the Indiana Supreme Court sanctioned his decision.

13   Federal law does not allow federally-assisted hospitals to decide that Down's Syndrome infants are not worth treating, much less to decide to starve them to death. Accordingly, I have directed the Departments of Justice and Health and Human Services to apply civil rights regulations to protect handicapped newborns. All hospitals receiving federal funds must post notices which will clearly state that failure to feed handicapped babies is prohibited by federal law. The basic issue is whether to value and protect the lives of the handicapped, whether to recognize the sanctity of

human life. This is the same basic issue that underlies the question of abortion.

The 1981 Senate hearings on the beginning of human life 14 brought out the basic issue more clearly than ever before. The many medical and scientific witnesses who testified disagreed on many things, but not on the *scientific* evidence that the unborn child is alive, is a distinct individual, or is a member of the human species. They did disagree over the *value* question, whether to give value to a human life at its early and most vulnerable stages of existence.

Regrettably, we live at a time when some persons do *not* value 15 all human life. They want to pick and choose which individuals have value. Some have said that only those individuals with "consciousness of self" are human beings. One such writer has followed this deadly logic and concluded that "shocking as it may seem, a newly born infant is not a human being."

A Nobel Prize winning scientist has suggested that if a handi- 16 capped child "were not declared fully human until three days after birth, then all parents could be allowed the choice." In other words, "quality control" to see if newly born human beings are up to snuff.

Obviously, some influential people want to deny that every 17 human life has intrinsic, sacred worth. They insist that a member of the human race must have certain qualities before they accord him or her status as a "human being."

Events have borne out the editorial in a California medical 18 journal which explained three years before *Roe* v. *Wade* that the social acceptance of abortion is a "defiance of the long-held Western ethic of intrinsic and equal value for every human life regardless of its stage, condition, or status."

Every legislator, every doctor, and every citizen needs to recog- 19 nize that the real issue is whether to affirm and protect the sanctity of all human life, or to embrace a social ethic where some human lives are valued and others are not. As a nation, we must choose between the sanctity of life ethic and the "quality of life" ethic.

I have no trouble identifying the answer our nation has always 20 given to this basic question, and the answer that I hope and pray it will give in the future. America was founded by men and women who shared a vision of the value of each and every individual. They stated this vision clearly from the very start in the Declaration of Independence, using words that every schoolboy and schoolgirl can recite:

> We hold these truths to be self-evident, that all men are created equal, that they are endowed by their Creator with certain unalienable rights, that among these are life, liberty, and the pursuit of happiness.

21   We fought a terrible war to guarantee that one category of mankind—black people in America—could not be denied the inalienable rights with which their Creator endowed them. The great champion of the sanctity of all human life in that day, Abraham Lincoln, gave us his assessment of the Declaration's purpose. Speaking of the framers of that noble document, he said:

> This was their majestic interpretation of the economy of the Universe. This was their lofty, and wise, and noble understanding of the justice of the Creator to His creatures. Yes, gentlemen, to all His creatures, to the whole great family of man. In their enlightened belief, nothing stamped with the divine image and likeness was sent into the world to be trodden on. . . . They grasped not only the whole race of man then living, but they reached forward and seized upon the farthest posterity. They erected a beacon to guide their children and their children's children, and the countless myriads who should inhabit the earth in other ages.

He warned also of the danger we would face if we closed our eyes to the value of life in any category of human beings:

> I should like to know if taking this old Declaration of Independence, which declares that all men are equal upon principle and making exceptions to it where will it stop. If one man says it does not mean a Negro, why not another say it does not mean some other man?

22   When Congressman John A. Bingham of Ohio drafted the Fourteenth Amendment to guarantee the rights of life, liberty, and property to all human beings, he explained that *all* are "entitled to the protection of American law, because its divine spirit of equality declares that all men are created equal." He said the rights guaranteed by the amendment would therefore apply to "any human being." Justice William Brennan, in another case decided only the

year before *Roe* v. *Wade*, referred to our society as one that "strongly affirms the sanctity of life."

Another William Brennan—not the Justice—has reminded us 23 of the terrible consequences that can follow when a nation rejects the sanctity of life ethic:

> The cultural environment for a human holocaust is present whenever any society can be misled into defining individuals as less than human and therefore devoid of value and respect.

As a nation today, we have *not* rejected the sanctity of human life. 24 The American people have not had an opportunity to express their view on the sanctity of human life in the unborn. I am convinced that Americans do not want to play God with the value of human life. It is not for us to decide who is worthy to live and who is not. Even the Supreme Court's opinion in *Roe* v. *Wade* did not explicitly reject the traditional American idea of intrinsic worth and value in all human life; it simply dodged this issue.

The Congress has before it several measures that would enable 25 our people to reaffirm the sanctity of human life, even the smallest and the youngest and the most defenseless. The Human Life Bill expressly recognizes the unborn as human beings and accordingly protects them as persons under our Constitution. This bill, first introduced by Senator Jesse Helms, provided the vehicle for the Senate hearings in 1981 which contributed so much to our understanding of the real issue of abortion.

The Respect Human Life Act, just introduced in the ninety- 26 eighth Congress, states in its first section that the policy of the United States is "to protect innocent life, both before and after birth." This bill, sponsored by Congressman Henry Hyde and Senator Roger Jepsen, prohibits the federal government from performing abortions or assisting those who do so, except to save the life of the mother. It also addresses the pressing issue of infanticide which, as we have seen, flows inevitably from permissive abortion as another step in the denial of the inviolability of innocent human life.

I have endorsed each of these measures, as well as the more 27 difficult route of constitutional amendment, and I will give these initiatives my full support. Each of them, in different ways, attempts to reverse the tragic policy of abortion-on-demand imposed by the Supreme Court ten years ago. Each of them is a decisive way to affirm the sanctity of human life.

28   We must all educate ourselves to the reality of the horrors taking place. Doctors today know that unborn children can feel a touch within the womb and that they respond to pain. But how many Americans are aware that abortion techniques are allowed today, in all fifty states, that burn the skin of a baby with a salt solution, in an agonizing death that can last for hours?

29   Another example: two years ago, the *Philadelphia Inquirer* ran a Sunday special supplement on "The Dreaded Complication." The "dreaded complication" referred to in the article—the complication feared by doctors who perform abortions—is the *survival* of the child despite all the painful attacks during the abortion procedure. Some unborn children *do* survive the late-term abortions the Supreme Court has made legal. Is there any question that these victims of abortion deserve our attention and protection? Is there any question that those who *don't* survive were living human beings before they were killed?

30   Late-term abortions, especially when the baby survives, but is then killed by starvation, neglect, or suffocation, show once again the link between abortion and infanticide. The time to stop both is now. As my administration acts to stop infanticide, we will be fully aware of the real issue that underlies the death of babies before and soon after birth.

31   Our society has, fortunately, become sensitive to the rights and special needs of the handicapped, but I am shocked that physical or mental handicaps of newborns are still used to justify their extinction. This administration has a Surgeon General, Dr. C. Everett Koop, who has done perhaps more than any other American for handicapped children, by pioneering surgical techniques to help them, by speaking out on the value of their lives, and by working with them in the context of loving families. You will not find his former patients advocating the so-called "quality-of-life" ethic.

32   I know that when the true issue of infanticide is placed before the American people, with all the facts openly aired, we will have no trouble deciding that a mentally or physically handicapped baby has the same intrinsic worth and right to life as the rest of us. As the New Jersey Supreme Court said two decades ago, in a decision

upholding the sanctity of human life, "a child need not be perfect to have a worthwhile life."

Whether we are talking about pain suffered by unborn children, 33 or about late-term abortions, or about infanticide, we inevitably focus on the humanity of the unborn child. Each of these issues is a potential rallying point for the sanctity of life ethic. Once we as a nation rally around any one of these issues to affirm the sanctity of life, we will see the importance of affirming this principle across the board.

Malcolm Muggeridge, the English writer, goes right to the heart 34 of the matter: "Either life is always and in all circumstances sacred, or intrinsically of no account; it is inconceivable that it should be in some cases the one, and in some the other." The sanctity of innocent human life is a principle that Congress should proclaim at every opportunity.

It is possible that the Supreme Court itself may overturn its 35 abortion rulings. We need only recall that in *Brown* v. *Board of Education* the court reversed its own earlier "separate-but-equal" decision. I believe if the Supreme Court took another look at *Roe* v. *Wade*, and considered the real issue between the sanctity of life ethic and the quality of life ethic, it would change its mind once again.

As we continue to work to overturn *Roe* v. *Wade*, we must also 36 continue to lay the groundwork for a society in which abortion is not the accepted answer to unwanted pregnancy. Pro-life people have already taken heroic steps, often at great personal sacrifice, to provide for unwed mothers. I recently spoke about a young pregnant woman named Victoria, who said, "In this society we save whales, we save timber wolves and bald eagles and Coke bottles. Yet, everyone wanted me to throw away my baby." She has been helped by Sav-a-Life, a group in Dallas, which provides a way for unwed mothers to preserve the human life within them when they might otherwise be tempted to resort to abortion. I think also of House of His Creation in Coatesville, Pennsylvania, where a loving couple has taken in almost two hundred young women in the past ten years. They have seen, as a fact of life, that the girls are *not* better off having abortions than saving their babies. I am also reminded of the remarkable Rossow family of Ellington, Connecticut, who have opened their hearts and their home to nine handicapped adopted and foster children.

37   The Adolescent Family Life Program, adopted by Congress at the request of Senator Jeremiah Denton, has opened new opportunities for unwed mothers to give their children life. We should not rest until our entire society echoes the tone of John Powell in the dedication of his book, *Abortion: The Silent Holocaust,* a dedication to every woman carrying an unwanted child: "Please believe that you are not alone. There are many of us that truly love you, who want to stand at your side, and help in any way we can." And we can echo the always-practical woman of faith, Mother Teresa, when she says, "If you don't want the little child, that unborn child, give him to me." We have so many families in America seeking to adopt children that the slogan "every child a wanted child" is now the emptiest of all reasons to tolerate abortion.

38   I have often said we need to join in prayer to bring protection to the unborn. Prayer and action are needed to uphold the sanctity of human life. I believe it will not be possible to accomplish our work, the work of saving lives, "without being a soul of prayer." The famous British member of Parliament William Wilberforce prayed with his small group of influential friends, the "Clapham Sect," for *decades* to see an end to slavery in the British empire. Wilberforce led that struggle in Parliament, unflaggingly, because he believed in the sanctity of human life. He saw the fulfillment of his impossible dream when Parliament outlawed slavery just before his death.

39   Let his faith and perseverance be our guide. We will never recognize the true value of our own lives until we affirm the value in the life of others, a value of which Malcolm Muggeridge says: " . . . however low it flickers or fiercely burns, it is still a Divine flame which no man dare presume to put out, be his motives ever so humane and enlightened."

40   Abraham Lincoln recognized that we could not survive as a free land when some men could decide that others were not fit to be free and should therefore be slaves. Likewise, we cannot survive as a free nation when some men decide that others are not fit to live and should be abandoned to abortion or infanticide. My administration is dedicated to the preservation of America as a free land, and there is no cause more important for preserving that freedom than affirming the transcendent right to life of all human beings, the right without which no other rights have any meaning.

STUDY QUESTIONS

1. Of the many arguments Reagan offers in this essay, what is his core argument for the conclusion that abortion is wrong?
2. At various places Reagan calls the fetus a "child," a "human life," and a "baby." What evidence does Reagan provide that these words are true indicators of a fetus's status?
3. Reagan connects abortion to the attitudes that lead to infanticide and slavery. Why does he think the "freedom of choice" position on abortion stems from these same attitudes? (Consider, for example, the "dreaded complication" that Reagan mentions in paragraph 29.)
4. In paragraphs 9 and 11, Reagan raises what he calls "the real issue" or "question" of abortion. Why does he think the question is *not* when human life begins?
5. How do you think Reagan would respond to the criteria of personhood presented in the selection by Mary Anne Warren (p. 297)?
6. Throughout the essay, Reagan quotes well-known individuals and authorities. Do these quotations supplement or replace argument?

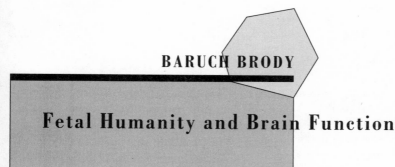

BARUCH BRODY

Fetal Humanity and Brain Function

Baruch Brody is Leon Jaworski Professor of Biomedical Ethics, Director of the Center for Ethics, Medicine, and Public Issues, and Professor of Medicine and Community Medicine at Baylor College of Medicine in Houston, Texas. In the following selection, Brody argues that while a fetus is not a human being from the point of conception, it becomes one early in the pregnancy. His strategy in this essay is unusual, since he reasons backwards from the conditions for death to a conclusion about when human life begins.

1   The question which we must now consider is the question of fetal humanity. Some have argued that the fetus is a human being with a right to life (or, for convenience, just a human being) from the moment of conception. Others have argued that the fetus only becomes a human being at the moment of birth. Many positions in between these two extremes have also been suggested. How are we to decide which is correct?

2   The analysis which we will propose here rests upon certain metaphysical assumptions which I have defended elsewhere. These assumptions are: (a) the question is when has the fetus acquired all the properties essential (necessary) for being a human being, for when it has, it is a human being; (b) these properties are such that

[Baruch Brody, "Fetal Humanity and the Theory of Essentialism," in Robert Baker and Frederick Elliston, eds., *Philosophy and Sex*. Buffalo, N.Y.: Prometheus Books, 1975, pp. 348–352.]

the loss of any one of them means that the human being in question has gone out of existence and not merely stopped being a human being; (c) human beings go out of existence when they die. It follows from these assumptions that the fetus becomes a human being when it acquires all those characteristics which are such that the loss of any one of them would result in the fetus's being dead. We must, therefore, turn to the analysis of death.

We will first consider the question of what properties are essential to being human if we suppose that death and the passing out of existence occur only if there has been an irreparable cessation of brain function (keeping in mind that that condition itself, as we have noted, is a matter of medical judgment). We shall then consider the same question on the supposition that [Paul] Ramsey's more complicated theory of death (the modified traditional view) is correct.   3

According to what is called the brain-death theory, as long as there has not been an irreparable cessation of brain function the person in question continues to exist, no matter what else has happened to him. If so, it seems to follow that there is only one property—leaving aside those entailed by this one property—that is essential to humanity, namely, the possession of a brain that has not suffered an irreparable cessation of function.   4

Several consequences follow immediately from this conclusion. We can see that a variety of often advanced claims about the essence of humanity are false. For example, the claim that movement, or perhaps just the ability to move, is essential for being human is false. A human being who has stopped moving, and even one who has lost the ability to move, has not therefore stopped existing. Being able to move, and a fortiori moving, are not essential properties of human beings and therefore are not essential to being human. Similarly, the claim that being perceivable by other human beings is essential for being human is also false. A human being who has stopped being perceivable by other humans (for example, someone isolated on the other side of the moon, out of reach even of radio communication) has not stopped existing. Being perceivable by other human beings is not an essential property of human beings and is not essential to being human. And the same point can be made about the claims that viability is essential for being human, that independent exist-   5 ence is essential for being human, and that actual interaction with other human beings is essential for being human. The loss of any of these properties would not mean that the human being in question had gone out of existence, so none of them can be essential to that human being and none of them can be essential for being human.

6   Let us now look at the following argument: (1) A functioning brain (or at least, a brain that, if not functioning, is susceptible of function) is a property that every human being must have because it is essential for being human. (2) By the time an entity acquires that property, it has all the other properties that are essential for being human. Therefore, when the fetus acquires that property it becomes a human being. It is clear that the property in question is, according to the brain-death theory, one that is had essentially by all human beings. The question that we have to consider is whether the second premise is true. It might appear that its truth does follow from the brain-death theory. After all, we did see that the theory entails that only one property (together with those entailed by it) is essential for being human. Nevertheless, rather than relying solely on my earlier argument, I shall adopt an alternative approach to strengthen the conviction that this second premise is true: I shall note the important ways in which the fetus resembles and differs from an ordinary human being by the time it definitely has a functioning brain (about the end of the sixth week of development). It shall then be evident, in light of our theory of essentialism, that none of these differences involves the lack of some property in the fetus that is essential for its being human.

7   Structurally, there are few features of the human being that are not fully present by the end of the sixth week. Not only are the familiar external features and all the internal organs present, but the contours of the body are nicely rounded. More important, the body is functioning. Not only is the brain functioning, but the heart is beating sturdily (the fetus by this time has its own completely developed vascular system), the stomach is producing digestive juices, the liver is manufacturing blood cells, the kidney is extracting uric acid from the blood, and the nerves and muscles are operating in concert, so that reflex reactions can begin.

8   What are the properties that a fetus acquires after the sixth week of its development? Certain structures do appear later. These include

the fingernails (which appear in the third month), the completed vocal chords (which also appear then), taste buds and salivary glands (again, in the third month), and hair and eyelashes (in the fifth month). In addition, certain functions begin later than the sixth week. The fetus begins to urinate (in the third month), to move spontaneously (in the third month), to respond to external stimuli (at least in the fifth month), and to breathe (in the sixth month). Moreover, there is a constant growth in size. And finally, at the time of birth the fetus ceases to receive its oxygen and food through the placenta and starts receiving them through the mouth and nose.

I will not examine each of these properties (structures and functions) to show that they are not essential for being human. The procedure would be essentially the one used previously to show that various essentialist claims are in error. We might, therefore, conclude, on the supposition that the brain-death theory is correct, that the fetus becomes a human being about the end of the sixth week after its development. 9

There is, however, one complication that should be noted here. There are, after all, progressive stages in the physical development and in the functioning of the brain. For example, the fetal brain (and nervous system) does not develop sufficiently to support spontaneous motion until some time in the third month after conception. There is, of course, no doubt that that stage of development is sufficient for the fetus to be human. No one would be likely to maintain that a spontaneously moving human being has died; and similarly, a spontaneously moving fetus would seem to have become human. One might, however, want to claim that the fetus does not become a human being until the point of spontaneous movement. So then, on the supposition that the brain-death theory of death is correct, one ought to conclude that the fetus becomes a human being at some time between the sixth and twelfth week after its conception. 10

But what if we reject the brain-death theory, and replace it with its equally plausible contender, Ramsey's theory of death? According to that theory—which we can call the brain, heart, and lung theory of death—the human being does not die, does not go out of existence, until such time as the brain, heart and lungs have irreparably ceased functioning naturally. What are the essential features of being human according to this theory? 11

12   Actually, the adoption of Ramsey's theory requires no major modifications. According to that theory, what is essential to being human, what each human being must retain if he is to continue to exist, is the possession of a functioning (actually or potentially) heart, lung, or brain. It is only when a human being possesses none of these that he dies and goes out of existence; and the fetus comes into humanity, so to speak, when he acquires one of these.

13   On Ramsey's theory, the argument would now run as follows: (1) The property of having a functioning brain, heart, or lungs (or at least organs of the kind that, if not functioning, are susceptible of function) is one that every human being must have because it is essential for being human. (2) By the time that an entity acquires that property it has all the other properties that are essential for being human. Therefore, when the fetus acquires that property it becomes a human being. There remains, once more, the problem of the second premise. Since the fetal heart starts operating rather early, it is not clear that the second premise is correct. Many systems are not yet operating, and many structures are not yet present. Still, following our theory of essentialism, we should conclude that the fetus becomes a human being when it acquires a functioning heart (the first of the organs to function in the fetus).

14   There is, however, a further complication here, and it is analogous to the one encountered if we adopt the brain-death theory: When may we properly say that the fetal heart begins to function? At two weeks, when occasional contractions of the primitive fetal heart are present? In the fourth to fifth week, when the heart, although incomplete, is beating regularly and pumping blood cells through a closed vascular system, and when the tracings obtained by an ECG exhibit the classical elements of an adult tracing? Or after the end of the seventh week, when the fetal heart is functionally complete and "normal"?

15   We have not reached a precise conclusion in our study of the question of when the fetus becomes a human being. We do know that it does so some time between the end of the second week and the end of the third month. But it surely is not a human being at the moment of conception and it surely is one by the end of the third month. Though we have not come to a final answer to our question, we have narrowed the range of acceptable answers considerably.

16   [In summary] we have argued that the fetus becomes a human

being with a right to life some time between the second and twelfth week after conception. We have also argued that abortions are morally impermissible after that point except in rather unusual circumstances. What is crucial to note is that neither of these arguments appeal to any theological considerations. We conclude, therefore, that there is a human-rights basis for moral opposition to abortions.

STUDY QUESTIONS

1. The overall structure of Brody's argument is as follows:

> A human goes out of existence when it dies.
> A human dies when feature z is no longer present.
>
> Therefore, feature z is essential to being a human.
> Fetuses have feature z at time t.
>
> Therefore, fetuses are humans at time t.
>
> Therefore, abortions are immoral after time t.

What premises are assumed between the final two lines of the overall argument?

2. Brody considers two theories about when death occurs: the brain-death theory and Ramsey's heart-lungs-brain theory. In paragraph 11, Brody states that the two theories are "equally plausible." On what evidence does he make this judgment?

3. In discussing Ramsey's theory of death (paragraphs 11 through 13), Brody makes an inference like the following:

> One is not dead unless one's heart, lungs, and brain are not functioning (paragraph 11).
>
> If one has a functioning heart, lungs, or brain, then one is alive (paragraph 13).

Let's symbolize the predicates as follows:

> $Hx = x$ has a functioning heart
> $Lx = x$ has functioning lungs
> $Bx = x$ has a functioning brain

$Ax = x$ is alive

Does the following symbolization capture the form of this inference?

$(x) [\sim(\sim Hx \cdot \sim Lx \cdot \sim Bx) \supset Ax]$

$(x) [(Hx \lor Lx \lor Bx) \supset Ax]$

If not, what is the correct symbolization? Is the inference valid?

4. If we compare Brody's essay with Mary Anne Warren's "On the Moral and Legal Status of Abortion" (p. 297), we get two different accounts of the defining features of human beings. What is the fundamental point of disagreement that gives rise to the different definitions?

LAURENCE H. TRIBE

Opposition to Abortion Is Not Based on Alleged Rights to Life

Laurence H. Tribe was born in Shanghai in 1941. He is Tyler Professor of Constitutional Law at Harvard Law School. In the following selection, excerpted from his book Abortion: The Clash of Absolutes, *Tribe offers an analysis of the premises underlying opposition to abortion.*

1   Most of those who regard abortion as, at best, a necessary evil would nonetheless make an exception permitting abortion in cases of rape

[Laurence H. Tribe, excerpts from *Abortion: The Clash of Absolutes.* New York: W. W. Norton, 1990, pp. 231–234, references deleted.]

and incest. (This exception is really about rape. Most cases of incest probably involve an older relative and a young child, and so in most people's experience, incest is really a particular kind of rape.) Although polling numbers on abortion are notoriously sensitive to the wording of the questions (the *New York Times* has observed that "one of every six Americans says simultaneously that abortion is murder and that it is sometimes the best course"), the polls do reveal this truth quite starkly.

One nationwide poll, for example, showed that 40 percent of the American public oppose abortion when it is sought because "the mother is an unmarried teenager whose future life might be seriously affected." Yet 81 percent favor abortion "if the woman became pregnant because of rape or incest." Only 17 percent oppose abortion in such cases. This suggests that almost 60 percent of those who oppose abortion for the unmarried teenager would support it in cases of rape or incest.

Regional polls corroborate the hypothesis that people who generally oppose abortion would nonetheless permit it in cases of rape and incest. For example, polls in Florida in the weeks after the *Webster* decision showed that although 59 percent of the registered voters said they agreed that during the first trimester of pregnancy the decision to have an abortion "should be left entirely to a woman and her doctor," 53 percent of those polled said that abortion should be "illegal" when sought because the woman's family "has a very low income and cannot afford to have any more children," and 60 percent said that abortion should not be permitted where sought because "the pregnancy would interfere with the mother's work or education." Still, 78 percent of those polled thought abortion should be available in cases where the pregnancy resulted from rape or incest. Only 13 percent said it should not. This suggests that more than 75 percent of the people who oppose abortion in circumstances of economic or personal hardship may well accept it in cases of rape and incest.

A similar poll in Utah found that, although 58 percent of the adult population thought abortion should not be available "to women who choose it in the first trimester" and 68 percent thought it should not be available to women who choose it in the second trimester, prior to viability, again an overwhelming majority (81 percent) agreed that abortion should be available in cases of rape and incest. Only 11 percent disagreed. This suggests that up to 80 percent of Utah residents who oppose abortion on request in the first trimester of pregnancy may nonetheless support the availability of abortion in cases of rape and incest.

5   Support of a rape exception makes plain that most people's opposition to abortion, unlike their opposition to murder, *can* be overridden. It therefore suggests that antiabortion sentiment is not *entirely* rooted in a belief that abortion constitutes the killing of an innocent human being. It is hard to see how any such justification for limiting abortion could plausibly be put forward by anyone who thinks that abortion should be permitted in cases of rape. A fetus conceived as a result of a violent rape is no less innocent than one conceived in a mutually desired act of love. The fetus obviously is not responsible for the circumstances surrounding its conception. Yet the vast majority of people who oppose abortion would permit such a fetus to be destroyed, even if they were rewriting from scratch the constitutional rules governing this thorny topic.

6   If support for a rape and incest exception suggests that most opposition to abortion is *not* entirely about the destruction of innocent human life it might also reveal something about the views, conscious or unconscious, that lie at the heart of the belief that in general, access to abortion should be restricted.

7   Surely there should be nothing abhorrent about the *particular* fetuses that are the products of rapes. It is true that a position in favor of denying criminals the right to reproduce has at times been expressed in the United States—for example in the Oklahoma law struck down in the 1940s by the Supreme Court in *Skinner v. Oklahoma*, a law that provided for the sterilization of anyone previously found guilty two or more times of "felonies involving moral turpitude." But a desire to deny the rapist his child could hardly explain a willingness to make abortion available to women who have been raped. And any notion that the fetus itself is tainted by a kind of "original sin" seems most implausible. After all, when the woman who has been raped *chooses* to give birth to the rapist's child rather than to abort, she is commended, not condemned.

8   Right-to-life advocates who would allow abortion for a woman who becomes pregnant after a rape are probably reacting out of compassion for the woman; they don't think she should have to live through having her rapist's child develop within her. But the only

thing to distinguish that from any other unwanted pregnancy is the nature of the sexual activity out of which the pregnancy arose. A fetus resulting from rape or (in most cases) from incest is the product of a sex act to which the woman did not consent. It is only the *nonconsensual nature of the sex* that led to her pregnancy that could make abortion in the case of rape seem justified to someone who would condemn all other abortions not needed to save the pregnant woman's life.

This in turn suggests that one's opposition to such *other* abor- 9
tions reflects a sense that continued pregnancy is simply the price women must pay for engaging in *consensual sex*. The lack of sympathy toward women who have experienced contraceptive failure suggests that many of us have no discomfort at the idea that women who choose to have sex simply cannot be allowed to avoid *some* risk of a pregnancy that they will just have to carry to term.

As we have seen, this feeling may be partly rooted in the belief 10
that in general, this is the way of nature. In this view, opposition to abortion may reflect an ambivalence about the use of technology in general, in this case medical technology, to overcome that which always before seemed "natural": that sex would lead to pregnancy and pregnancy to childbirth.

But notice how often this feeling about abortion is held by people 11
who generally welcome the energetic uses of new technologies. Especially if such people regard nervousness about nuclear reactors or computers or other "unnatural" developments as silly or childish, their aversion to abortion rights would seem to reflect a deeply held *sexual* morality, in which pregnancy and childbirth are seen as a punishment that women in particular must endure for engaging in consensual sex. The fact that opposition to abortion rights may in large part be about sexual morality is reflected, too, in the attitude, noted earlier, of those who oppose abortion and seem willing to do almost anything to stop it—*except* take the effective pregnancy-reducing step of providing birth control education and better contraceptives.

At least to *these* "pro-life" activists, it seems to be more important 12
to prevent the marginal increase in sexual activity that they believe will follow from sex education and the availability of birth control than to lower the number of abortions being performed. Theirs is

thus a position in which sexual morality is primary, with any claim of a fetus's right to life taking a very distant backseat.

STUDY QUESTIONS

1. Tribe's core argument is as follows: If the opposition to abortion were based on the rights of the fetus, then opponents would not allow an exception for pregnancies resulting from rape; but they do allow an exception for rape; hence opposition to abortion is not based on the rights of the fetus. Identify the argument for each of the premises in Tribe's core argument.

2. Tribe cites data from a number of polls to support the conclusion that most people who generally oppose abortion would make exceptions in cases of rape. Are the polls he cites representative enough to support this conclusion?

3. What is Tribe's best explanation for why many of those opposed to abortion will allow exceptions in cases of rape?

4. What other explanations does Tribe consider and reject? Are they the only possible explanations?

5. Does Tribe say anything in this passage that would be a problem for those opposed to abortion in all cases?

6. Does Tribe prove his conclusion that much opposition to abortion is not based on the view that a fetus has a right to life?

MARY ANNE WARREN

On the Moral and Legal Status of Abortion

Mary Anne Warren, author of Gendercide *and* The Nature of Woman, *is a professor of philosophy at San Francisco State University in California. In the following selection, she defends a woman's right to abortion.*

The question which we must answer in order to produce a satisfactory solution to the problem of the moral status of abortion is this: How are we to define the moral community, the set of beings with full and equal moral rights, such that we can decide whether a human fetus is a member of this community or not? What sort of entity, exactly, has the inalienable rights to life, liberty, and the pursuit of happiness? Jefferson attributed these rights to all *men*, and it may or may not be fair to suggest that he intended to attribute them *only* to men. Perhaps he ought to have attributed them to all human beings. If so, then we arrive, first, at Noonan's problem of defining what makes a being human, and, second, at the equally vital question which Noonan does not consider, namely, What reason is there for identifying the moral community with the set of all human beings, in whatever way we have chosen to define that term?

[Mary Anne Warren, Part II of "On the Moral and Legal Status of Abortion." *The Monist* 57 (January 1973), pp. 52–61.]

1. On the Definition of 'Human'

2   One reason why this vital second question is so frequently over-looked in the debate over the moral status of abortion is that the term 'human' has two distinct, but not often distinguished, senses. This fact results in a slide of meaning, which serves to conceal the fallaciousness of the traditional argument that since (1) it is wrong to kill innocent human beings, and (2) fetuses are innocent human beings, then (3) it is wrong to kill fetuses. For if 'human' is used in the same sense in both (1) and (2) then, whichever of the two senses is meant, one of these premises is question-begging. And if it is used in two different senses then of course the conclusion doesn't follow.

3   Thus, (1) is a self-evident moral truth,[1] and avoids begging the question about abortion, only if 'human being' is used to mean something like "a full-fledged member of the moral community." (It may or may not also be meant to refer exclusively to members of the species *Homo sapiens.*) We may call this the *moral* sense of 'human.' It is not to be confused with what we will call the *genetic* sense, i.e., the sense in which *any* member of the species is a human being, and no member of any other species could be. If (1) is acceptable only if the moral sense is intended, (2) is non-question-begging only if what is intended is the genetic sense.

4   In "Deciding Who is Human," Noonan argues for the classification of fetuses with human beings by pointing to the presence of the full genetic code, and the potential capacity for rational thought. It is clear that what he needs to show, for his version of the traditional argument to be valid, is that fetuses are human in the moral sense, the sense in which it is analytically true that all human beings have full moral rights. But, in the absence of any argument showing that whatever is genetically human is also morally human, and he gives none, nothing more than genetic humanity can be demonstrated by the presence of the human genetic code. And, as we will see, the *potential* capacity for rational thought can at most show that an entity has the potential for *becoming* human in the moral sense.

---

1. Of course, the principle that it is (always) wrong to kill innocent human beings is in need of many other modifications, e.g., that it may be permissible to do so to save a greater number of other innocent human beings, but we may safely ignore these complications here.

2. Defining the Moral Community

Can it be established that genetic humanity is sufficient for moral humanity? I think that there are very good reasons for not defining the moral community in this way. I would like to suggest an alternative way of defining the moral community, which I will argue for only to the extent of explaining why it is, or should be, self-evident. The suggestion is simply that the moral community consists of all and only *people*, rather than all and only human beings;[2] and probably the best way of demonstrating its self-evidence is by considering the concept of personhood, to see what sorts of entity are and are not persons, and what the decision that a being is or is not a person implies about its moral rights.

What characteristics entitle an entity to be considered a person? This is obviously not the place to attempt a complete analysis of the concept of personhood, but we do not need such a fully adequate analysis just to determine whether and why a fetus is or isn't a person. All we need is a rough and approximate list of the most basic criteria of personhood, and some idea of which, or how many, of these an entity must satisfy in order to properly be considered a person.

In searching for such criteria, it is useful to look beyond the set of people with whom we are acquainted, and ask how we would decide whether a totally alien being was a person or not. (For we have no right to assume that genetic humanity is necessary for personhood.) Imagine a space traveler who lands on an unknown planet and encounters a race of beings utterly unlike any he has ever seen or heard of. If he wants to be sure of behaving morally toward these beings, he has to somehow decide whether they are people, and hence have full moral rights, or whether they are the sort of thing which he need not feel guilty about treating as, for example, a source of food.

How should he go about making this decision? If he has some anthropological background, he might look for such things as religion, art, and the manufacturing of tools, weapons, or shelters, since

---

2. From here on, we will use 'human' to mean genetically human, since the moral sense seems closely connected to, and perhaps derived from, the assumption that genetic humanity is sufficient for membership in the moral community.

these factors have been used to distinguish our human from our prehuman ancestors, in what seems to be closer to the moral than the genetic sense of 'human.' And no doubt he would be right to consider the presence of such factors as good evidence that the alien beings were people, and morally human. It would, however, be overly anthropocentric of him to take the absence of these things as adequate evidence that they were not, since we can imagine people who have progressed beyond, or evolved without ever developing, these cultural characteristics.

9   I suggest that the traits which are most central to the concept of personhood, or humanity in the moral sense, are, very roughly, the following:

(1) consciousness (of objects and events external and/or internal to the being), and in particular the capacity to feel pain;
(2) reasoning (the *developed* capacity to solve new and relatively complex problems);
(3) self-motivated activity (activity which is relatively independent of either genetic or direct external control);
(4) the capacity to communicate, by whatever means, messages of an indefinite variety of types, that is, not just with an indefinite number of possible contents, but on indefinitely many possible topics;
(5) the presence of self-concepts, and self-awareness, either individual or racial, or both.

10   Admittedly, there are apt to be a great many problems involved in formulating precise definitions of these criteria, let alone in developing universally valid behavioral criteria for deciding when they apply. But I will assume that both we and our explorer know approximately what (1)–(5) mean, and that he is also able to determine whether or not they apply. How, then, should he use his findings to decide whether or not the alien beings are people? We needn't suppose that an entity must have *all* of these attributes to be properly considered a person; (1) and (2) alone may well be sufficient for personhood, and quite probably (1)–(3) are sufficient. Neither do we need to insist that any one of these criteria is *necessary* for personhood, although once again (1) and (2) look like fairly good

candidates for necessary conditions, as does (3), if 'activity' is construed so as to include the activity of reasoning.

All we need to claim, to demonstrate that a fetus is not a person, is that any being which satisfies *none* of (1)–(5) is certainly not a person. I consider this claim to be so obvious that I think anyone who denied it, and claimed that a being which satisfied none of (1)–(5) was a person all the same, would thereby demonstrate that he had no notion at all of what a person is—perhaps because he had confused the concept of a person with that of genetic humanity. If the opponents of abortion were to deny the appropriateness of these five criteria, I do not know what further arguments would convince them. We would probably have to admit that our conceptual schemes were indeed irreconcilably different, and that our dispute could not be settled objectively.

I do not expect this to happen, however, since I think that the concept of a person is one which is very nearly universal (to people), and that it is common to both proabortionists and antiabortionists, even though neither group has fully realized the relevance of this concept to the resolution of their dispute. Furthermore, I think that on reflection even the antiabortionists ought to agree not only that (1)–(5) are central to the concept of personhood, but also that it is a part of this concept that all and only people have full moral rights. The concept of a person is in part a moral concept; once we have admitted that x is a person we have recognized, even if we have not agreed to respect, x's right to be treated as a member of the moral community. It is true that the claim that x is a *human being* is more commonly voiced as part of an appeal to treat x decently than is the claim that x is a person, but this is either because 'human being' is here used in the sense which implies personhood, or because the genetic and moral senses of 'human' have been confused.

Now if (1)–(5) are indeed the primary criteria of personhood, then it is clear that genetic humanity is neither necessary nor sufficient for establishing that an entity is a person. Some human beings are not people, and there may well be people who are not human beings. A man or woman whose consciousness has been permanently obliterated but who remains alive is a human being which is no longer a person; defective human beings, with no appreciable mental capacity, are not and presumably never will be people; and a fetus is a human being which is not yet a person, and which therefore cannot coherently be said to have full moral rights. Citizens of the next century should be prepared to recognize highly advanced, self-aware robots or computers, should such be developed, and intelligent inhabitants of other worlds, should such be found, as people in the fullest sense, and to respect their moral rights. But to ascribe full moral rights to an entity which is not a person is as absurd as to ascribe moral obligations and responsibilities to such an entity.

3. Fetal Development and the Right to Life

14   Two problems arise in the application of these suggestions for the definition of the moral community to the determination of the precise moral status of a human fetus. Given that the paradigm example of a person is a normal adult human being, then (1) How like this paradigm, in particular how far advanced since conception, does a human being need to be before it begins to have a right to life by virtue, not of being fully a person as of yet, but of being *like* a person? and (2) To what extent, if any, does the fact that a fetus has the *potential* for becoming a person endow it with some of the same rights? Each of these questions requires some comment.

15   In answering the first question, we need not attempt a detailed consideration of the moral rights of organisms which are not developed enough, aware enough, intelligent enough, etc., to be considered people, but which resemble people in some respects. It does seem reasonable to suggest that the more like a person, in the relevant respects, a being is, the stronger is the case for regarding it as having a right to life, and indeed the stronger its right to life is. Thus we ought to take seriously the suggestion that, insofar as "the human individual develops biologically in a continuous fashion . . . the rights of a human person might develop in the same way."[3] But

---

3. Thomas L. Hayes, "A Biological View," *Commonweal*, 85 (March 17, 1967), 677–78; quoted by Daniel Callahan, in *Abortion, Law, Choice, and Morality* (London: Macmillan & Co., 1970).

we must keep in mind that the attributes which are relevant in determining whether or not an entity is enough like a person to be regarded as having some of the same moral rights are no different from those which are relevant to determining whether or not it is fully a person—i.e., are no different from (1)–(5)—and that being genetically human, or having recognizably human facial and other physical features, or detectable brain activity, or the capacity to survive outside the uterus, are simply not among these relevant attributes.

Thus it is clear that even though a seven- or eight-month fetus 16 has features which make it apt to arouse in us almost the same powerful protective instinct as is commonly aroused by a small infant, nevertheless it is not significantly more personlike than is a very small embryo. It is *somewhat* more personlike; it can apparently feel and respond to pain, and it may even have a rudimentary form of consciousness, insofar as its brain is quite active. Nevertheless, it seems safe to say that it is not fully conscious, in the way that an infant of a few months is, and that it cannot reason, or communicate messages of indefinitely many sorts, does not engage in self-motivated activity, and has no self-awareness. Thus, in the *relevant* respects, a fetus, even a fully developed one, is considerably less personlike than is the average mature mammal, indeed the average fish. And I think that a rational person must conclude that if the right to life of a fetus is to be based upon its resemblance to a person, then it cannot be said to have any more right to life than, let us say, a newborn guppy (which also seems to be capable of feeling pain), and that a right of that magnitude could never override a woman's right to obtain an abortion, at any stage of her pregnancy.

There may, of course, be other arguments in favor of placing legal 17 limits upon the stage of pregnancy in which an abortion may be performed. Given the relative safety of the new techniques of artifically inducing labor during the third trimester, the danger to the woman's life or health is no longer such an argument. Neither is the fact that people tend to respond to the thought of abortion in the later stages of pregnancy with emotional repulsion, since mere emotional responses cannot take the place of moral reasoning in determining what ought to be permitted. Nor, finally, is the frequently heard argument that legalizing abortion, especially late in the pregnancy, may erode the level of respect for human life, leading, perhaps, to an increase in unjustified euthanasia and other crimes. For this threat, if it is a threat, can be better met by educating people to the kinds of moral distinctions which we are making here than by limiting access to abortion (which limitation may, in its disregard for the rights of women, be just as damaging to the level of respect for human rights).

18   Thus, since the fact that even a fully developed fetus is not personlike enough to have any significant right to life on the basis of its personlikeness shows that no legal restrictions upon the stage of pregnancy in which an abortion may be performed can be justified on the grounds that we should protect the rights of the older fetus; and since there is no other apparent justification for such restrictions, we may conclude that they are entirely unjustified. Whether or not it would be *indecent* (whatever that means) for a woman in her seventh month to obtain an abortion just to avoid having to postpone a trip to Europe, it would not, in itself, be *immoral,* and therefore it ought to be permitted.

4. Potential Personhood and the Right to Life

19   We have seen that a fetus does not resemble a person in any way which can support the claim that it has even some of the same rights. But what about its *potential,* the fact that if nurtured and allowed to develop naturally it will very probably become a person? Doesn't that alone give it at least some right to life? It is hard to deny that the fact that an entity is a potential person is a strong prima facie reason for not destroying it; but we need not conclude from this that a potential person has a right to life, by virtue of that potential. It may be that our feeling that it is better, other things being equal, not to destroy a potential person is better explained by the fact that potential people are still (felt to be) an invaluable resource, not to be lightly squandered. Surely, if every speck of dust were a potential person, we would be much less apt to conclude that every potential person has a right to become actual.

Still, we do not need to insist that a potential person has no right 20
to life whatever. There may well be something immoral, and not
just imprudent, about wantonly destroying potential people, when
doing so isn't necessary to protect anyone's rights. But even if a
potential person does have some prima facie right to life, such a
right could not possibly outweigh the right of a woman to obtain an
abortion, since the rights of any actual person invariably outweigh
those of any potential person, whenever the two conflict. Since this
may not be immediately obvious in the case of a human fetus, let
us look at another case.

Suppose that our space explorer falls into the hands of an alien 21
culture, whose scientists decide to create a few hundred thousand or
more human beings, by breaking his body into its component cells,
and using these to create fully developed human beings, with, of
course, his genetic code. We may imagine that each of these newly
created men will have all of the original man's abilities, skills,
knowledge, and so on, and also have an individual self-concept, in
short that each of them will be a bona fide (though hardly unique)
person. Imagine that the whole project will take only seconds, and
that its chances of success are extremely high, and that our explorer
knows all of this, and also knows that these people will be treated
fairly. I maintain that in such a situation he would have every right
to escape if he could, and thus to deprive all of these potential people
of their potential lives; for his right to life outweighs all of theirs
together, in spite of the fact that they are all genetically human, all
innocent, and all have a very high probability of becoming people
very soon, if only he refrains from acting.

Indeed, I think he would have a right to escape even if it were 22
not his life which the alien scientists planned to take, but only a year
of his freedom, or, indeed, only a day. Nor would he be obligated to
stay if he had gotten captured (thus bringing all these people-po-
tentials into existence) because of his own carelessness, or even if he
had done so deliberately, knowing the consequences. Regardless of
how he got captured, he is not morally obligated to remain in
captivity for *any* period of time for the sake of permitting any
number of potential people to come into actuality, so great is the
margin by which one actual person's right to liberty outweighs
whatever right to life even a hundred thousand potential people
have. And it seems reasonable to conclude that the rights of a

woman will outweigh by a similar margin whatever right to life a
fetus may have by virtue of its potential personhood.

23   Thus, neither a fetus's resemblance to a person, nor its potential
for becoming a person provides any basis whatever for the claim
that it has any significant right to life. Consequently, a woman's
right to protect her health, happiness, freedom, and even her life,[4]
by terminating an unwanted pregnancy, will always override whatever right to life it may be appropriate to ascribe to a fetus, even a
fully developed one. And thus, in the absence of any overwhelming
social need for every possible child, the laws which restrict the right
to obtain an abortion, or limit the period of pregnancy during which
an abortion may be performed, are a wholly unjustified violation of
a woman's most basic moral and constitutional rights.[5]

STUDY QUESTIONS

1. In paragraph 3, Warren says that 'human' has two senses.
   What are they? And what is the distinction Warren makes in
   paragraph 5 between people and human beings?
2. What is the point of the thought experiment in paragraphs 7
   and 8 involving the space traveler who encounters aliens on
   an unknown planet? Does Warren uses it as part of her
   argument?
3. In paragraph 15, Warren rejects four attributes as candidates
   for determining that a fetus has rights. What are they, and
   on what grounds does she reject them?
4. In paragraph 16, Warren argues that even if a fetus has some
   degree of a right to life, "a right of that magnitude could
   never override a woman's right to obtain an abortion, at any
   stage of her pregnancy." Has she yet argued that a woman
   has a right to obtain an abortion? Where does she present her
   reasons justifying a woman's right to abortion?

4. That is, insofar as the death rate, for the woman, is higher for childbirth
than for early abortion.

5. My thanks to the following people, who were kind enough to read and
criticize an earlier version of this paper: Herbert Gold, Gene Glass, Anne
Lauterbach, Judith Thomson, Mary Mothersill, and Timothy Binkley.

5. In the selection by Ronald Reagan (p. 275), abortion is linked to a lack of respect for human life and thus to crimes such as infanticide and slavery. Does Warren respond to the following objection: "Since you think that a woman may have an abortion at any point during her pregnancy, and since a fetus one day before birth and an infant one day after birth are not significantly different in their attributes, your position logically implies that infanticide is acceptable"?

6. What is the point of the example in paragraph 21 involving the space explorer who falls into the hands of aliens who wish to clone him?

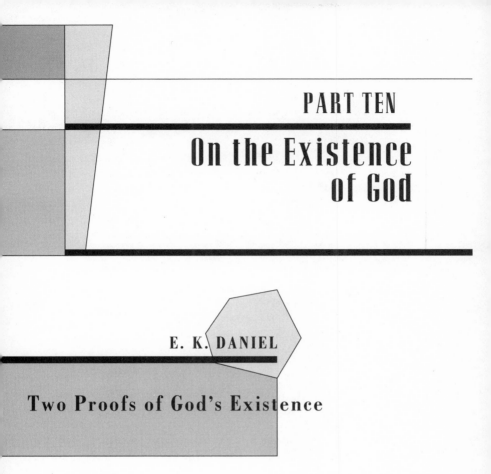

PART TEN

On the Existence of God

E. K. DANIEL

Two Proofs of God's Existence

*In the following selection, excerpted from a longer essay on
proofs offered for the existence of God, Daniel presents and defends two traditionally powerful theistic arguments.*

In section I, I said that my defense of theism will proceed by way
of defending the classical arguments for the existence of God. I also
said that my defense of the arguments would follow an earlier
defense of them by Julian Hartt.

1

[E. K. Daniel, excerpt from "A Defense of Theism," in E. D. Klemke, A. David
Kline, and Robert Hollinger, eds., *Philosophy: The Basic Issues*, 3rd ed. New York:
St. Martin's Press, 1990, pp. 269–272.]

2   Hartt's defense of these . . . arguments is extremely interesting and worthy of careful study. He mentions that: (a) there are several all-pervasive, broad characteristics of the world (universe)—or features of the world—which we experience; (b) each of the three *a posteriori* arguments focuses on one (or more) of these features; and (c) in each case, the feature(s) can only be explained by, and thus necessitate(s) the existence of, a being who is transcendent to the universe: God.

3   What are these features? And which of the three arguments focuses on which feature? We may put this in the form of a table:

Argument	*Feature (of universe)*
1. First-Cause (Cosmological)	finitude; contingency
2. Design (Teleological)	purposiveness; purposeful adaptation and arrangement

Again, in Hartt's view, these are objective features of the world (universe) which we experience, and each necessitates the existence of a (transcendent and infinite) God.

4   1. *The First-Cause (Cosmological) Argument.* The first-cause argument calls attention to and begins with the feature of *finitude and the related feature of contingency.* The argument also makes use of and rests on the notion of a *first cause* in connection with those features. Thus we find three variations. These different themes can give rise to several forms of the first-cause argument, or all of them can be included in a single argument. I propose to defend the cosmological argument by reformulating it as follows:

> Everything in the universe is finite.
>
> Whatever is finite is limited.
>
> Hence, whatever is limited cannot be the cause of its own existence.
>
> Everything in the universe is contingent.
>
> Whatever is contingent is dependent on something else for its existence.

Hence, whatever is contingent cannot be the cause of its own existence.

The totality of things making up the universe is also finite and contingent.

Thus, the totality (universe) must also have a cause for its existence.

Since it cannot be the cause of its own existence, the cause must be something external to the universe.

That is, since the universe cannot contain the reason for its existence within itself, the reason for its existence must be something external to it.

Hence, there must exist an infinite and self-subsistent (non-contingent) being who is the cause of the universe.

Unlike that which is finite and contingent, such a being must exist necessarily.

Such a being is commonly called God.

Therefore, there exists an infinite, necessary, and uncaused cause—God.

Someone may object: But why does the universe as a totality need a cause or explanation? Why can it not have existed infinitely in time? I reply: let us suppose it did. Then what the cosmological argument seeks is to provide answers to some questions: (1) Why does anything exist at all? (2) Why does it exist as it does rather than some other way? Or (1) Why is there a world at all? (2) Why is there this kind of universe rather than some other one? The answer is: Because of the purpose of an unlimited, infinite, and necessary being—an ultimate first cause which is itself uncaused—God.

In summary: Why does the fact that the universe is finite and contingent necessitate God's existence? The answer is that whatever is finite is limited. Hence, it cannot cause itself. And whatever is contingent is dependent on something else for its existence. Hence, it cannot be the cause of its own existence. The universe—as well as everything in it—is finite and contingent. There is nothing about it to indicate that it could be the cause of its own existence. Since it cannot be the cause of its own existence, it must have been caused by something else—a being external to the universe. Therefore, such a being must exist: an unlimited, necessary, and uncaused cause—God.

7   2. *The Design (Teleological) Argument.* The design argument calls attention to another feature of the universe, that of *purposiveness,* or purposeful adaptation of means to ends.

8   The word *teleological* comes from the Greek word *telos,* meaning purpose or goal. Theism is a teleological metaphysics through and through. Hence, it is understandable and natural for there to be arguments which focus on the notion of purpose. Among them is the teleological argument for the existence of God. This argument claims that the many features of design, purpose, and adaptation in the universe are indications of a Cosmic Intelligence or Mind—God—which designed, planned, and brought the universe into existence, I propose to defend the teleological argument by reformulating it as follows:

> Suppose that while walking along an ocean beach, or a barren field, we come upon an object, such as a watch.
>
> If we examine the watch, we find that it shows evidence of purpose and design.
>
> We detect orderliness and intricacy.
>
> We find an adaptation of means to ends (the parts are arranged to work together to enable the hands to move and to enable us to tell time).
>
> All of this is evidence of rationality and design.
>
> Hence, there exists a rational being who designed and brought the watch into being.

Similarly:

> Look out at the universe and the things within it.
>
> The universe also shows evidence of design and purpose.
>
> We detect orderliness and intricacy.
>
> Moreover, we find a marvelous adaptation of means to ends.
>
> An example of such adaptation is the existence of two sexes for the end of procreation or the structure of the eye for the end of seeing.
>
> All this is also evidence of rationality and design.
>
> Hence, there must exist a rational being who designed and brought the universe into existence.
>
> That is, there must exist a Cosmic Designer—God.

It may be objected: But could not the universe have resulted from chance? I reply: Although there may be chance _in_ the universe, the universe _itself_ is not the product of chance but of _intelligent purpose_. The environment in which we find ourselves is not a fortuitously functioning mechanism; nor is it an organism. It is imbued with purpose. Everyone admits that humans show evidence of mind and purposive behavior—as in designing and making a house. But we cannot suppose that purposeful activity is limited to humans and that everything else in nature is blind or the result of sheer chance. Why not? Because _our_ minds, our intelligent planning, have not made the universe. Therefore, there must exist a being who designed the universe and brought it into existence.

9

In summary: Why does the fact that the universe is purposeful necessitate God's existence? The reason is that whatever is purposeful shows signs of intelligence—mind. Hence, what is purposive cannot have come about accidentally, or from something non-purposive. Hence, the only way to explain the purposiveness in the universe is: It got here because of the thought, design, and activity of a Cosmic Intelligence—God.

10

STUDY QUESTIONS

1. The first step of the First Cause argument goes like this:

   Everything in the universe is finite.

   Whatever is finite is limited.

   Hence, whatever is limited cannot be the cause of its own existence.

   What assumed premise does this argument depend on?

2. For each of the remaining steps in the First Cause argument, determine whether they depend on assumed premises.

3. The design argument proceeds by making an analogy from a watch and the universe. How many points of similarity between the watch and the universe does the analogy depend on?

4. The design argument can be diagrammed as follows:

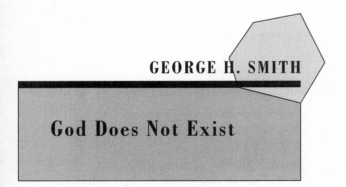

(1) The watch is   +   (2) The watch requires an
    orderly   intelligent desiger

(3)   +   (4) The universe is orderly

(5) The universe requires an intelligent designer.

What inductive generalization is required at (3) in order to complete the argument?

5. Does it make sense to suppose that if God exists, he must be orderly and intricate, and his parts must show an adaption of means to ends? If so, does the design argument lead us to suppose that God must have been designed by a rational being?

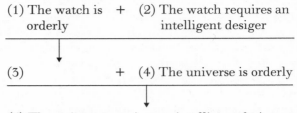

GEORGE H. SMITH

God Does Not Exist

George H. Smith is a senior research fellow at the Institute for Humane Studies at George Mason University in Virginia. He is the author of Atheism, Ayn Rand, and Other Heresies, *and*

[George H. Smith, excerpt from Chapter 3 of *Atheism: The Case Against God.* Buffalo, N.Y.: Prometheus Books, 1979, pp. 81–87, references deleted.]

Atheism: The Case Against God, *from which the following is excerpted.*

Briefly, the problem of evil is this: If God does not know there is   1
evil, he is not omniscient. If God knows there is evil but cannot
prevent it, he is not omnipotent. If God knows there is evil and can
prevent it but desires not to, he is not omnibenevolent. If, as the
Christian claims, God is all-knowing and all-powerful, we must
conclude that God is not all-good. The existence of evil in the
universe excludes this possibility.

There have been various attempts to escape from the problem of   2
evil, and we shall briefly consider the more popular of these. But
one point requires emphasis. The Christian, by proclaiming that
God is good, commits himself to the position that man is capable of
distinguishing good from evil—for, if he is not, how did the Christian arrive at his judgment of "good" as applied to God? Therefore,
any attempt to resolve the problem of evil by arguing that man
cannot correctly distinguish good from evil, destroys the original
premise that it purports to defend and thus collapses from the
weight of an internal inconsistency. If the human standards of good
and evil are somehow invalid, the Christian's claim that God is good
is equally invalid.

One general theological approach to the problem of evil consists   3
of the claim that evil is in some way unreal or purely negative in
character. This argument, however, is so implausible that few
Christians care to defend it. The first problem with it, as Antony
Flew notes, is: "If evil is really nothing then what is all the fuss
about sin about: nothing?"

In *Some Dogmas of Religion,* John McTaggart quickly disposes   4
of the claim that evil is in some way unreal:

> Supposing that it could be proved that all that we think evil was in
> reality good, the fact would still remain that we think it evil. This
> may be called a delusion or a mistake. But a delusion or mistake is
> as *real* as anything else. A savage's erroneous belief that the earth is
> stationary is just as real a fact as an astronomer's correct belief that
> it moves. The delusion that evil exists, then, is real. But then . . . it
> seems certain that a delusion or an error which hid from us the
> goodness of the universe would itself be evil. And so there would be
> real evil after all. . . . However many times we pronounce evil unreal,

we always leave a reality behind, which in its turn is to be pro-
nounced evil.

5   As for the argument that evil is purely negative, a privation of
the good (as disease may be said to be the absence of health),
Wallace Matson provides this illuminating example in *The Existence of God:*

> It may console the paralytic to be told that paralysis is mere lack of
> mobility, nothing positive, and that insofar as he *is,* he is perfect. It
> is not clear, however, that this kind of comfort is available to the
> sufferer from malaria. He will reply that his trouble is not that he
> lacks anything, but rather that he has too much of something,
> namely, protozoans of the genus *Plasmodium.*

6   Any attempt to absolve God of the responsibility for evil by
claiming that, in the final analysis, there is no such thing as evil is,
as Matson puts it, "an unfunny joke." This approach merely ends
up by negating our human standards of good and evil, which, as
previously indicated, undercuts the argument at its root.

7   Another common effort to reconcile God and evil is to argue that
evil is the consequence of man's freely chosen actions. God, through
his gift of free will, gave man the ability to distinguish and choose
between good and evil, right and wrong. As a free agent, man has
the potential to reach a higher degree of perfection and goodness
than if he were a mere robot programmed to behave in a given
manner. Thus it is good that man has free will. But this entails the
opportunity for man to select evil instead of good, which has been
the case in the instances of torture, murder, and cruelty which some
men inflict upon others. The responsibility for these actions, however, rests with man, not with God. Therefore, concludes the Christian, evil does not conflict with the infinite goodness of God.

8   While this approach has some initial plausibility, it falls far short
of solving the problem of evil. We are asked to believe that God
created man with the power of choice in the hope that man would
voluntarily pursue the good, but that man thwarts this desire of God
through sin and thus brings evil upon himself. But, to begin with,
to speak of frustrating or acting contrary to the wishes of an
omnipotent being makes no sense whatsoever. There can be no
barriers to divine omnipotence, no obstacles to thwart his desires, so
we must assume that the present state of the world is precisely as

God desires it to be. If God wished things to be other than they are, nothing could possibly prevent them from being other than they are, man's free will notwithstanding. In addition, we have seen that free will is incompatible with the foreknowledge possessed by an omniscient being, so the appeal to free will fails in this respect as well. In any case, God created man with full knowledge of the widespread suffering that would ensue, and, given his ability to prevent this situation, we must presume that God desired and willed these immoral atrocities to occur.

It is unfair to place the responsibility for immoral actions on man's free will in general. Individual men commit atrocities, not the bloodless abstraction "man." Some men commit blatant injustices, but others do not. Some men murder, rob, and cheat, but others do not. Some men choose a policy of wanton destructiveness, but others do not. And we must remember that crimes are committed by men against other men, innocent victims, who cannot be held responsible. The minimum requirement for a civilized society is a legal system whereby the individual liberties of men are protected from the aggressive activities of other men. We regard the recognition and protection of individual rights as a moral necessity, and we condemn governments that fail to provide a fair system of justice. How, then, are we to evaluate a God who permits widespread instances of injustice when it is easily within his power to prevent them? The Christian believes in a God who displays little, if any, interest in the protection of the innocent, and we must wonder how such a being can be called "good."

The standard reply to this objection is that God rewards the virtuous and punishes the wicked in an afterlife, so there is an overall balance of justice. An extreme variation of this tactic was reported in the *New York Times* of September 11, 1950. Referring to the Korean War, this article states: "Sorrowing parents whose sons have been drafted or recalled for combat duty were told yesterday in St. Patrick's Cathedral [by Monsignor William T. Greene] that death in battle was part of God's plan for populating 'the kingdom of heaven.'"

This approach is so obviously an exercise in theological rationalization that it deserves little comment. If every instance of evil is to be rectified by an appeal to an afterlife, the claim that God is all-good has no relevance whatsoever to our present life. Virtually any immoral action, no matter how hideous or atrocious, can be explained away in this fashion—which severs any attempt to discuss the alleged goodness of a creator from reference to empirical evidence. More importantly, no appeal to an afterlife can actually eradicate the problem of evil. An injustice always remains an injustice, regardless of any subsequent efforts to comfort the victim. If a father, after beating his child unmercifully, later gives him a lollipop as compensation, this does not erase the original act or its evil nature. Nor would we praise the father as just and loving. The same applies to God, but even more so. The Christian may believe that God will punish the perpetrators of evil and compensate the victims of injustice, but this does not explain why a supposedly benevolent and omnipotent being created a world with evildoers and innocent victims in the first place. Again, we must assume that there are innocent victims because God desires innocent victims; from the standpoint of Christian theism, there is simply no other explanation. If an omnipotent God did not want innocent victims, they could not exist—and, by human standards, the Christian God appears an immoral fiend of cosmic dimensions.

12   Even if we overlook the preceding difficulties, the appeal to free will is still unsuccessful, because it encompasses only so-called *moral* evils (*i.e.*, the actions of men). There remains the considerable problem of *physical* evils, such as natural disasters, over which man has no control. Why are there floods, earthquakes and diseases that kill and maim millions of persons? The responsibility for these occurrences obviously cannot be placed on the shoulders of man. From an atheistic standpoint, such phenomena are inimical to man's life and may be termed evil, but since they are the result of inanimate, natural forces and do not involve conscious intent, they do not fall within the province of moral judgment. But from a Christian perspective, God—the omnipotent creator of the natural universe—must bear ultimate responsibility for these occurrences, and God's deliberate choice of these evil phenomena qualifies him as immoral.

13   There is an interesting assortment of arguments designed to explain the existence of natural evils. Some theologians argue that evil exists for the sake of a greater good; others maintain that apparent evils disappear into a universal harmony of good. Although something may appear evil to man, we are assured by the

Christian that God is able to view the overall perspective, and any apparent evil always turns out for the best. These approaches share the premise that man cannot understand the ways of God, but this simply pushes us into agnosticism. It will not do for the Christian to posit an attribute of God and, when asked to defend that attribute, contend that man cannot understand it.

If we are incorrect in calling natural disasters, diseases and other   14
phenomena evil, then man is incapable of distinguishing good from evil. But if this is the case, by what standard does the Christian claim that God is good? What criterion is the Christian using?

If man cannot pass correct moral judgments, he cannot validly   15
praise *or* condemn anything—including the Christian God. To exclude God from the judgment of evil is to exclude him from the judgment of good as well; but if man can distinguish good from evil, a supernatural being who willfully causes or permits the continuation of evil on his creatures merits unequivocal moral condemnation.

Some Christians resort to incredible measures to absolve their   16
God from the responsibility for evil. Consider this passage from *Evil and the God of Love* in which John Hick attempts to reconcile the existence of an omnibenevolent deity with the senseless disasters that befall man:

> . . . men and women often act in true compassion and massive generosity and self-giving in the face of unmerited suffering, especially when it comes in such dramatic forms as an earthquake or a mining disaster. It seems, then, that in a world that is to be the scene of compassionate love and self-giving for others, suffering must fall upon mankind with something of the haphazardness and inequity that we now experience. It must be apparently unmerited, pointless, and incapable of being morally rationalized. For it is precisely this feature of our common human lot that creates sympathy between man and man and evokes the unselfish kindness and goodwill which are among the highest values of personal life.

Aside from displaying a low regard for man's "highest values"   17
and their origins, Hick illustrates an important point: *There is virtually nothing which the Christian will accept as evidence of God's evil.* If disasters that are admittedly "unmerited, pointless, and incapable of being morally rationalized" are compatible with the

"goodness" of God, what could possibly qualify as contrary evidence? The "goodness" of God, it seems, is compatible with any conceivable state of affairs. While we evaluate a man with reference to his actions, we are not similarly permitted to judge God. God is immune from the judgment of evil as a matter of principle.

18 Here we have a concrete illustration of theological "reasoning." Unlike the philosopher, the theologian adopts a position, a dogma, and then commits himself to a defense of that position come what may. While he may display a willingness to defend this dogma, closer examination reveals this to be a farce. His defense consists of distorting and rationalizing all contrary evidence to meet his desired specifications. In the case of divine benevolence, the theologian will grasp onto any explanation, no matter how implausible, before he will abandon his dogma. And when finally pushed into a corner, he will argue that man cannot understand the true meaning of this dogma.

19 This brings us to our familiar resting place. The "goodness" of God is different in kind from goodness as we comprehend it. To say that God's "goodness" is compatible with the worst disasters imaginable, is to empty this concept of its meaning. By human standards, the Christian God cannot be good. By divine standards, God may be "good" in some unspecified, unknowable way—but this term no longer makes any sense. And so, for the last time, we fail to comprehend the Christian God.

STUDY QUESTIONS

1. In the first paragraph, Smith presents a brief account of the problem of evil. As stated, the argument relies on some assumed premises. Rewrite the argument, filling in the assumed premises, and determine whether it is valid.

2. For the rest of the selection Smith proceeds by considering a number of attempts to reconcile the existence of the Christian God with the existence of evil, and arguing that they all fail. How many distinct attempts at reconciliation does Smith consider? Can you think of any others?

3. In paragraph 18, Smith concludes that theologians who de-

fend the Christian God against the problem of evil are not really reasoning but rather "rationalizing all contrary evidence." Judging from the strength of the various responses to the problem of evil, how much evidence does Smith have for this claim?

ACKNOWLEDGMENTS

Caroline Bird. Excerpts from *The Case Against College*. New York: David McKay Co., 1975, pp. 3–13, 20–23, 62–66, 70–74, 77–79, 83, 90–91, 93–94, 97–98, 106–108, 110, 112, 116–117, 122.

Cesare Bonesana. "Torture." Excerpt from James A. Farrar, *Crimes and Punishments*. London: Chatto & Windus, 1880, pp. 148–152.

Justice Louis Brandeis. Dissenting opinion, *New State Ice Co.* v. *Liebmann*, 463 U.S. 262 (1931). Pp. 262–311, footnotes omitted.

Justice William Brennan. Section III of concurring opinion in *Furman* v. *Georgia* 408 U.S. 285–305 (1972).

Baruch Brody. "Fetal Humanity and the Theory of Essentialism." In Robert Baker and Frederick Elliston, eds., *Philosophy and Sex*. Buffalo, NY: Prometheus Books, 1975, pp. 348–352.

Vincent Bugliosi. Excerpt from *Outrage: The Five Reasons Why O. J. Simpson Got Away With Murder*. W. W. Norton & Co., 1996, pp. 20–22.

Johnnie L. Cochran, with Tim Rutten. Excerpt from *Journey to Justice*. New York: Ballantine Books, 1996, pp. 338–351.

E. K. Daniel. Excerpt from "A Defense of Theism." In E. D. Klemke, A. David Kline, and Robert Hollinger, eds. *Philosophy: The Basic Issues*, 3rd ed. St. Martin's, 1990, pp. 269–272.

Charles Darwin. Excerpts from "Recapitulation." *On the Origin of Species*. A Facsimile of the First Edition. Harvard University Press, 1966, pp. 459, 466–469.

Alan M. Dershowitz, "Shouting 'Fire!' " *Atlantic Monthly,* January 1989, pp. 72–74.

Steven Durland, excerpt from "Censorship, Multiculturalism, and Symbols." *High Performance* (Fall 1989).

John Enright, "What is Poetry?" *Objectively Speaking,* Autumn 1989.

Marsha Familiaro Enright, "Con Molto Sentimento." *Objectivity* 2:3 (1996), 117–151.

Sigmund Freud, *Civilization & Its Discontents,* transl. James Strachey. W. W. Norton, 1952, pp. 58–59.

Linda Gorman, "Minimum Wages." *The Fortune Encyclopedia of Economics,* ed. David Henderson. Warner, 1993, pp. 499–503.

Stephen J. Gould, "Sex, Drugs, Disasters, and the Extinction of Dinosaurs." *The Flamingo's Smile.* New York: W. W. Norton, pp. 417–426.

Michael Harrington, excerpt from *The Other America.* Pelican, 1971, pp. 187–190.

Henry Hazlitt, excerpt from Chapter XI of *Economics in One Lesson.* Westport, Conn.: Arlington House, 1946, 1962, 1979, pp. 75–77.

Jesse Helms, Amendment 420: The NEA Should Not Fund Obscenity. U.S. Senate, July 26, 1989. Reprinted in Bolton, Richard, ed. *Culture Wars,* New Press 1992, pp. 73–77.

Carl Hempel, excerpt from *Philosophy of Natural Science.* Prentice-Hall, 1966, pp. 3–6.

Robert Hughes, "A Loony Parody of Cultural Democracy," *Time,* August 14, 1989.

Thomas Jefferson, "The Declaration of Independence."

Don B. Kates, Jr., "Handgun Bans—Facts to Fight With." *Annual Guns and Ammo, 1984.* Los Angeles: Petersen.

Michael Levin, "The Case for Torture." *Newsweek,* June 7, 1982, p. 13.

Liberty Network Association, "The New World Order." Mailing from Liberty Network Association, c/o 13223 Black Mountain Road, 1–311, San Diego, California 92129.

Niccolò Machiavelli, "On Cruelty and Clemency: Whether It is Better to be Loved or Feared." Section XVII of *The Prince,* transl. Robert M. Adams. New York: W. W. Norton, 1977, pp. 47–49.

Hosea L. Martin, "A Few Kind Words for Affirmative Action." *The Wall Street Journal,* April 25, 1991, op-ed page.

H. L. Mencken. "The Penalty of Death," from *Prejudices, Fifth Series.* Alfred A. Knopf, 1926; copyright renewed 1954 by H. L. Mencken, pp. 22–27.

Lisa H. Newton. "Bakke and Davis: Justice, American Style." *National Forum (The Phi Beta Kappa Journal)* LVIII, no. 1 (Winter 1978), pp. 22–23.

Murdock Pencil. "Salt Passage Research: The State of the Art." *Journal of Communication,* Autumn 1976, pp. 31–36.

Ronald Reagan. *Abortion and the Conscience of the Nation.* Nashville: Thomas Nelson Publishers, 1984, pp. 15–16, 18–19, 21–25, 27–36, 38.

Jean-Jacques Rousseau. Excerpt from *Emile,* transl. Eleanor Worthington. Boston: Ginn, Heath & Co. 1883, pp. 52–54.

David Rubinstein. "Don't Blame Crime on Joblessness," *The Wall Street Journal,* November 9, 1992, op-ed page.

Robert Samuelson. "Highbrow Pork Barrel," *Washington Post,* August 16, 1989.

Isaac Shapiro. "The Dispute over the Minimum Wage," *Dissent* 1989, pp. 18–20.

Max Shulman. "Love Is a Fallacy," *The Many Loves of Dobie Gillis.* New York: Doubleday, 1951.

John Henry Sloan, Arthur L. Kellermann, Donald T. Reay, James A. Ferris, Thomas Koepsell, Frederick P. Rivara, Charles Rice, Laurel Gray, and James LoGerfo. "Handgun Regulations, Crime, Assaults, and Homicide: A Tale of Two Cities," *New England Journal of Medicine* 319, Nov. 10, 1988, pp. 1256–1262.

George H. Smith. Excerpt from Chapter 3 of *Atheism: The Case Against God.* New York: Prometheus, 1979, pp. 81–87.

Justice Potter Stewart. *Gregg* v. *Georgia* 428 U.S. 153 (1976), excerpts from parts III, IV, and V.

Sissel Seteras Stokes. From "Letters to the Editor," *Bloomington* (Indiana) *Herald-Telephone,* September 6, 1987.

Sheila Tobias. Excerpts from Chapter 3 of *Overcoming Math Anxiety.* New York: W. W. Norton, 1978, pp. 70–72, 74, 77–88, 91–96.

Laurence H. Tribe. Excerpt from *Abortion: The Clash of Absolutes.* New York: W. W. Norton, 1990, pp. 231–234.

Mary Anne Warren. Part II of "On the Moral and Legal Status of Abortion." *The Monist* 57 (January 1973), pp. 52–61.

John H. Wigmore. "The Borden Case." *American Law Review* 37 (1893), pp. 806–814.